T0340045

Reconstructing Marxism

Reconstructing Marxism

Essays on Explanation and the Theory of History

ERIK OLIN WRIGHT,
ANDREW LEVINE
& ELLIOTT SOBER

VERSO

London · New York

First published by Verso 1992
© Erik Olin Wright, Andrew Levine and Elliott Sober 1992
All rights reserved

Verso
UK: 6 Meard Street, London W1V 3HR
USA: 29 West 35th Street, New York, NY 10001–2291

Verso is the imprint of New Left Books

British Library Cataloguing in Publication Data
A catalogue record for this book is available from the British Library

Library of Congress Cataloging-in-Publication Data
A catalogue record for this book is available from the Library of Congress

Typeset in Times by Leaper & Gard Limited, Bristol
Printed in Great Britain by Biddles Ltd

ISBN: 978-0-86091-554-6

To
Michael Burawoy
and
Richard Lewontin

Contents

Preface

The following essays address historical materialism, Marx's theory of history and issues in the philosophy of social science relevant to Marxist theory. In the political atmosphere of the early 1990s, a book devoted to these topics may seem anachronistic. Recent events in countries once officially designated "Marxist", and changing intellectual fashions elsewhere, will lead many readers to wonder why Marxist ideas should still be taken seriously. We address these concerns by making some Marxist ideas objects of critical attention, and we try to counter the current disinclination to take Marxism seriously by arguing for the continuing timeliness of the project Marx began.

We have called this book *Reconstructing Marxism* because we find pertinent the metaphor it suggests. However many renovations the Marxist edifice now requires, we think that it is an edifice with reasonably solid foundations, located in the right neighborhood. A title suggested in a quip by Philippe Van Parijs was *Recycling Marxism*. In our view, this goes too far in its recommendation that we demolish the building, salvaging some remnants for future use, but discarding the bulk of what was once there, as though it were so much useless (perhaps even "toxic") waste. We do not believe that Marxism is in such a state of disrepair as to warrant recycling. In our view, the old structure, reconstructed, may still be humanity's best hope for understanding the social world, and for changing it.

We regret, however, that our title may seem to promise more than we deliver. Our brief for *reconstructing* Marxist positions is more programmatic than substantive. We argue that a theory of history with a conceptual structure like the one Marx proposed, but with vastly diminished explanatory pretensions, is surprisingly plausible. We also suggest that the prospects for Marxist class analysis are eminently favorable, despite the unfortunate fact that Marxists have too often taken up untenable positions in some generally ill-conceived methodological controversies. But in the end, only empirical corroboration can vindicate Marxist claims; this is a task we do not undertake at all. For better or worse, the essays assembled here are almost exclusively philosophical in scope. They therefore only approach the point where the arduous and open-ended task of *reconstructing* Marxism, in the fullest sense of the expression, can finally begin.

The essays that comprise this book were written over a period of ten years within an emerging intellectual current that has come to be known as "analytical Marxism". We discuss this style of Marxist theorizing in Chapter 1, and reflect on its implications for the Marxist agenda in Chapter 8. In the course of that period our preoccupations have changed, moving from a focus on some core themes of traditional Marxism to a more general engagement with problems in the philosophy of social science. The first essay in the series (Chapter 2), written in 1979, is concerned exclusively with Marx's theory of history and G.A. Cohen's attempt to reconstruct and defend it. The second essay to be written (Chapter 4) connects Marxist and neo-Weberian perspectives on the theory of history by discussing Anthony Giddens's critique of historical materialism. In the next essay chronologically (Chapters 3 and 5), the main task is to clarify some of the senses in which a theory of history can be "historical". This essay compares Marx's theory of history with Darwin's account of evolution. Historical materialism anchors this essay, but Marx's theory is not these chapters' exclusive focus. The fourth essay to be written (Chapter 6) discusses methodological individualism and micro-reductionism. The deployment of individualistic analyses in Marxism is more the occasion here than its central concern. Finally, the last essay in this series (Chapter 7) discusses what it means to claim that some causes are more important than others. The role of "causal primacy" arguments in Marxism is only one of a number of illustrations we deploy. Indeed, in our choice of illustrations we sometimes stray far from radical social theory altogether.

This shift of preoccupation from narrowly Marxist themes towards more general issues in the philosophy of social science is to some extent symptomatic of the intellectual trajectory of analytical Marxism during the 1980s. A decade ago, most analytical Marxists were concerned with the traditional core of Marxist theory: exploitation, class, historical materialism, the transition from feudalism to capitalism, the possibilities for socialism. By the end of the 1980s, the topics had widened to include many of the central questions of mainstream social philosophy and social science. While analytical Marxists continue to engage these issues in distinctively Marxist ways, the principal concerns of most of them have long ceased to be Marxism as such.

It might seem that this shift in focus signals a move away from Marxism altogether. Some critics of analytical Marxism believe that it is headed in precisely this direction. We disagree. Reconstructing Marxism will inevitably erode the boundaries separating Marxism from some of its rivals. But in the present conjuncture, this eventuality is indispensable for strengthening the theoretical capacity of Marxism itself.

Six of the eight chapters in this book are based on essays originally published as articles. When we decided to collect them together, we planned to limit our revisions to deletions of redundancies and corrections of minor errors. Once we had assembled them, however, and determined what needed to be done to make them cohere, we realized that we had learned more than we had thought in the course of the past decade. Much of what we had once considered settled needed to be reworked. As a result, all of the previously published essays have been revised in varying degrees. Chapter 1 is an amalgam of two previous essays. Chapters 2 and 4 have been substantially altered. Chapter 5 is a much expanded spin-off from an earlier essay. In Chapters 3 and 6, revisions mainly involved reorganizations, clarifications and amendments.

Chapter 1 is based, in part, on "What is Analytical Marxism?" (Wright), *Socialist Review* 89/4 (December 1989), pp. 37–56; and "What is a Marxist Today?" (Levine) in *Analyzing Marxism: New Essays on Analytical Marxism*, Robert Ware and Kai Nielsen, eds, *Canadian Journal of Philosophy*, supplementary volume 15 (1989), pp. 29–58.

Chapter 2 is a substantially revised version of "Rationality and Class Struggle" (Levine and Wright), *New Left Review* 123 (1980), pp. 47–68. The current version is based, in part, on a descendant of the original paper published as Chapter 5 of *Arguing for Socialism* (Levine) (London: Routledge & Kegan Paul, 1984; 2nd edition, London: Verso, 1988).

Chapters 3 and 5 are based on "What's Historical About Historical Materialism" (Levine and Sober), *The Journal of Philosophy* 82, 6 (June 1985), pp. 304–26; and the revisions of that paper published as Chapter 5 of *The End of the State* (Levine) (London: Verso, 1987).

Chapter 4 is a substantially revised version of "Giddens's Critique of Marx" (Wright), *New Left Review* 138 (1983), pp. 11–36. A somewhat different version entitled "Models of History's Trajectory" was published in David Held and John B. Thompson, eds, *Anthony Giddens and His Critics* (Cambridge: Cambridge University Press, 1989).

Chapter 6 is a slightly revised version of "Marxism and Methodological Individualism" (Levine, Sober and Wright), *New Left Review* 162 (1987), pp. 67–84.

Chapters 7 and 8 appear here for the first time.

We are grateful to the editors of each of the journals in which the ancestors of these chapters first appeared for permission to draw on this material.

G.A. Cohen read and commented on versions of Chapters 1, 2, 7 and 8 with a degree of attention that can only be described as heroic. His comments forced a complete rethinking of the issues involved in Chapter 7 and substantial rewriting of the other three chapters. No doubt, he would still disagree with much of what we have written. However, there would be much more to disagree with in our book but for his criticisms. Sam Bowles, Robert Brenner, Michael Burawoy, Jon Elster, Robert Hauser, Daniel Hausman, Richard Lewontin, Richard Miller, Philippe Van Parijs, Adam Przeworski, John Roemer, Arthur Stinchcombe and Robert Van der Veen have provided invaluable comments, and we have benefited, separately and together, from discussions with Ronald Aminzade, Alan Carling, Margaret Levy and Joel Rogers, among many others.

Erik Olin Wright
Andrew Levine
Elliott Sober

1

Marxism:
Crisis or Renewal?

It has become commonplace nowadays to speak of a crisis—and even of the end—of Marxism. This dire forecast can hardly be explained just by the cultural hegemony exercised by Marxism's ideological opponents. Real conditions—internal theoretical developments, changes in intellectual culture and, above all, transformed political circumstances—contribute to the impression that this once central tradition of radical social theory and practice is in a process of collapse.

Certainly, extraordinary changes have taken place in societies once ruled by Communist parties officially identified with Marxism. A few years ago, the "Marxism" of these parties was the official ideology of a third of the planet. Now, with Communist parties everywhere renouncing much of their previous theory and practice, and with their role in the societies they once ruled becoming increasingly precarious, Marxism appears to have fallen victim to the fate it officially forecast for its rivals—it has been swept, apparently, into the "dustbin of history".

Moreover, the major part of the left in advanced capitalist countries and even in much of the Third World appears to have largely shed its historical affiliation with the Marxist tradition. Not only have Marxist revolutionary aspirations been marginalized, even as distant political objectives within most progressive movements, but programs for social reform inspired by Marxist understandings of the social world and Marxist visions of ideal social arrangements no longer shape left political practice.

These transformations, compounded by developments internal to Marxist theory and to the intellectual culture in which it exists, have led many Marxists to turn away from the Marxist tradition or to move "beyond" it. Thus many of those who have remained on the left have

1

gravitated towards one or another form of "post-Marxism".[1] Further-more, among radicals who continue to identify with Marxism, there is no longer any firm consensus on what Marxism is. Of course, there have always been doctrinal divisions among self-identified Marxists. But there was once a common core of theoretical agreement: the labor theory of value provided a critical tool for analyzing capitalism; historical materialism supplied a proper account of epochal historical change; class structure and class struggle were fundamental explanatory concepts. This essential core is now itself contested. Many who identify with the Marxist tradition today reject the labor theory of value, are skeptical of historical materialism's plausibility and regard classes as only one of many determinants of state policies, prevailing ideologies and other traditional Marxist explananda.

This declining intellectual consensus, coincident with the collapse of authoritarian state socialist regimes, has fostered the sense of crisis that has now become pervasive. However, recent years have also witnessed considerable theoretical innovation and progress. We believe that, on balance, the current period is much more a time of theoretical matu-ration than imminent senescence; and that, so far from approaching its natural death, a reconstructed Marxism, less grandiose but also far sounder than any of its ancestors, will emerge from this period of theoretical transformation.

The essays in this book aim to further this process of reconstruction. As such, they occupy a particular historical location. Very generally, they fall within the intellectual current that has come to be known as "analytical Marxism".[2] Analytical Marxism emerged in the 1970s as an

---

1. The term "post-Marxism" has come to designate a theoretical-political posture that sees itself transcending Marxism rather than categorically opposing it. *Post*-Marxists are therefore quite different from many of the *exploitation*-Marxists of the 1950s, who in abandoning Marxism often became militant anti-communist apologists for capitalism. Representative examples of post-Marxist work include, Jean L. Cohen, *Class and Civil Society: the limits of Marxian critical theory* (Amherst: University of Massachusetts Press, 1982); Michael Albert and Robin Hahnel, *Marxism and Socialist Theory* (Boston: South End Press, 1981); Ernesto Laclau and Chantal Mouffe, *Hegemony and Socialist Strategy: towards a radical democratic politics* (London: Verso, 1985).

2. Some representative works within the analytical Marxist theoretical current are: G.A. Cohen, *Karl Marx's Theory of History: a defense* (Princeton, NJ: Princeton University Press, 1978); John Roemer, *A General Theory of Exploitation and Class* (Cambridge, MA: Harvard University Press, 1982); Adam Przeworski, *Capitalism and Social Democracy* (Cambridge: Cambridge University Press, 1985); Erik Olin Wright, *Classes* (London: Verso, 1985); Robert Brenner, "The Agrarian Roots of European Capitalism", in T.H. Aston and C.H.E. Philpon, eds, *The Brenner Debate* (Cambridge: Cambridge University Press, 1985), pp. 213–327; Jon Elster, *Making Sense of Marx* (Cambridge: Cambridge University Press, 1985); Sam Bowles and Herbert Gintis, *Democracy and Capitalism* (New York: Basic Books, 1986); Andrew Levine, *Arguing for*

alternative to the Marxisms that had existed in the West for most of this century. Since the demise of what is now called "the Marxism of the Second International" around the time of the First World War, Marxism as an intellectual tradition existed primarily either as Communist Party orthodoxy or as a heterogeneous mix of tendencies identified as "Western Marxism".[3] Analytical Marxism has developed as a way of furthering what, in Chapter 8, we call the Marxist agenda, while trying to avoid the limitations of both these styles of Marxist theorizing.

Within this current, analytical philosophy, empirical social science and neoclassical economic analysis have been joined with traditional Marxist theoretical and political concerns. As a strategy for reconstructing Marxism, analytical Marxism above all aspires to clarify rigorously foundational concepts and assumptions and the logic of theoretical arguments built on those foundations. Of course, nearly all theorists, and certainly all Marxists, share these aims to some extent. But like analytical philosophers generally, analytical Marxists place these values at the very center of their intellectual project, sometimes to the virtual exclusion of other objectives characteristic of earlier Marxisms. In particular, analytical Marxists are impatient with vague programmatic schemes of an all-encompassing sort and with views that elude precise formulation. As analytical Marxism has emerged as a distinct current, sweeping philosophical pronouncements have given way to more modest but tractable theorizing. Positions have been carefully elaborated, assessed, revised and, in some cases, abandoned. In consequence, many traditional Marxist claims have been shown to be vulnerable or unsustainable, and the theoretical line of demarcation between Marxism

---

Socialism, 2nd edition (London: Verso, 1988) and *The End of the State* (London: Verso, 1987); Richard W. Miller, *Analyzing Marx: morality, power and history* (Princeton, NJ: Princeton University Press, 1984); Joshua Cohen and Joel Rogers, *On Democracy* (London: Penguin, 1983); and Allen Wood, *Karl Marx,* (London: Routledge & Kegan Paul, 1981).

3. We use the term "Western Marxism" in the widely accepted sense introduced by Merleau-Ponty and made more current by Perry Anderson. See Maurice Merleau-Ponty, *Adventures of the Dialectic,* trans. Joseph Bien (Evanston, IL.: Northwestern University Press, 1973), pp. 30–58; and Perry Anderson, *Considerations on Western Marxism* (London: NLB, 1976). Roughly, the term denotes that current of theorizing that runs through the work of Georg Lukács, Karl Korsch, Antonio Gramsci, the "critical theorists" of the Frankfurt School (Adorno, Horkheimer, Marcuse et al.), existentialist Marxists (Sartre, Merleau-Ponty), structuralist Marxists (Althusser, Balibar), and so on. Politically, Western Marxism has opposed the official Marxism of the Soviet Union and the Western European Communist parties—though, in some cases, only implicitly. Philosophically, Western Marxism is shaped in varying ways by "continental" philosophical currents—neo-Hegelianism, above all—and tends to focus programmatically on grand reconstructions of Marxist philosophy.

and some of its traditional rivals has been somewhat blurred. We believe, nevertheless, that the Marxist theoretical project is advanced by this process of clarification, deflation and reconstruction.

Analytical Marxism has its roots in English-speaking intellectual culture, and its content is conditioned by historical circumstances peculiar mainly to North America and Great Britain. There have never been mass political movements identified with Marxism anywhere in the English-speaking world. Philosophers, social scientists and historians who have identified with Marxism within these countries have therefore been less directly involved in significant political events than has been common for Marxists elsewhere. In addition, in the United States particularly, Marxist theory was, for many years, effectively repressed and marginalized. Thus English-speaking Marxism, throughout its history, has existed in much more of a political vacuum than official Communism or Western Marxism in many other parts of the world. To be sure, by the 1970s, pressures supporting the exclusion of Marxist theory from university culture had largely subsided in the United States. But this liberalization only reinforced the "academic", politically disengaged character of Marxist theory in the English-speaking world.

While Marxism in Britain and the United States has been peripheral to the principal Marxist theoretical currents of the twentieth century, it has not been altogether excluded. Great Britain has long had a flourishing tradition of Marxist historical writing, and there have been important Trotskyist and independent Marxist theorists in the United States and elsewhere. Official Communism and every strain of Western Marxist theory have had proponents, and many of the great Western Marxists have lived as refugees or emigrés in English-speaking countries. On balance, though, there has not been a continuing Marxist intellectual tradition, and what did exist was largely extinguished in the period preceding the 1960s. Thus analytical Marxism, in so far as it is rooted in English-speaking culture, represents a new departure, if not quite a fresh start. It is, in the main, a consequence of the New Left movements of the 1960s and their continuations.

For want of an indigenous tradition, it was necessary, at first, for these political movements to *import* Marxism from Western Europe. In the late 1960s and into the 1970s, continental European Marxism had a tremendous impact on radical intellectuals in Britain and the United States. These importations have exhibited a remarkable tenacity. For nearly a decade, Althusserian Marxism in Britain and the United States survived the demise of the Althusserian project in France, and critical theory in the Frankfurt School tradition still flourish among some philosophers, literary scholars and legal theorists.

Some radicals—not all of them Marxists—continue to look to France and Germany for intellectual sustenance. In recent years, however, intellectual life in Europe, particularly in France, has veered even more sharply to the right than has English-speaking intellectual culture, and Marxism has declined even more dramatically as a dynamic theoretical practice. Where Marxism had once been hegemonic in Europe, theoretical work came increasingly under the influence of theorists of culture, language and power (e.g. Foucault and Derrida) who were at odds with Marxist positions. If Marxist intellectuals in the United States and Britain were to contribute to a positive reconstruction of Marxism (rather than simply join in its demolition), it was unlikely that they would find their inspiration in the theoretical fashions that were current in Europe.

By the end of the 1970s, however, there had been nearly fifteen years of intensive theoretical development among British and American radical intellectuals, and an increasing awareness of the limitations not just of Communist orthodoxy, but of Western Marxism too. It was also evident that a substantial body of work had already been produced, owing no clear allegiance to either tendency. It was in this context that some writers who would now be deemed analytical Marxists came to see themselves as proponents of a new intellectual research program.

From the point of view of the Marxist tradition, perhaps the most controversial feature of analytical Marxism is its wholesale embrace of conventional scientific and philosophical norms. Throughout its history, Marxism has had a problematic relation with "science". On the one hand, some Marxists have been expressly hostile to scientific values, viewing science—or at least the positivists' view of science—as a means for ideological domination and an enemy of human emancipation. On the other hand, Marxists who have declared themselves "scientific socialists" and claimed for Marxism the status of a full-fledged "science of society" have often seriously transgressed scientific norms. "Scientific Marxism" has too often masked a rigid ideology in which all the answers were known in advance, a Marxology that canonized the classical texts and isolated central Marxist claims from revision or transformation. Instead of constituting a theoretical apparatus capable of learning new things about the world, self-styled scientific Marxism has often been a closed system of thought that reaffirms itself through selective observation and interpretation. We, like analytical Marxists generally, reject both of these positions.

The view that Marxism should, without embarrassment, subject itself to the conventional standards of social science and analytical philosophy implies a rejection of the thesis that Marxism as a social theory deploys a distinctive methodology that differentiates it radically from "bourgeois social science". Such methodological claims involve a familiar list of contrasts: Marxism is dialectical, historical, materialist, anti-positivist and holist, while bourgeois social theory is undialectical, ahistorical, idealist, positivist and individualist. Some of these specific ideas are addressed in the essays that follow, particularly in Chapters 5 and 6. Analytical Marxists are quite skeptical of the value of such claims, believing them to be generally grounded in obscurantist assertions rather than coherent arguments.[4]

It would be difficult to overestimate the role obscurantism has played in defending claims for Marxism's methodological distinctiveness. Consider, for example, the idea that Marxist theory, in contrast to rival views, is *dialectical*. It is notoriously unclear what this widely repeated claim means. The additional assurance that Marx somehow set the dialectic "on its feet" hardly helps; and neither do the other characterizations that commentators have proffered. Aficionados can, of course, identify and produce dialectical explanations. Arguably, Marx himself did precisely that. Moreover, it does seem that the skillful use of dialectical metaphors can serve worthwhile heuristic purposes. But it is one thing to be fluent in a suggestive idiom, something else to deploy a distinctive methodology.[5]

This is not to say that all of the specific elements traditionally subsumed under the expression "Marxist method" should be rejected out of hand. The point is that in order to be useful, such elements have to be translated into a language of causes, mechanisms and effects, rather than left as elusive philosophical principles. Take the notion of "contradiction", a key element of the purported dialectical method. One way of explicating this concept in conventional causal language is to treat a contradiction as a situation in which there are multiple conditions for the reproduction of a system which cannot all be simultaneously

---

4. Perhaps the strongest statement of this skepticism was made by Jon Elster in the first chapter of his book, *Making Sense of Marx*, where he categorically denounces all such claims to a distinctive Marxist method, which he identifies with the unfortunate influence of Hegelian philosophy on Marx's work.

5. To support this dismissive assessment, it would be necessary to analyze purported examples of dialectical reasoning—an arduous task that is beyond the scope of this work. For now, we will assert that dialectical accounts either restate what could perfectly well be expressed in less esoteric ways, or else they are unintelligible. If there were in fact a distinctive and explanatorily useful dialectical method, it ought by now—after the best efforts of so many for so long—to have become more apparent. That it has not is good (if not conclusive) reason for holding that there is no dialectical method at all. What there is, at best, is a way of organizing and directing thinking at a pre-theoretical level, which, in some cases, facilitates the discovery of insights that can be well expressed in terms consonant with the norms of scientific culture. We take the view propounded by R. Lewontin and R. Levins, in *The Dialectical Biologist* (Cambridge, MA: Harvard University Press, 1985) to exemplify this modest interpretation of the utility of "dialectical thinking".

satisfied. Alternatively, a contradiction can be viewed as a situation in which the unintended consequences of a strategy subvert the accomplishment of its intended goals.[6] Or finally, a contradiction can be viewed as an underlying social antagonism that produces conflicts: if a social relation has certain properties, which have an intrinsic tendency to generate conflict, one might say that the conflict is generated by a contradiction. There may be advantages or disadvantages to each of these formulation. In all of these cases, however, "contradiction" is not treated as a philosophically driven way of interpreting the essence of a process, but as a way of explicating the interactions among a set of causal mechanisms. This kind of translation of an element of Marxist method into a language of causal mechanisms is essential if the explanations generated using the element are to be scientifically intelligible.[7]

One result of freely deploying the intellectual resources of mainstream philosophy and social science is that analytical Marxism tends to blur received understandings of what distinguishes Marxism from "bourgeois" theory. In consequence, the analytical current can serve as a *means for exiting from* as well as a *means for reconstructing* Marxist theory. The strong antipathy to mainstream methodological principles characteristic of much traditional Marxism acted as a kind of cognitive barrier to intellectual cooptation and dilution of radical commitment. Once that barrier is removed, it is much easier gradually to slide away from the core substantive preoccupations and arguments of the Marxist tradition. The Marxism in analytical Marxism is thus more precarious than it was in earlier currents of Marxist thought.

We believe that the risks entailed by this precariousness must be taken if Marxism is to remain a relevant and powerful part of radical intellectual and political culture. In the end, however, the only justification for this orientation is the results it provides. Like other research programs, analytical Marxism cannot be justified a priori. We hope that the essays that follow will provide at least a partial vindication of our stance.

---

6. This is the meaning of contradiction preferred by Jon Elster. See his book, *Logic and Society* (New York: John Wiley, 1978), as well as *Making Sense of Marx*, for discussions of this view of contradiction.

7. The same arguments can be made for the methodological claims of "structuralist" Marxism. Structuralist methodology is either perfectly standard, despite its self-representations, or else wildly implausible, as would be conceded nowadays by many of its former adherents. To defend this claim would also require an arduous analysis of purported structuralist explanations: those of Althusser and his co-thinkers and their disciples throughout the world, particularly in Britain and the United States during the gestation period of the analytical Marxist current. In lieu of the requisite investigation, it is worth noting that, when pressed to elucidate methodological positions, structuralists, like traditional dialecticians, advert to vague and unhelpful metaphors of dubious cogency.

PART I

The Theory of History

Introduction

Any attempt at reconstructing Marxism must contend with the Marxist theory of history—historical materialism. Very few Marxists today would accept the highly deterministic version of historical materialism that dominated the Marxism of the Second International and then the Marxism of the Communist parties established after the Bolshevik Revolution. In the orthodox version of the theory, human history was held to follow a well-defined trajectory of stages, driven by the development of the forces of production (roughly, technological capacity) and their interactions with relations of production (roughly, real property relations). Within that trajectory, capitalism was seen as the highest form of class society, and communism was the culmination of the internal contradictions of capitalism.

While the orthodox theory has relatively few adherents today, historical materialism remains important for two reasons. First, even Marxists who reject the substantive theses of historical materialism derive many of their core concepts from it—among others, forces of production, relations of production and modes of production. Also, the idea that class struggle is crucial to understanding social change is grounded in historical materialist claims. If historical materialism were rejected altogether, these concepts and ideas would lack adequate foundations. Historical materialism also continues to be relevant because its central intuition remains implicit throughout contemporary Marxism: that the epochal sweep of human history is not a random walk, but a coherent structure, which can be made the object of a theory. History is not simply a chain of events strung together; it is characterized by fundamental, underlying tendencies that give social change directionality and make certain kinds of futures more likely than others. The idea that history itself can be the object of theory thus remains alive in the Marxist tradition even though the orthodox account of an inevitable sequencing of epochal stages has been broadly rejected.

Our objective in the chapters on the theory of history that follow is to contribute to the reconstruction of the Marxist theory by clarifying the structure of classical historical materialism and identifying ways in which it might be rendered more plausible. We shall begin, in Chapter 2, by examining and criticizing in some detail the most sustained defense of the classical theory extant: G.A. Cohen's *Karl Marx's Theory of History: a Defense.* Chapter 3 attempts to provide a deeper account of the explanatory agenda of historical materialism by comparing it with another prominent "theory of history", the Darwinian theory of biological evolution. We shall be interested in the sense in which each of these theories is "historical". We shall argue that historical materialism is a much more ambitious historical theory than the theory of evolution; historical materialism attempts to develop a theory of the overall trajectory of human history and not simply to account for the causal processes that explain each change within that trajectory. Chapter 4 then examines a general critique of the very enterprise of a theory of history by focusing on some claims advanced by a prominent non-Marxist social theorist, Anthony Giddens. Finally, in Chapter 5, we shall explore some ways in which the explanatory ambitions of historical materialism might be circumscribed in order to make the theory more plausible while still retaining its essential character and core insights. In the end, we cannot definitively defend the kind of historical materialism we describe. Our considered attitude towards historical materialism is therefore agnostic, though optimistic. The defense of historical materialism depends, ultimately, on the evidence of history; and it is still not sufficiently clear what would be involved in supporting or infirming historical materialist claims. We do hope, however, that what we are able to say on behalf of historical materialism will help clarify an agenda for future work on the problem.

2

Classical Historical Materialism

Although the inauguration of a new theory of history was one of Marx's major theoretical achievements, relatively few of his writings directly address this topic. It is mainly in unpublished texts (for example, *The German Ideology*) and writings not intended for publication (the *Grundrisse*) that we find express attempts to elaborate aspects of the theory. Elsewhere there are mainly intimations.[1] The one explicit and general discussion of historical materialism in Marx's own work occurs in a brief but celebrated passage in the Preface to *The Critique of Political Economy* (1859). Historical materialism, then, was not a principal focus of Marx's theoretical investigations. However, it is implicit in many of his investigations and is, in any case, a fundamental component of Marxist theory.

The 1859 Preface has come to enjoy a certain notoriety among Marxists. Its schematic assertions, while hardly transparent, seem disarmingly simple. In it Marx argues that the overall course of human history can be divided into a series of distinct epochs, each characterized by a distinctive set of relations of ownership and control of productive resources, *social relations of production*. These relations of production explain critical properties of the society's political and ideological institutions, its *superstructure*, and are themselves explained by the level of development of the society's technology and overall organization of the production process, its *forces of production*. What gives history its direction is the causal structure that joins the forces of production, relations of production and the superstructure.

---

1. For discussion of some relevant passages from the Marxian corpus, see G.A. Cohen, *Karl Marx's Theory of History: A Defence* [*KMTH*] (Oxford and Princeton, NJ: Oxford University Press and Princeton University Press, 1978), pp. 142–50.

Because of the simple and deterministic character of its arguments, the 1859 Preface lent itself to easy adoption by the "orthodox" Marxisms of the Second and Third Internationals. In consequence, a brief and elliptical statement of a theory became frozen into dogma, immune from the often facile but sometimes trenchant criticisms leveled against it, and impervious to theoretical elaboration and clarification.

Sympathy for the actual positions advanced in the 1859 Preface, however, goes against the grain of much recent Marxist thought. The cutting edge of twentieth-century Western Marxism, as it has developed in more or less overt opposition to the official Marxism of the Communist parties, has tended to oppose the assertions of the Preface, though express opposition is seldom admitted. Western Marxists, including those most adamantly opposed to the substantive claims of Marx's theory of history, often profess allegiance to "historical materialism", even while they contest its fundamental positions.[2]

The reasons for opposition to historical materialism, or at least to its orthodox formulations, are readily apparent. There is, first of all, its determinist cast, which accords poorly with the general tendency of Western Marxist thought. Western Marxists have focused upon the role of human (individual and collective) agency in social transformation, a theme that, at best, enters at a lower level of abstraction from that at which historical materialism is pitched. There are also more immediately political grounds for opposition. Indisputably, the Preface accords causal primacy (of a sort it does not clearly explain) to the forces over the relations of production, suggesting the kind of "economistic" politics Western Marxists have opposed with virtual unanimity. Marx contended in the Preface, that "no social formation ever perishes before all the productive forces for which there is room in it have developed" and "new, higher relations of production never appear before the material conditions of their existence have matured in the womb of the old society itself". If these claims are right, it would seem that social transformation depends first on developing productive forces, and only then on revolutionizing production relations. Western Marxists, in contrast, have tended to emphasize the transformation of production relations,

---

2. A striking case in point is the work of Louis Althusser and his colleagues. For Althusser, "historical materialism" is expressly endorsed, but the term is used to designate Marxist social science in general. In Althusser's view, historical materialism does not even include a substantive theory of epochal historical change of the sort Marx advanced in the 1859 Preface. This radically redefined "historical materialism" is elaborated extensively by Etienne Balibar, Althusser's principal collaborator, in "The Fundamental Concepts of Historical Materialism", L. Althusser and E. Balibar, *Reading Capital* (London: New Left Books, 1970). On the Althusserians' version of historical materialism, see Andrew Levine, "Althusser's Marxism", *Economy and Society* 10, 3, 1981, pp. 243–83.

according comparatively little importance to the development of productive forces.

A straightforward reading of Marx's injunctions in the Preface would suggest the folly of attempting to build socialism in underdeveloped countries in the absence of successful socialist revolutions in the most advanced capitalist centers. This was in fact the position universally adhered to by the Marxists of the Second International—including, at first, even the Bolsheviks who, in overthrowing bourgeois rule in Europe's most backward capitalist country, sought to spark world revolution by attacking imperialism at its "weakest link". The failure of the revolution elsewhere in Europe, however, complicated efforts to develop a politics—and a political theory—based on the orthodox position. Stalin's notion of "socialism in one country", though literally opposed to what all Marxists believed before the October Revolution, could be interpreted as an attempt to develop a political response to the situation precipitated by the failure of the revolution in Germany and elsewhere. So too was Trotsky's opposing theory of Permanent Revolution. This is not the place to compare the success of these positions in translating the classical Marxist view of the primacy of productive forces into a politics appropriate for the world situation that developed after 1917. The point is just that, for both Stalin and Trotsky, what was crucially important in socialist transformation, and what must therefore have primacy in any socialist politics, are society's productive forces and their development.

The importance of developing productive forces has been emphasized by the Communist parties, as by many others. It inspired a political program wherever Soviet Communism exercised ideological influence, and varying degrees of dissent from Western Marxists outside and sometimes also inside these parties. The list of Soviet sins, committed for the sake of developing productive forces, is well known: the brutal collectivization of agricultural production, the hierarchical structure and "productivist" ideology that governs factories, the selective, technocratic and authoritarian structure of the educational system, the severe centralization of political power and, perhaps most important, the indefinite prolongation of police terror and the inexorable growth of bureaucratic domination. Needless to say, commitment to the theoretical positions of the 1859 Preface does not entail support for the political programs adopted by the leaders of the Soviet Union. In any case, the best Marxist thought in the West, with very few exceptions, has sought to distance itself from the Soviet experience; and therefore, sometimes inadvertently, sometimes deliberately, from the theoretical positions endorsed by Marxian officialdom.

For both theoretical and political reasons, therefore, most Western

Marxists have been hostile to historical materialism, rejecting it outright or abandoning its core theses while retaining a nominal commitment to the label. In this context, G.A. Cohen's seminal *Karl Marx's Theory of History: A Defense* (*KMTH*) was a remarkable achievement. In recent years, a number of writers have investigated the Marxist theory of history.[3] However, Cohen's book was the first to uncover and develop the causal structure of Marx's theory. There are, to be sure, differences between Cohen's position and Marx's—for instance, on the extent to which historical materialism is said to assert an order and necessity for transformations among pre-capitalist economic structures. Cohen's intent was not quite to defend Marx's express views, but to defend what he took to be defensible in Marx's view. In any case, the theory of history presented and defended in *Karl Marx's Theory of History* is nearly Marx's own. With this caution, and in view of its fidelity to orthodox understandings of historical materialism, we shall identify Cohen's with the *orthodox* view, and discuss his clearly elaborated positions, rather than Marx's own diffuse intimations of a systematic theory.

In our view, *Karl Marx's Theory of History* is at least as helpful for revealing flaws in classical historical materialism as for providing a defense of it. But to reflect on the orthodox theory's shortcomings is to begin to reconstruct the Marxist theory of history. We shall therefore launch our engagement with the Marxist theory of history by elaborating and then criticizing Cohen's arguments.

What Historical Materialism Claims

Orthodox historical materialism advances the following two, very general claims:

(1) that the level of development of productive forces in a society explains the set of social relations of production, the "economic structure", of that society; and

(2) that the economic structure of a society, its "economic base", explains that society's legal and political "superstructures" and forms of consciousness.

---

3. See, among others, Melvin Rader, *Marx's Interpretation of History* (Oxford: Oxford University Press, 1979); William H. Shaw, *Marx's Theory of History* (Palo Alto: Stanford University Press, 1979); John McMurtry, *The Structure of Marx's World View* (Princeton, NJ: Princeton University Press, 1978); and Allen Wood, *Karl Marx* (London: Routledge & Kegan Paul, 1981).

Cohen designates (1) the *Primacy Thesis*; (2) can be called the *Base/Superstructure Thesis*. In both cases, Cohen argues, the explanations in question are *functional explanations*. This is a novel, and controversial, way of understanding the causal relations in historical materialism. Marxists in general have been quite hostile to functionalism in sociology and have formally disavowed the use of functional explanations. Nevertheless, Cohen insists that such explanations lie at the heart of Marx's own analysis and provide the only coherent basis for the Primacy Thesis and the Base/Superstructure Thesis.

Functional explanations explain the existence or form of a given phenomenon by virtue of its beneficial effects on something else.[4] Consider, for example, Bronislaw Malinowski's explanation of the existence of magic rituals among the Trobriand Islanders. Such rituals are explained, Malinowski argued, by the fact that they reduce the fear and anxiety elicited by dangerous forms of fishing. The rituals are thus "functional" for creating the necessary psychological states in order for people to engage in fishing under those conditions (given the low level of technology), and their existence is explained by these beneficial effects.[5]

There is much debate in the philosophy of science as to the legitimacy of such functional explanations. They are often viewed as teleological or, at best, as elliptical forms of more conventional causal arguments. We shall not attempt to provide any defense of functional explanations as such in this discussion. We agree with Cohen that functional forms of explanation can be legitimate in social science provided that in principle a mechanism can exist which regulates the functional adaptations. As we shall see later, we believe Cohen's functional arguments for the primacy thesis are not convincing, but we shall not challenge the very enterprise of attempting to construct a functional account.

The heart of Cohen's book, then, is a functional argument about the relationship between the forces and relations of production; he pays much less attention to the parallel problem of the functional explanation of the superstructure by the economic base. Since the dynamic process that accounts for the trajectory of human history lies mainly in the forces/relations argument, we also shall focus on this part of the theory in what follows.

The pivot of Cohen's functional explanation links the level of development of the forces of production to the (functional) effects of the relations of production on the use and subsequent development of the

---

4. See Chapter 7, pp. 155–60, for more detailed discussion of functional explanation.
5. The use of this example to explicate the meaning of functional explanation comes from Arthur Stinchcombe, *Constructing Social Theories* (New York: Harcourt Brace Jovanovich, 1968).

forces. Specifically, Cohen writes, "the production relations are of a kind R at time t because relations of kind R are suitable to the use and development of the productive forces at t, given the level of development of the latter at t."[6] And again: "When relations endure stably, they do so because they promote the development of the forces.... The property of a set of productive forces which explains the nature of the economic structure embracing them is their disposition to develop within a structure of that nature."[7] Cohen's task is to give an account of the interconnection of forces and relations of production that makes this functional explanation defensible.

Cohen elaborates the structure of this functional explanation in terms of what he calls "dispositional facts" about the system. Consider the example of rituals among Trobriand Islanders. Even before the invention of rituals, it was a dispositional fact of the culture that rituals would be fear-reducing. This dispositional fact about the culture, along with some unspecified selection mechanism, is said to explain the presence of ritual:

(1) *dispositional fact*: [Ritual → reduced fear]

(2) *functional explanation*: [Ritual → reduced fear] → Ritual

Now, while it also is a dispositional fact of the society that fear produces ritual, this second dispositional fact does not explain fear. Thus:

(3) *dispositional fact*: [Fear → increased ritual]

(4) *false functional explanation*: [Fear → increased ritual] → fear

The fact that (2) is true while (4) is false implies that while a functional explanation of ritual by fear is correct, a symmetrical functional explanation of fear is not.[8]

Cohen's functional explanation of the relations of production by the forces of production can be represented in terms of dispositional facts.[9]

---

6. Cohen, *KMTH*, 160.

7. Ibid., p. 161. The second passage specifies the functional explanation differently from the first. In the first statement, the functional claim made reference to the effects of the production relations on the "use and development" of the productive forces; in the second statement, reference is only made to development. For reasons which we shall discuss presently, the first formulation is more satisfactory.

8. In Chapter 7, we shall argue that although one can *represent* a functional explanation in terms of dispositional facts and their effects, Cohen's proposal does not provide an adequate *definition* of what it is for something to have the function it does. We believe that the substance of Cohen's argument can be formulated in terms of the former claim.

9. This representation comes from Philippe Van Parijs, "Marxism's central puzzle", in T. Ball and J. Farr, eds, *After Marx* (Cambridge: Cambridge University Press, 1984).

Let PF = productive forces, and PR = production relations. The argument then is:

(1) *dispositional fact*: [PR → use and development of PF]
(2) *functional explanation*: [PR → use and development of PF] → PR
(3) *Primacy thesis*: Level PF → [PR → use and development PF] → PR

That is, the level of development of the forces of production explains which kinds of production relations would further enhance the development of the forces of production, and this (dispositional) fact explains which production relations actually pertain. This is a complex and elegant explanatory structure. Cohen's task is to provide an account of the reasoning that renders it plausible.

The Case for the Primacy Thesis

The case for the Primacy Thesis, in Cohen's reconstruction, can be decomposed into six subsidiary theses. In outline, the argument goes as follows: A given level of development of productive forces is compatible with only a limited range of social relations of production (Thesis 1). Since forces of production tend to develop over time (Thesis 2), the forces eventually reach a level at which they are no longer compatible with existing relations of production (Thesis 3). When such incompatibilities arise, the relations are said to "fetter" the forces of production. Because human beings are somewhat rational (in the sense that they are able to adapt means to ends), and because they face a compelling, transhistorical need to develop the productive forces (as the argument for Thesis 2 maintains), when the forces are fettered by the relations, human beings have an interest in transforming the relations. If they also have the necessary capacities (Thesis 4), they will be able to do so (Thesis 5), and to substitute new relations of production that are optimal for the further development of the productive forces (Thesis 6). In the rest of this section, we elaborate these claims; in the following section, we submit them to critical scrutiny.

(1) *The Compatibility Thesis*: "*A given level of productive power is compatible only with a certain type, or certain types, of economic structure.*"[10] The idea of compatibility between relations and forces of

---

10. *KMTH*, p. 158.

production is introduced in order to demonstrate the existence of reciprocal limits between the forces and relations of production: for a given level of development of productive forces, only certain forms of production relations are possible; for a given form of production relations, only a certain range of development of productive forces is possible. Limits, in this context, mean two different things. First, there is the idea that within a given set of production relations the forces of production can only develop to a certain extent. Beyond that point, further development would be unattainable within those relations. Thus, it might be argued that slavery and computer technology could not coexist, for in a slave society the forces of production would stagnate at a lower stage of development. The limits in this case are limits of material possibility.

The second sense holds that certain combinations of forces and relations of production cannot *stably* coexist. It is this sense of compatibility that Cohen has in mind when he asserts the incompatibility of slavery and computer technology. "Slavery ... could not be the general condition of producers in a society of computer technology, if only because the degree of culture needed in laborers who can work that technology would lead them to revolt successfully against slave status."[11] Cohen does not claim that computers could not emerge under slavery, but rather stresses the social instability of the hypothetical combination, slavery plus computers. It is this sense of reciprocal limits that is most important for historical materialism—for, in the historical materialist scheme, *in*compatibilities always emerge *within* existing production relations.[12]

Why, in general, would forces of production that *can* emerge within a set of relations of production be unable to coexist stably with those relations of production? Cohen does not attempt to answer this question directly. But it is relevant to note that implicitly he deploys two distinct notions of incompatibility: *use-incompatibility* and *development-incompatibility*.[13]

---

11. Ibid. This illustration is crucial for the development of Cohen's argument since he offers no general conceptual defense of the compatibility thesis, but simply affirms its truth through the use of this "obvious" example.

12. The use of the slavery plus computers example as the central illustration of "incompatibility" is somewhat infelicitous in these terms, precisely because, according to Cohen, computers could never emerge within slavery to generate the hypothesized instabilities. More to the point would have been the emergence of certain technologies within feudalism which helped to destabilize feudal property relations.

13. Despite the way Marxists sometimes talk, there is no pure dichotomy between compatible and incompatible combinations of forces and relations of production. Incompatibility is always a matter of *degree*. The greater the degree of incompatibility, the less stable is the coexistence of the forces and relations of production. The incompatibilities Cohen and Marx intend exist when the degree of incompatibility between forces and relations of production is so great that the stability of their interconnection comes into question.

Use-incompatibility is the simplest of these senses. It pertains whenever certain forces of production which can be generated within a set of production relations cannot be used—or effectively used—within those relations. This situation could come about for a variety of reasons. For example, the relations of production might generate obstacles that prevent direct producers from developing the necessary skills for using the forces of production (e.g. because of personal bondage to landlords). If such obstacles exist, then the necessary forms of labor power for deploying these forces of production might not be forthcoming. Eliminating these obstacles, in turn, would threaten the existing relations of production. Or, to take another example, use-incompatibility may occur when the use of particular forces of production within a given set of production relations undermines the capacity of exploiting classes to appropriate surplus from direct producers. Certain forces of production, for example, could enhance the autonomy of direct producers and increase their ability to resist exploitation, thereby rendering the combination of those forces and relations of production unstable. In such cases the use of the forces of production will tend to destabilize the relations of production.

Development-incompatibility is the notion stressed most by Cohen. If there is a material limit to the development of forces of production within a given set of production relations, there will eventually come a point at which those forces can develop no further. This was the first general sense of "limits", discussed above. But why should limits of material possibility for development constitute an *incompatibility* between the *level* of the forces of production attained and the relations of production? The Compatibility Thesis is about compatibilities between levels of the forces of production and forms of production relations. Development-incompatibility would occur when, for whatever reason, stagnation in the development of the forces of production destabilizes the social relations of production. We shall discuss the plausibility of this condition when we consider Thesis 3, the Contradiction Thesis, below.

These two forms of incompatibility of forces and relations of production are not independent of one another. Use-incompatibility, for example, may help explain development-incompatibility in so far as the ineffective use of existing forces of production may contribute to fettering further development of the forces. Nevertheless, since it could happen that certain forces of production are systematically underutilized and yet the forces of production could continue to develop, the two kinds of incompatibility should be considered analytically distinct.

Each of these forms of incompatibility implies a reciprocal set of limits imposed by the forces on the relations and the relations on the forces. Productive forces impose limits on the range of possible relations of production (since only certain relations will be stably reproduced by these forces), and relations of production impose limits on productive forces (since only certain productive forces can be used effectively, developed and exploited within those relations).

According to Cohen, the correspondences between sets of production relations or economic structures and levels of development of productive forces recognized by historical materialism is summarized in Table 2.1.

This table of correspondences is admittedly rough: it fails to distinguish among the various forms of pre-capitalist class societies, and it provides no precise criteria for distinguishing the different levels of productive development. None the less, it does provide an ordered sequence of social forms within an overall historical trajectory. *If* a compelling theory of the movement from one form to another could be produced, we would indeed have a powerful, if coarse-grained, theory of history.

The rationale for the correspondences asserted in Table 2.1 is plain enough. A class, for Marx, is constituted by its relation to other classes in the social process of appropriating an economic surplus. Class relations are thus impossible without some surplus. Hence, the first correspondence in the typology. Whenever a surplus exists, then, class society becomes *possible*. Indeed, on Cohen's account, class society becomes necessary, since it is only under conditions of class domination that a small surplus can be expanded—through "investment" in technological development and in new productive facilities—into a larger surplus. Individual producers would be unwilling to make the necessary sacrifices required for further developing productive forces under such conditions. Thus an exploiting class, which appropriates the economic surplus and uses it, or at least allows it to be used, to spur development, is essential for a rise in the level of development of productive forces given that those forces have already developed sufficiently to produce a

Table 2.1 Correspondence of Forces and Relations of Production*

Form of Economic Structure	Level of Productive Development
1. Pre-class society	No surplus
2. Pre-capitalist class society	Some surplus, but less than
3. Capitalist society	Moderately high surplus, but less than
4. Post-class society	Massive surplus

*This table is modified from Cohen, *Karl Marx's Theory of History*, p. 198.

small surplus. Pre-class society (primitive communism) is therefore incompatible with any level of development of productive forces capable of generating a small surplus. This is the basis for the second correspondence.

A small surplus, in turn, is incompatible with capitalist class relations. Capitalism requires a moderately high surplus (and thus a moderately developed level of the forces of production), in order to allow for "repeated introduction of new productive forces and thus for regular capitalist investment".[14] When a moderately high level of surplus is reached, pre-capitalist relations of production increasingly fetter the further development of productive forces, and therefore come to be superseded by distinctively capitalist social relations. Likewise a moderately high level of development of productive forces is incompatible with post-class society, a society of collective control of the surplus by the direct producers. Since the development of productive forces from moderate to high levels requires great deprivation and toil, the direct producers would never freely impose such sacrifices on themselves. Only a production system dominated by market imperatives, forcing a logic of accumulation on direct producers and owners of means of production, can accomplish this development. This constitutes the basis for the third correspondence.

The compatibility thesis thus maintains, albeit roughly, a systematic relation of correspondence between forces and relations of production. But it does not itself establish the primacy of productive forces. As Cohen writes:

> ... some Marxists who accept the primacy of the forces are content to equate it with the constraints they impose on the production relations. But that is unsatisfactory. For the constraint is symmetrical. If high technology rules out slavery, then slavery rules out high technology. Something must be added to mutual constraint to establish the primacy of the forces.[15]

The development thesis plays this role.

(2) *The Development Thesis: "The productive forces tend to develop throughout history"*.[16] The claim is that there is a *tendency* for forces of production to develop continuously, not that forces of production invariably do develop continuously. Thesis 2 is not falsified, though it is surely infirmed, by historical examples of stagnation and regression.

---

14. Cohen, *KMTH*, p. 198.
15. Ibid., p. 158.
16. Ibid., p. 134.

Likewise, it is corroborated, though not established definitively, by the many historical illustrations that can be adduced in its support.

In Cohen's reconstruction, and arguably also in Marx's view, the Development Thesis is supported by appeal to characteristics of the human condition, human capacities and human nature. These characteristics are conceived transhistorically.[17] Human beings, the argument goes, are at least somewhat rational, and "rational human beings who know how to satisfy compelling wants ... will be disposed to seize and employ the means to satisfaction of those wants."[18] Under conditions of relative scarcity, where few if any wants can be satisfied immediately or without effort, the development of productive forces becomes a "compelling want". Then, in as much as human beings "possess intelligence of a kind and degree which enables them to improve their situation",[19] humans will in fact seize the means for the satisfaction of this compelling want by recurrently and progressively developing the productive forces (assuming, of course, that no countervailing tendencies of greater strength or outside forces—like invasions or natural calamities—intervene). Thus there is a permanent, human impulse to try to improve humanity's abilities to transform nature to realize human wants. In consequence, there is a tendency for productive forces to develop. Furthermore, the development of productive forces will tend to be cumulative. Human beings are sufficiently rational that, having once improved their situation by developing the productive forces they find at hand, they will not revert to less developed forces, except under extraordinary circumstances beyond their control. In short, in virtue of

---

17. Marx is sometimes thought to have opposed transhistorical characterizations of human nature, largely in consequence of some well-known disparaging allusions to the contractarian tradition in some of his early writings, especially the Introduction to the *Critique of Hegel's Philosophy of Right*, and in the opening sentences of the 1857 Introduction to the *Grundrisse*, a text that also serves as the Introduction to *The Critique of Political Economy*, the text whose Preface provides the most direct formulation of historical materialism. In fact, Marx's transhistorical claims partly overlap with some tenets of traditional contractarianism. Probably the clearest account of the human condition and of human nature as conceived in the contractarian tradition is provided by David Hume in *A Treatise of Human Nature*, Book III, part 2, section 2; and *An Enquiry Concerning the Principles of Morals*, section III, part 1. A similar account can be gleaned from Book I, Chapter 13 of Thomas Hobbes's *Leviathan*. Some pertinent features of the situation they describe are relative equality among human beings in the distribution of mental and physical endowments—including the ability to adopt means to ends—and the relative scarcity of most of what nature provides for the satisfaction of human wants. In this tradition too, human nature is deemed to be self-interested—to the extent that individuals generally seek to maximize their distributive shares and to minimize burdensome toil. Marx, on Cohen's account, also appeals to relative scarcity and self-interest, though without claiming that human beings are *always* and *only* self-interested, and to a relatively equally distributed ability to adapt means to ends.

18. Cohen, *MKTH*, p. 152.

19. Ibid.

Figure 2.1 Interconnection of Compatibility Thesis,
Development Thesis and Contradiction Thesis

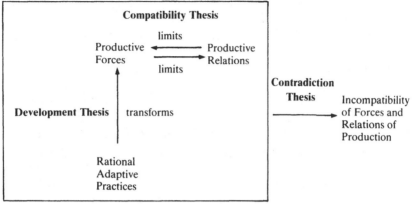

human nature and (rational) capacities, wherever (relative) scarcity prevails, as it always has, there is a tendency for human beings to try to improve their means for transforming nature (in accordance with their wants), and therefore a tendency for productive forces to develop continuously.

The Development Thesis introduces the asymmetry lacking in the Compatibility Thesis. These two together imply a further claim:

(3) *The Contradiction Thesis: Given the reciprocal limits that exist between forces and relations of production (the Compatibility Thesis), and the tendency of the productive forces to develop (the Development Thesis), with sufficient time, the productive forces will develop to a point where they are no longer compatible with the relations of production under which they had previously developed.*[20] The name is apt, if we understand "contradiction" to mean an untenable structural instability. The Contradiction Thesis holds that, as development proceeds, contradictions in this sense are bound to emerge. This thesis is represented in Figure 2.1.

We have already noted that there are two senses of incompatibility implicit in the Compatibility Thesis. In principle, the development of the forces of production could generate either or both of these incompatibilities. In most of Cohen's discussion he places the greatest emphasis on

---

20. In Cohen's words: "Given the constraints, with sufficient development of the forces the old relations are no longer compatible with them" (*KMTH*, p. 158).

development-incompatibility, but of the two forms of incompatibility this seems less likely to generate pervasive social instability, and thus perform the explanatory task it must within historical materialism. Imagine a situation in which development-fettering occurred at a level of development of the forces of production at which the forces and relations of production were still fully use-compatible. That is, further development of the forces of production was blocked, but the existing forces of production could be fully and effectively utilized within those relations. Why should this situation lead to a pervasive instability in the coexistence of those forces and relations of production? Unless people became acutely aware of forgone opportunities for reductions in toil, it seems unlikely that the combination would be at all precarious. In contrast, when use-incompatibility occurs, existing productive resources—not capacities for *future* development—are wasted or at least underdeployed. This is likely to be much more transparent to actors, and therefore use-incompatibilities are more likely to motivate those classes that are hurt by such underutilization of forces of production to try to establish a new articulation of forces and relations of production.

Development-fettering, therefore, seems unlikely, in and of itself, to be the central incompatibility embodied in the "contradiction of forces and relations of production". To the extent that it is implicated in such instabilities it is more likely to be as a symptom than as a driving force. Use-incompatibility between forces and relations of production is likely to contribute to a blockage of development of the forces of production; and the restoration of use-compatibility is likely to open up new possibilities for such development. But the fettering and unfettering of development as such is most plausibly a by-product of use-compatibility, rather than the pivotal incompatibility that explains transformations of the relations of production. This causal sequence is depicted in Figure 2.2.[21]

There is some evidence in Cohen's discussion that in fact, in spite of his emphasis on development-fettering, it is use-incompatibility that does much of the explanatory work. Thus he cites the following passages from Marx in support of the Primacy Thesis:

---

21. Shifting the emphasis in the Primacy Thesis from development-incompatibility to use-incompatibility helps solve a problem Cohen confronts in his analysis of advanced capitalism. Cohen notes that there is no evidence that capitalism blocks the development of the forces of production, but that it does prevent the rational deployment of the forces of production. Thus, at current levels of capitalist development, it should be possible to reduce work-time drastically or to transform alienating labor into meaningful work, but the requirements of capitalist production relations militate against the implementation of these changes. In *KMTH*, Cohen depicts this situation as a "distinctive contradiction" of late capitalism, implying that "fettering" has taken on a new aspect in the present context. We would argue, in contrast, that in all stages of the historical materialist trajectory, it is use-fettering that destabilizes social relations; and that development-fettering, if it occurs, is only a by-product of use-fettering.

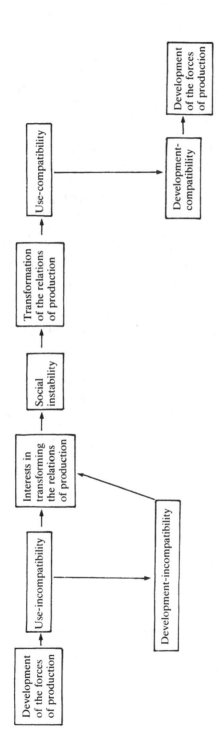

Figure 2.2 Causal Linkage between Development of Forces of Production, Use-incompatibility and Development-incompatibility

As the main thing is not to be deprived of the fruits of civilization, of the *acquired* productive forces, the traditional forms in which they were produced must be smashed.... in order that they may not be deprived *of the result attained,* and forfeit the fruits of civilization, they are obliged from the moment when their mode of intercourse no longer *corresponds to the productive forces acquired,* to change their traditional social forms.[22]

In both passages, the emphasis is on incompatibilities between the use of existing forces of production and existing social relations, not on the future development of the productive forces.[23] If development-fettering occurred *without* use-incompatibility, people would not face the loss of "productive forces acquired" or be "deprived of the fruits of civilization". They would only lose future opportunities. It is hard to imagine a mechanism that could cause this loss to register as an interest compelling epochal social change. Certainly, neither Cohen nor Marx have proposed one. On the other hand, if use-incompatibility occurs, regardless of the status of development-incompatibility, then people face such a loss. If the Primacy Thesis is sound, therefore, it seems likely that it is rooted in the problems of use-compatibility and exploitation-compatibility of the forces and relations of production rather than development-compatibility.

In an essay entitled "Fettering" published a decade after *Karl Marx's Theory of History,* Cohen recognizes that use-fettering is a more plausible basis for predicting transformations of relations of production than is development-fettering.[24] In this essay, however, he proposes a third concept of fettering, "net fettering", which Cohen feels to be superior to both development-fettering and use-fettering. A set of relations of production are said to be "net fettering" of the forces of production when the *growth in the effective use* of forces of production would proceed more rapidly under alternative relations. Net fettering is thus a multiplicative function of the rate of growth of productive power and the degree to which a given level of productive power is effectively deployed. It thus combines aspects of both development-fettering and use-fettering.

---

22. Cohen, *KMTH,* p. 159. The first quotation is from *The Poverty of Philosophy;* the second from a letter of Marx to Annenkov written in 1846.

23. It is worth noting that in some of Cohen's formulations of the Primacy Thesis, use-compatibility figures equally with development-compatibility. Thus Cohen writes: "the production relations are of a kind R at time t because relations of kind R are suitable *to the use* and *development* of the productive forces at t, given the level of development of the latter at t" (*KMTH,* p. 160). In his subsequent discussion, however, use-compatibility is largely displaced by development-compatibility.

24. See G.A. Cohen, *History, Labour and Freedom: themes from Marx* (Oxford: Clarendon Press, 1988), Chapter 6, pp. 109–23.

We are skeptical of the argument that net fettering is more likely to provide solid grounds for the contradiction thesis than is use-fettering. As in the case of development-fettering, for net fettering to constitute a destabilizing force actors must have an understanding of what the future *trajectory* of development of productive forces is likely to be under alternative social systems; in this case, however, the counterfactual describing this alternative trajectory has to be melded with a second counterfactual, the degree to which the future productive forces will be effectively deployed. In contrast, use-fettering involves the cognitively simpler idea that existing productive resources are ineffectively used or wasted under existing social relations whereas they would not be so used under alternative social arrangements. This kind of fettering is much more likely to be implicated in crisis conditions and revolutionary motivations than the complex counterfactuals implied by net fettering.

The Contradiction Thesis asserts the inevitability of intensifying incompatibilities between forces and relations of production. The contradictions that result might in principle be resolved by a downward adaptation of the productive forces, a regression sufficient to restore compatibility. But this resolution is ruled out by the Development Thesis. Thus the contradictions that inevitably occur can be resolved only through a transformation of the relations of production. Such transformations will take place, however, only if there are historical agents capable of producing them. Hence:

(4) *The Capacity Thesis: Where there is an "objective" interest in transforming the relations of production to restore compatibility with the forces of production, the capacity for bringing that change about will ultimately be brought into being.* The Capacity Thesis figures implicitly in the derivation of the Primacy Thesis.[25] The fettering of the forces of production generates "incompatibilities" because fettering is an affront to basic human interests. If production relations are to change, then, it will likely be in consequence of the intentional struggles of actors with an interest in their transformation. But for these struggles to succeed, the actors must have the capacity to realize their interests. Hence the Capacity Thesis.

Class capacities for struggle--the organizational, ideological and material resources available to class agents—are not *identical* with class

---

25. Strictly speaking, the Capacity Thesis may not be required for the Primacy Thesis. It might be possible, for example, to imagine a selection-mechanism that translates interests in transformation into successful transformations in a way that does not involve the capacity of actors to struggle intentionally for their interests. The transformation of production relations could occur entirely "behind the backs" of actors. No one, however, has proposed such a mechanism.

interests in the *outcomes* of struggles. But in the orthodox historical materialist view, where interests in transforming class relations become generalized, as the Contradiction Thesis predicts, the capacities for effecting a transformation will be generated, at least in the long run.

The idea the Capacity Thesis expresses has been most directly defended by Marxists in its application to socialist revolution. For the ascendant working class under capitalism, the emergence of revolutionary, transformative interests helps generate the capacity for revolutionizing society. Workers are able to attract allies because of the universal interests their struggles embody, and the formation of coalitions strengthens the capacities for struggle of all insurgent groups. At the same time, according to the received view, the capacity of the bourgeoisie to forge alliances and mobilize support declines as their class project becomes associated with stagnation and crisis. In addition, under capitalism, development itself enhances the capacities of workers to transform production relations—by bringing workers together into factories, by educating them technically and politically, and by instilling a propensity for discipline and organization of a sort necessary for defeating capitalism definitively. Thus, in the traditional Marxist account, the capacities of the working class are enhanced by capitalist development both because the increasingly universalistic quality of their class interests fosters class alliances and because the development of the forces of production directly enhances their organizational power. If Thesis 4 were to be defended generally, a comparable story would have to be told for each of the epochal historical transformations historical materialism postulates.

(5) *The Transformation Thesis: When forces and relations of production are incompatible (as they will eventually become, so long as class society persists), the relations will change in such a way that compatibility between forces and relations of production will be restored.*

Where contradictions between forces and relations of production emerge, the resolution will always be in favor of the forces, not the relations; it is the relations of production that yield. "Why", Cohen asks, "should the fact that the relations restrict the forces foretell their doom, if not because it is irrational to persist with them given the price in lost opportunity to further inroads against scarcity?"[26] Assuming that the

---

26. Cohen, *KMTH*, p. 152. It is worth noting that Cohen restricts his explanation of the transformation of the relations to the problem of overcoming a development-incompatibility: it is *lost opportunity* rather than *present welfare* that drives social change. But Cohen is mistaken. Since the mechanism by which development is fettered is likely to be the growing use-incompatibility of the forces and relations of production, the motivational base for overturning the relations of production is more likely found in a diminution of present welfare, not in lost opportunities.

people with an interest in transforming the relations have the capacity to do so (Thesis 4), then Thesis 5 follows from Theses 2 and 3 (which follows, in turn, from Theses 1 and 2).

The Transformation Thesis "foretells the doom" of relations of production that fetter productive forces, but by itself it does not predict what new relations will replace the old. It only implies that, whatever these relations are, they will be compatible with the level of development of the productive forces. But historical materialism, in its orthodox version, aims at a more powerful explanation: it aims to account for the actual production relations that replace the ones that have been transformed. For the forces to explain the relations in this sense, we must be able to specify the outcome of the transformations Thesis 5 predicts. Hence:

(6) *The Optimality Thesis. When the relations of production are transformed, they will be replaced by relations of production that are functionally optimal for the use and further development of the productive forces.*

In Cohen's words, "the relations which obtain at a given time are the relations *most suitable* for the forces to develop at that time, given the level they have reached by that time."[27] The rationale for this claim derives from the Development Thesis in conjunction with the Transformation Thesis and the Capacity Thesis. Assuming that the relevant actors have the capacity to transform the relations to accord with their interests, and given that their interest in transforming the relations comes from a rational desire for the effective use of the forces, it would be irrational to replace the old relations with anything short of relations of production that are optimal for the further development of the productive forces. In so far as the capacity to transform the relations implies a capacity to transform them optimally, optimal outcomes will result.

Without the Optimality Thesis, the force of the Primacy Thesis would be reduced, for it would no longer be the case that the level of development of the forces of production would explain (functionally) the actual relations of production, but only the absence of incompatible relations. This is why Cohen insists on the Optimality Thesis vehemently, even in the face of obvious counterexamples. Pre-capitalist class relations, for the most part, can hardly be said to have encouraged the development of productive forces. None the less, Cohen argues, they may have been optimal for their time. "Even a set of relations which is not the means whereby the forces within it develop," Cohen insists, "may be optimal

---

27. Cohen, *KMTH*, p. 171.

for the development of the forces during the period when it obtains."[28]
In this sense, as some commentators have remarked, historical materialism maintains that, in the long run, as compatibilities are established or
restored, the world constituted by forces and relations of production, is
the best of all possible worlds.[29]

It is a tenet of the standard view that capitalism is the optimal and,
therefore, necessary form of economic structure appropriate for the
rapid development of modern industry, and is therefore a prerequisite
for socialism—the first stage of communism, an economic structure
beyond class divisions. This claim, once believed by all Marxists, is of
course opposed to the view that became standard in official Marxist
circles after the October Revolution, according to which development
from a relatively low base is also possible under socialism. Seventy years
after the event, the old orthodoxy again seems on the mark. It is a tenet
of historical materialism that a high level of development, a massive
surplus, is a necessary condition for socialism—not a task to be achieved
under socialism. Classical Marxism therefore opposed "premature"
attempts at socialist construction, and denied the possibility of non-
capitalist roads to the material conditions for communism. It is in this
spirit that Cohen insisted that "premature attempts at revolution, whatever their immediate outcome, will eventuate in a restoration of capitalist society".[30] It would be an exaggeration to claim that the wholesale
embrace of capitalism by Eastern European state socialist societies vin-
dicates the orthodox theory. But the orthodox theory arguably does
predict this eventuality.[31]

With the Optimality Thesis, the case for the Primacy Thesis is
complete. The productive forces functionally explain the relations of
production, since only those relations will persist which optimally
provide for the use and development of the forces. Since the forces of
production have a tendency to develop, and since there are limits to
development within all hitherto existing social relations, eventually the
relations of production become incompatible with the continued use and
development of the forces. When this happens, the relations will be
transformed to restore optimality.

---

28. Ibid.
29. Cf. Joshua Cohen, "Review of *KMTH*", *The Journal of Philosophy* lxxxv, 4
(1983).
30. Cohen, *KMTH*, p. 206.
31. In this respect, it is worth noting a contrast with "bourgeois" accounts of "totalitar-
ianism", in their application to the Soviet Union and other state socialist societies. On that
view, the state and party apparatus was thought sufficiently powerful to prevent capitalist
restoration, except of course in consequence of exogenous assaults on the "political superstructure" such as might arise through defeat in war.

The Case for the Primacy Thesis—Criticized

The Compatibility Thesis

The Compatibility Thesis makes two interconnected claims: (a) that for any given level of development of productive forces there are limits on compatible relations of production; and (b) that for all pre-socialist production relations there is an upper limit beyond which the further development of productive forces generates incompatibilities. We have already suggested that (a) is difficult to fault. So long as we can imagine production relations that would be incompatible with some specified level of development of the forces of production, that claim is sustainable. (b), however, is more problematic. In particular, why must there be a ceiling to the level of development of the forces of production within capitalist production relations? Or, more generally: why can't there be class-based production relations capable of developing productive forces indefinitely?

Orthodox historical materialists would support (b), in the case of capitalism, by invoking the inevitability of progressively more serious accumulation crises under capitalism. According to the view standard in Marxist political economy until recently, a rising organic composition of capital—roughly, a rising capital intensity within production—activates a general tendency for the rate of profit to fall.[32] The decline in the rate of profit creates tendencies towards crisis within capitalist economies for a variety of reasons: a low average rate of profit makes the economy more vulnerable to random shocks; the rate of bankruptcies of firms increases as the rate of profit declines, since more firms will have negative profits; increases in bankruptcies disrupt demand, thus causing otherwise profitable firms to lose money. The recurrence and deepening of these crisis tendencies mean that existing forces of production become chronically underutilized (thus use-incompatibility). Furthermore, since investment in new technologies is paid for out of profits in a capitalist economy, the secular decline in profits will ultimately dampen the development of the

---

32. In standard Marxist accounts, the organic composition of capital, q, is defined as the ratio of constant capital, c, the labor "embodied" in means of production, over the sum of constant and variable capital, v, the capital required to reproduce labor power. Thus $q = c/(c+v)$. In other words, the organic composition of capital is a measure of the extent to which labor is furnished with means of production in the production process. The rate of profit, p, is defined as the ratio of surplus value, s, to total capital outlay. Thus $p = s/(c+v)$. Finally, the rate of surplus value, e (for exploitation), is defined as the ratio of surplus value to variable capital: $e = s/v$. Combining these definitions, it follows that $p = e(1-q)$; and accordingly, that as the value of q, the organic composition of capital, rises, the value of p, the rate of profit, declines. See Paul M. Sweezy, *The Theory of Capitalist Development: Principles of Marxian Political Economy* (New York: Monthly Review Press, 1942).

forces of production (thus development-incompatibility). The declining rate of profit, the argument goes, therefore erodes the capacity for capitalism to use its existing forces of production effectively and to generate advances in the level of development of the forces of production beyond a certain point. Capitalism thereby generates its own fetters.

It is now clear, as most Marxist political economists realize, that this traditional Marxist account of the inevitability of accumulation crises under capitalism cannot be sustained. The claim is empirically unfounded and theoretically defective.[33] Cohen's reconstruction of Marx's theory of history, accordingly, rejects any appeal to the inevitability of capitalist breakdown (as conceived in standard, Marxist political economy).[34] Cohen defends (b) in a way arguably consistent with the spirit of orthodox historical materialism, though plainly at variance with its strict letter.

Cohen argues that capitalism, in promoting production for exchange rather than use, uses techological innovation to expand output, rather than to extend leisure time, where leisure is understood "as release from burdensome toil". Cohen writes:

> As long as production remains subject to the capitalist principle, the output increasing option will tend to be selected and implemented in one way or another ... Now the consequence of the increasing output which capitalism necessarily favors is increasing consumption. Hence the boundless pursuit of consumption goods is a result of a production process oriented to exchange-values rather than consumption-values. It is the Rockefellers who ensure that the Smiths need to keep up with the Jones.[35]

The boundless pursuit of consumer goods generates an incompatibility between forces and relations of production, not because productive power as such is fettered, but because it is irrationally deployed with respect to basic human interests:

> The productive technology of capitalism begets an unparalleled opportunity of lifting the curse of Adam and liberating men from toil, but the production relations of capitalist economic organization prevent the opportunity from

---

33. See Geoff Hodgson, "The Theory of the Falling Rate of Profit", *New Left Review* 84, (March/April 1974); and Ian Steedman, *Marx after Sraffa* (London: New Left Books, 1977), Chapter 9. A more sustained and technical account of these issues can be found in John Roemer, *Analytical Foundations of Marxian Economic Theory* (Cambridge: Cambridge University Press, 1981), Chapters 3–6.

34. In *KMTH* Cohen insists that none of his arguments depends upon any "specifically labor-theoretical account of value"; and in a later essay, "The Labor Theory of Value and the Concept of Exploitation", *Philosophy and Public Affairs* 8, 2 (1979), pp. 338–60, Cohen argues for the incoherence of the labor theory of value, thereby underscoring the independence of his account of historical materialism from traditional Marxian crisis theory.

35. Cf. Cohen, *KMTH*, p. 306.

being seized.... It brings society to the threshold of abundance and locks the door. For the promise of abundance is not an endless flow of goods, but a sufficiency produced with a minimum of unpleasant exertion.[36]

Capitalist production relations become irrational, in Cohen's view, with respect to a general notion of improving the human condition. They therefore do not "fetter" the development of these forces. Nor are capitalist relations incompatible with the full productive utilization of those forces of production.[37] Rather, the fettering in question concerns the irrational deployment of the forces of production, irrational with respect to some general notion of human welfare. Before advanced capitalism, human interests were advanced straightforwardly by augmenting the level of development of the forces of production. In advanced capitalism, where the forces of production are already sufficiently developed to support socialist relations of production, human interests are furthered by the rational deployment of the forces of production that already exist. Under capitalism, therefore, "fettering" is ultimately a matter of impeding the realization of fundamental human interests through the rational use of the productive forces, not blockage *per se* of their development or their productive use.

We agree that this shift in the notion of fettering is justified. The problem, however, is that it undermines the explanatory power of the Compatibility Thesis. The key idea of the Compatibility Thesis is that certain combinations of forces and relations of production cannot stably coexist; and that a society with a sufficiently incompatible combination would be unreproducible. This was the bite of the slavery and computers example. In the case of the consumption bias of capitalism, however, in order for there to be a genuine incompatibility between forces and relations of production, claims need to be made not only about the irrationality of the consumerist preferences engendered by capitalism, but also about the long-term unsustainability of these preferences. While it is not far-fetched to imagine an eventual disenchantment with consumerism in the advanced capitalist countries, we would need a much more elaborate theory of the process of preference formation and transformation than is currently available before we could confidently predict that an erosion of consumerism would be a sufficiently powerful force to create a fundamental instability in capitalism itself. In the absence of such a claim, there is no grounding for the idea that the development of the forces of production within capitalism has an inherent tendency to lead to a system-threatening contradiction between the forces and

---

36. Ibid., pp. 306–7.
37. By "full productive utilization" we mean that there are no underutilized productive capacities, not that capacities are used to meet human needs in a rational way.

relations of production. But without such grounding, it is not clear that the Compatibility Thesis holds for capitalism.

The Development Thesis

We believe (1) that, in general, technical progress has a *cumulative* character, since knowledge gained through technical progress is generally not forgotten; and (2) that throughout history, even if technological progress was rare and uneven, the probability of technological advances was generally greater than the probability of technological regressions. (1) and (2) together justify the claim that there exists a tendency for the forces of production to develop continuously. Thus we think the Development Thesis is broadly plausible.

What is less clear is how *strong* this developmental tendency is. The Development Thesis accomplishes a critical task within Cohen's defense of historical materialism: given the Compatibility Thesis, the Development Thesis provides a basis for believing that eventually incompatibilities between the forces and relations of production will occur. This expectation, however, presupposes that there cannot in the long run be social forces strong enough to block the development of the forces of production permanently, before they reach the point of use- or exploitation-incompatibility with the existing relations of production. The Development Thesis could be true and yet, in certain social structural situations, the tendency for the forces of production to develop in history could still be blocked by some other, more powerful tendency. A "tendency" need not always prevail.[38]

What is at issue is the relative *causal potency* of the forces of production and the superstructure in shaping the relations of production.[39] Neither Marx nor Cohen offers any convincing general reasons why the destabilizing effects on the relations of production caused by the developmental tendency of the forces of production is necessarily more powerful than the stabilizing tendency of the superstructure. But this is, ultimately, what the Primacy Thesis claims.[40] Human rational capacities, intelligence and natural scarcity explain the tendency of the force of production to develop; and development eventually destabilizes the relations of production. But the superstructure stabilizes production

---

38. See Cohen, *KMTH*, p. 135.

39. As we argue in Chapter 7, "causal potency" is always a claim about the relative impact of two causes on the same explanandum, in this case the forces of production and superstructures on the relations of production. It is often impossible to give a precise meaning to the claim that X is a more powerful cause of Y than Y is of X when they both cause each other, since the units of "effect" for X on Y and Y on X are radically heterogeneous.

40. Cf. Chapter 7 below.

relations. In order to conclude that there will be an overall epochal trajectory of social changes of the kind historical materialism postulates, a case must be made that, in general, the tendency for the forces of production to develop is a more potent cause of the destabilization of production relations than the superstructure is of their stabilization. We think this claim is plausible. However, no argument to this effect is provided by Cohen or indeed by any other orthodox treatment of historical materialism.

The Contradiction Thesis

If the developmental tendencies postulated in the Development Thesis are insufficiently strong, there could be class societies in which there are no endogenous tendencies for incompatibilities to develop between forces and relations of production. Or alternatively, incompatibilities might occur, but superstructures might be sufficiently powerful to neutralize them.

Consider the "Asiatic mode of production", mentioned by Marx in the *Grundrisse* and elsewhere, and much discussed by Marxists. If the Asiatic mode of production is a coherent concept with some possible applicability to concrete social formations, we have a counter-example, provided by Marx himself, to the Contradiction Thesis.[41] According to some Marxists, in the Asiatic mode of production the social form of production relations and the attendant form of the state generate a permanent tendency towards stagnation.[42] The productive forces

---

41. It could be the case that even though the development of the forces of production is fettered in the Asiatic mode of production, this fact would not impugn the Contradiction Thesis. The fettering could be due to causal processes distinct from the relations of production. In this case, what would be called into question is the applicability of historical materialism to this specific example, not the cogency of historical materialism's central claims. This rather different account of the implications for historical materialism of the Asiatic mode of production is noted and briefly discussed in Chapter 3. We should note that, for the present purpose, we are agnostic on the viability of the concept. Marx's characterization of Asian societies could well be false. Then these social formations would not constitute, even potentially, counter-examples to historical materialism. We mention the Asiatic mode of production here only to illustrate a gap in the theoretical argument itself, namely that it lacks a persuasive account of the inevitability of contradictions between forces and relations of production.

42. Marx's most direct remarks on the Asiatic and other precapitalist modes of production occur in the *Grundrisse*, and are conveniently collected in Karl Marx, *Pre-Capitalist Economic Formations*, ed. Eric J. Hobsbawm, (New York: International Publishers, 1964). For some discussions of the Asiatic mode of production, see Karl A. Wittfogel, *Oriental Despotism* (New Haven, CT: Yale University Press, 1963), Chapter 9; Wolfram Eberhard, *Conquerors and Rulers: Social Forces in Medieval China* (Leiden: E.E. Brill, 1970); Hélène Carrere d'Encausse and Stuart Schram, *Marxism and Asia* (London: Allen Lane, 1969); Maurice Godelier, "La notion de 'mode de production asiatique'", in CERM, *Sur le "Mode de production asiatique"* (Paris: Editions Sociales, 1969); and Barry Hindess and Paul Q. Hirst, *Pre-Captialist Modes of Production* (London: Routledge & Kegan Paul, 1975).

develop to a point and then stop developing. In the Asiatic mode of production, there is definite development-fettering by the relations of production, but not use-incompatibility. While the relations fetter the further development of the forces there is no contradiction, and thus no endogenous imperative for transformation. Therefore, the Asiatic mode of production can continue indefinitely (accompanied by stagnation of productive forces, not continuous development).

In the Marxist view, imperatives for change are represented as objective class interests. Incompatibilities between forces and relations of production are destabilizing because they generate class interests in transformation. The Contradiction Thesis effectively presupposes the development, within the "womb" of the old society, of a new class, with objective interests in reorganizing the development of the forces of production under its rule. Thus if no revolutionary class is brought into being, there is no endogenous basis for change. This is apparently the situation when the Asiatic mode of production dominates social formations. For example, in classical China, according to the traditional Marxist account, there was no class capable of advancing the level of development of productive forces. For many reasons—among others, the centralization of state power, the pattern of town/countryside relations, the absorption of merchants into the ruling class, and even the technical system of agricultural production—there was no proto-capitalist class, no bourgeoisie. And the peasantry was so fragmented and dispersed into organic peasant communities, having little contact with one another, that it too was unable to function as a revolutionary class, whatever its "objective" interests might have been in eliminating the mandarin ruling class. It was only with the assault of Western capitalism upon the Chinese social structure, an *exogenous* intervention, that the power of the traditional ruling class was finally broken.

Incompatibility leads to contradiction only if there exist class actors capable of becoming bearers of a new social order, an order that would unfetter the forces of production. Whether or not such a new class exists, however, depends upon specific historical forms taken by prevailing social relations of production, and not, as the orthodox view maintains, upon a dynamic invested in the forces of production as such—a dynamic derived, ultimately, from transhistorical human interests and capacities.

It appears, in other words, that orthodox historical materialism takes the transition from feudalism to capitalism in Western Europe as paradigmatic of epochal social transformations generally. In European feudalism, a new ruling class, the bourgeoisie, did develop in the womb of the old society. And this new class was, as the Primacy Thesis requires, interested in and capable of developing productive forces.

Even though there remain considerable debates over the extent to which endogenous developments within feudalism undermined its reproducibility, nevertheless it does constitute a case within which the contradiction thesis has plausibility.[43] It is more problematic, however, to see this thesis as plausible across all possible pre-capitalist forms of production relations.

The Capacity Thesis

The emergence of collective actors with interests in transforming the relations of production under conditions of fettering explains transformation of the relations only if those actors also have a capacity to pursue their interests effectively. The absence of an adequate theory of class capacity constitutes an important weakness of historical materialism, particularly in its applications to capitalist society. Even if the Compatibility Thesis, the Development Thesis and the Contradiction Thesis were correct, progressive transformations of the relations of production would follow only if the Capacity Thesis holds.

Marxists have traditionally held that the working class under capitalism can in principle organize a socialist economy. But does the working class have the capacity actually to overthrow capitalism itself? If it does not yet have this capacity, *must* it eventually develop the means for fulfilling its "historical mission"?

Marx himself was exuberantly, and naively, optimistic in this regard. Cohen, reconstructing Marx's position more than a century later, after so many failed hopes, is more cautious. Still, he does present a general argument in support of the view that class capacities for change follow from class interests in change, that is, from the intensification of

---

43. Many non-Marxists, and some Marxists, have suggested that the imperative to develop the forces of production was not the principal cause for the rise of the bourgeoisie and the emergence of capitalism. Far more crucial, some have argued, were such particularities of European geopolitical conditions as the pattern of town/countryside relations (a quite different pattern from the Chinese), the fragmentation and decentralization of political authority (again, in contrast to the Chinese case), the specific structure of agrarian property within the broadly feudal type of production relations, the discovery of the Americas, accidents of geographical location, and so on. But these and similar factors are either characteristics of the particular social structure of European feudalism or else exogenous factors. They are not reducible to the level of development of the forces of production. For influential Marxist discussions of the transition from feudalism to capitalism that place little stress on the contradiction of forces and relations of production as such, see Perry Anderson, *Lineages of the Absolutist State* (London: New Left Books, 1974); and Immanuel Wallerstein, *The Modern World-System: Capitalist Agriculture and the Origins of the European World-Economy in the Sixteenth Century* (New York and London: Academic Press, 1974). See also T. H. Ashton, ed., *The Brenner Debate: Agrarian Class Structure and Economic Development in Pre-Industrial Europe* (Cambridge: Cambridge University Press, 1985).

contradictions between forces and relations of production. Specifically, he holds that ruling classes blocking the development of productive forces will lose support from outside their class, while ascending classes, capable in principle of liberating the forces of production from the social relations that fetter their further development, will gain allies and support. Capacities arise along with interests, because (rational) people will cast their lot with classes that promise a better future.

Another argument, specific to the development of working-class capacities, is linked to an account of economic crises under capitalism. Cohen writes:

> In our view, Marx was not a breakdown theorist, but he did hold that once capitalism is fully formed, then each crisis it undergoes is worse than its predecessor. But the forces improve across periods which include crises in which they stagnate. Hence they are more powerful just before a given crisis than they were before any earlier one.... Therefore, socialism grows more and more feasible as crises get worse and worse (but not *because* they get worse and worse). There is no economically legislated final breakdown, but what is de facto the last depression occurs when there is a downturn in the cycle *and* the forces are ready to accept a socialist structure *and* the proletariat is sufficiently class conscious and organized.

This third, crucial condition, Cohen notes, "is not entirely independent. The maladies of capitalism and the development of the forces under it stimulate proletarian militancy."[44]

The more general argument—that people will cast their lot with the class that promises a better future—is plausible only if we assume that people generally understand their situation and have reasonable expectations about the consequences for themselves of living under radically different social relations, and, above all, that people can translate their interests into the requisite organizational and material means for implementing them. None of these claims is self-evident.

The more specific argument for the development of working-class capacities confronts less evident difficulties. The claim that socialism becomes increasingly feasible as productive forces grow seems unproblematic. However the claim that crises become ever more intense is far from clear. In virtue of what processes do crises become ever more intense? If, like Cohen, we deny traditional Marxist accounts of capitalist breakdown, what is left to justify the claim of ever intensifying crises? At best, this claim stands in need of further argument. The related claim that the proletariat will become sufficiently class conscious

---

44. Cohen, *KMTH*, pp. 203–4 and p. 204, note 2.

and organized to implement new, socialist relations of production is hardly established by appeal to an "objective" interest in transforming capitalism into socialism. Disillusionment with bourgeois class rule is not sure to lead to the revolutionary formation of the proletariat. Disillusionment is, at most, a necessary condition for revolutionary class consciousness and organization; it is hardly sufficient.

Furthermore, if the inevitability of capitalist breakdown is denied, disillusionment is not even very likely to occur. Were it the case that crisis tendencies inexorably lead to permanent stagnation, the case for the inevitability of the working class becoming capitalism's "gravediggers" would be more plausible. Given ever increasing immiseration and a horizon of deteriorating conditions, revolutionary organization—and a revolutionary will—might be likely to develop, just as Marx, in his more optimistic moments, thought. But if we agree with Cohen that the distinctive contradiction of advanced capitalism is evident not in stagnation and immiseration, but in the irrational deployment of productive resources, then the automatic development of class consciousness seems a good deal less plausible. An increasingly irrational deployment of productive forces will not by itself lead workers to revolutionary opposition to capitalism. In a privatized consumer society of the sort characteristic of advanced capitalism, workers plainly have much more to lose than their chains.

Claims for the inevitable development of working-class capacities arising out of the "fettering" of the forces of production under capitalism are doubly inadequate: first, because class capacities are determined by a variety of factors irreducible to the development of the forces of production, and second, because technological change itself can systematically undermine the capacities for struggle of the working class.

The capacity of the working class to forge effective organizations for struggle depends upon a wide range of economic, political and ideological factors. At the economic level, for example, labor market segmentation and the development of complex job hierarchies and internal labor markets can undermine the unity of the working class, at least with respect to immediate, market-related issues. The economic fragmentation of the working class is further intensified when it coincides with—and reinforces—racial, ethnic and sexual divisions. While there are indeed tendencies favoring the homogenization and degradation of labor of the sort Marx investigated, and while these tendencies may contribute to the growth of working-class capacities, there are also important counter-tendencies promoting differentiation and segmentation that undermine these capacities.

It has been argued that the capitalist state also contributes to the erosion of working-class capacities by disorganizing subordinate classes, undermining the class character of working-class parties and deflecting political programs from revolutionary towards reformist objectives.[45] Finally, on the ideological level, the class capacities of the working class are undermined by mechanisms rooted in capitalist production and distribution itself, as Marx recognized long ago (capital and commodity fetishism); and in the multitude of ideological or broadly cultural institutions that impose individualist and consumerist values—values that militate against the formation of revolutionary class consciousness and contribute to the disorganization of the working class and its integration into the prevailing order.

Needless to say, there are tendencies counteracting each of the debilitating tendencies just noted. But unless it can be shown that the development of the forces of production *necessarily* defeats each of these disorganizing processes (in the long run), there is no reason to hold that the fettering of the forces of production under capitalism—manifest, as Cohen would have it, in their increasingly irrational deployment—will inevitably lead to a growth in the revolutionary capacity of the working class; and therefore to socialism.

It might even be doubted whether the development of the forces of production under capitalism increases the class capacities of the working class at all. While it is likely, as Marx stressed, that the factory system, the distinctively capitalist form of organization of the production process, does improve communications among workers by drawing large numbers of workers together and breaking down (some) forms of craft and skill divisions within the working class, it is also evident that technical change—especially in advanced capitalism—can weaken working-class capacities. The global telecommunications revolution, combined with dramatic improvements in transportation systems, has made it easier for the bourgeoisie to organize production globally—in "world market factories". This phenomenon, so far from bringing workers together, exacerbates national and regional divisions within the working class and isolates technical coordination from direct production. The tendency towards monopolization of technical knowledge within managerial strata closely linked to the bourgeoisie materially and ideologically has undermined the capacity of the direct producers to organize production. These and similar aspects of modern capitalism may not have the debilitating effect on working-class capacities sometimes ascribed to

---

45. See, for example, Nicos Poulantzas, *Political Power and Social Classes* (London: New Left Books, 1973); and Adam Przeworski, "Social Democracy as an Historical Phenomenon", *New Left Review* 122 (1980).

them. But it is clear that there is no unequivocal and automatic connection, even of a tendential character, between technical change and development under capitalism and the growth of working-class capacities for the revolutionary transformation of capitalism into socialism.

What holds for the emergence of working-class capacities under capitalism surely pertains more generally. There is no necessary connection between the development of an objective interest in epochal social change on the part of a class and the development of class capacities for bringing about epochal transformations. An objective interest in moving from one mode of production to another is not sufficient, even in the long run, for revolutionizing modes of production. But if class capacities do not, in the end, derive from the development of productive forces—if class capacities are radically irreducible to class interests—it is unwarranted, finally, to impute to these productive forces the kind of primacy orthodox historical materialism ascribes to them.

Subordinating class capacities for action to class interests in the outcomes of actions is a consequence of the individualist style of argument Marx sometimes lapsed into, despite his many disparaging allusions to contractarians and other "individualists". By abstracting human beings and their interests from the social and historical conditions in which these interests are formed and sustained, orthodox historical materialism (implicitly) maintains that structural conditions for the translation of interests into actions are derived from these interests themselves. However, this claim is almost certainly false. What the best Marxian social science of this century has shown repeatedly is that the major determinants of political action are irreducible, social determinations. Human beings may be generally interested in augmenting the level of development of productive forces, yet thwarted permanently from acting upon that interest. There may be insurmountable social constraints blocking epochal historical change. An abstracted, ahistorical account of human interests and rationality will not, it seems, provide a basis for explaining the historical efficacy of these constraints, nor even for acknowledging their existence.[46]

The Transformation Thesis and The Optimality Thesis

Even if the Capacity Thesis were true, the Transformation and Optimality Theses would be questionable, especially as they apply to the transition to socialism in developed capitalist societies. Suppose that workers do have the capacity to overthrow capitalism and establish socialism.

---

46. In Chapter 6 we argue that these claims are compatible with what is defensible in individualistic stances in social science and with a proper ontology of the social world.

They still might not do so because of the costs of the struggle.[47] Rational actors do not act simply on the basis of the benefits associated with outcomes; they also take the expected costs of the process needed to obtain those outcomes into account. At one point, Cohen acknowledges this problem. In criticizing the view that the vote by workers for bourgeois parties demonstrates that they are captivated by bourgeois ideology, Cohen writes:

> This answer no doubt gives a part of the truth, in exaggerated form. But it is important to realize that it is not the whole truth. For it neglects the costs and difficulties of carrying through a socialist transformation. Workers are not so benighted as to be helpless dupes of bourgeois ideology, nor all so uninformed as to be unaware of the size of the socialist Project. Marxist tradition expects revolution only in crisis, not because then alone will workers realize what burden capitalism puts upon them, but because when the crisis is bad enough the dangers of embarking on a socialist alternative become comparatively tolerable.[48]

This comment, however, is not developed in *Karl Marx's Theory of History*, nor is it integrated into Cohen's account of the "distinctive" contradiction of advanced capitalism. Capitalism might be wasteful and irrational, but still not engender such a deep crisis that the costs of a revolutionary struggle for socialism become "comparatively tolerable".

To focus on the costs borne by individuals who participate in revolutionary upheavals is to raise the ubiquitous "free-rider problem". In general, revolutionary transformations are "public goods" in the sense that their benefits necessarily spill over to (many) individuals regardless of the individuals' contribution to them. Thus, in socialist revolutions, if Marxists are right, the social changes the revolution implements do not just benefit revolutionary militants but virtually everyone not in the ruling class. Then if rationality is identified with a means–ends calculus of costs and benefits, it is hard to see why anyone would ever participate in revolutionary struggles. Everyone would want to be a free-rider. However, this problem vanishes if it is understood that people participate in revolutionary struggles not simply for individual-instrumental reasons, but for expressive reasons too. Class struggles, especially when they take on revolutionary dimensions, are not just means for enhancing one's own distributive share. They are processes that enable people to express values, solidarities, anger and ideological commitments. If people are committed to values that can only be expressed through

---

47. Cf. Adam Przeworski, *Capitalism and Social Democracy* (Cambridge: Cambridge University Press, 1985), Chapter 5.
48. Cohen, *KMTH*, p. 245.

struggle, then it is impossible to be a bystander and still receive "benefits" from the struggle.

It is incumbent on Marxists to produce a proper account of revolutionary motivation. Orthodox historical materialism holds that the fettering of productive capacities explains the inevitable emergence of revolutionary motivations, but neither Cohen nor any other orthodox historical materialist has provided a satisfactory rationale for this claim. It would seem that none can be offered within the strict purview of historical materialism. Except when workers literally have "nothing to lose but their chains", a richer theory of revolutionary motivation than historical materialism provides is needed.

In defense of the orthodox theory, it should be noted that productive forces undoubtedly do play a role in determining the costs of revolutionary struggle. One reason that revolutions have typically followed in the wake of major wars is that wars undermine the repressive capacity of defeated states, and therefore reduce the costs of revolutionary activity. Also the defeat of a state at war is, at least in some cases, linked to the stagnation of its productive forces, relative to those of other states. The problem at hand, however, is not whether the fettering of productive forces has *some* effect on the emergence of revolutionary agents, but whether a general theory of revolutionary agency can be derived directly from an account of the level of development of productive forces and their fettering. We believe that in general it cannot.

In advanced capitalism, even with fettered productive forces, it is not clear why the repressive capacity of the state should decline, why it should lose the loyalty of the police and military in the face of social conflict. It is even less clear why the irrational deployment of productive forces should generate incentives for individuals to risk their lives, or even their standards of living for a period of time, in order to be "lifted from the curse of Adam". Workers may come to believe that socialism would be in their interest, but this does not imply that they will also believe that it is in their interests to suffer the costs of destroying capitalism even when they have the organizational capacity to succeed in this endeavor. Socialist transformations may well be possible. But if they are, it is not simply a consequence of the fettering of the productive forces.

Conclusion

If the criticisms we have raised are correct, then the Primacy Thesis in the form advanced by Cohen cannot be sustained. But this conclusion does not imply a rejection of the importance of technological development in a theory of social change. Technological development is undoubtedly a critical factor for opening up new historical possibilities. Therefore an account of the level and type of development is almost certainly indispensable for conceptualizing possible alternatives to existing social orders.

What we would question is the contention that explanatory primacy, without any qualification whatsoever, should be accorded to the productive forces. At the very least, historical materialism, as Marx sketched it in the 1859 Preface and as Cohen reconstructed it in *Karl Marx's Theory of History*, must be supplemented by a theory of class capacities—or at least an account of the development of working-class capacities under capitalism. In all likelihood, such a theory would have to be based directly on an analysis of social relations of production, the state and ideology—and perhaps also on human interests distinct from the one in which orthodox historical materialism invests the entire dynamic of epochal historical change.[49]

Socialist political strategies must contend directly with the obstacles in the way of developing appropriately revolutionary class capacities: the institutional form of the capitalist state, divisions within the working class and between that class and its potential allies, and mechanisms of ideological domination and deflection. Such obstacles are irreducible to the forces of production. Thus the fettering of these forces in no way ensures the eventual erosion of the obstacles to working-class capacities. A revolutionary theory which sees the building of working-class capacities as an inevitable outcome of technological development, and which fails to grasp the specificity of the role of social structural constraints in the formation of class capacities, will, we think, be incapable of informing revolutionary practice constructively.

Our doubts about the Primacy Thesis, in its orthodox form, do not by any means imply a rejection of the core insights of historical materialism. We believe that the Transformation Thesis, and even the Optimality Thesis, can be incorporated in modified form in a more complex model of historical trajector*ies*. What is needed is the elaboration of a range of possible outcomes, each conditional on the presence of other, relatively independent causal processes. Classical historical materialism charts one normatively salient path of epochal social change, contingent upon the coincident development and fettering of class capacities. But there almost certainly are alternative paths, contingent upon other conditions, within a more open theory of historical trajectories. While we cannot offer such a theory, we shall try to indicate something of its structure in Chapter 5.

---

49. Plausible candidates might include, among others, interests in freedom, community and self-realization.

3

What is Historical about
Historical Materialism?

It is widely held that, in the eighteenth and nineteenth centuries, history came into its own as a proper object of scientific scrutiny, and that the writings of Darwin and Marx were decisive in this regard. To be sure, theories of nature and society had always allowed for change. But before Darwin and Marx the predominant view was that stasis, not change, was the natural state of systems. Darwin and Marx definitively reversed this conception, discovering a primary disposition to change in the nature of the objects they described. For them, stasis remained a theoretical possibility, but one requiring special explanation.

While both Darwinism and Marxism constitute revolutionary breaks with earlier conceptions of natural and human history, and while there are important conceptual affinities joining Darwin's theory of evolution and Marx's theory of history, it has not been sufficiently appreciated how these theories differ—precisely in the sense they count as *historical.* Evolutionary theory and historical materialism exemplify different strategies for making history an object of theoretical investigation. By reflecting on these differences, we can gain some purchase on the kind of theory historical materialism is, and appreciate the very special sense in which Marx did indeed construct an *historical* theory. Marx's theory of history must, of course, be judged by standards that could be applied in principle to any purported explanatory program. However, there are special features of the theory that require identification before a proper assessment can be made. The comparison with evolutionary theory is particularly useful for bringing these special features into focus.

In the next section we shall explain the sense in which the Darwinian theory of evolution constitutes a theory of the *history* of living things. This will be followed by a brief recapitulation of the core arguments of historical materialism. In the following two sections, we shall then compare the characteristic historicity of each theory, first by examining the differences in each theory's core explanandum, and then by examining the structure of each theory's explanations. The chapter will conclude with a discussion of the particularly controversial character of historical materialism's empirical claims.

The Historical Character of Evolutionary Theory

Whenever theories of change are applied to account for particular instances of change, the resulting explanations are, in one transparent sense, *historical.* What are explained are the vicissitudes of some explanandum between two moments of time. In this minimal respect even the physics of billiard balls would count as an historical theory.

It has been thought that evolutionary theory is historical in a stronger sense. David Hull,[1] adapting ideas that Gustav Bergmann advanced concerning psychology,[2] suggests that a theory is historical when "knowledge of the past is *necessary* to predict the future. Knowledge of the present alone will not do." Although this criterion singles out an interesting structural property a theory might have (roughly, the Markov property), it is not satisfied by the standard models that comprise evolutionary theory. In population genetics, for example, the gene and genotype frequencies of a population at a given time, plus the array of evolutionary forces that then impinge on the population, uniquely determine the future state or the probability distribution of possible future states of the population. The past impinges on the future only in so far as it has affected the present.

This leaves open the question of the degree to which possible variation in past history can produce different states in the present. Natural populations are often said to be "historical" for this reason. Dobzhansky showed how a population's response to selection depends on its genetic composition; since different local populations of the *Drosophilia* species he was working with were found to differ genetically, he concluded that the "outcome of such experiments depends upon the geographical origin of the ancestors of the experimental animals".[3] Similarly, Lewontin argued that the present genetic configuration of a population depends

---

1. David Hull, *Philosophy of Biological Science* (Englewood Cliffs, NJ: Prentice-Hall, 1974), p. 83.

2. Gustav Bergmann, *Philosophy of Science* (Madison: University of Wisconsin Press, 1957).

3. In Ronald Munson, ed., *Man and Nature* (New York: Delta Books, 1971), p. 194. Quoted in Hull, *Philosophy of Biological Science*, p. 85.

"not only on the static probability distribution of environments, but *on their historical sequence as well* ... if the historical order in which populations occur is a significant variable in population adaptation, then an element of uniqueness is introduced."[4]

Both Dobzhansky's and Lewontin's arguments show, in effect, which properties of a system need to be included in a theory that thoroughly explains that system's possible changes of state. It would not be difficult to describe non-biological systems that have analogous properties. For example, the present state of a steel ball might depend not just on which forces impinged on it, but on the order in which these forces occurred. If the ball is magnetized before it is passed through an electrical field, the result may be different from what would obtain if the ball were magnetized only afterwards.

It is often thought that evolving populations are much more complicated than the systems treated in billiard ball physics; a large number of parameters need to be taken into account if the trajectory of the system is to be plotted. We do not contest this difference, but think it fails to establish a sense in which evolutionary theory is *historical*—or more historical than billiard ball physics. A dynamical equation with one independent variable and an equation with several do not, in that respect, count as qualitatively different. Both may theorize about change in the same way.

Another sort of proposal has been made concerning what makes evolutionary theory "historical". Morton Beckner held that a theory is historical when it contains an historical concept.[5] He suggests that "hungry" is such a concept, since its application to an organism at one time logically implies something about that organism's past. Strictly speaking, Beckner's example is not quite apt, since "hunger" refers to an organism's physiological state at one time without itself implying anything about its previous history. Even so, Beckner is correct in noting that evolutionary theory deploys historical concepts. "Adaptation" is a case in point, since that term is standardly applied only to traits that arose by a process of natural selection.[6] However, this way of showing

---

4. "Is Nature Probable or Capricious?" *Bioscience* 16 (1966), pp. 25–6; quoted in Hull, ibid., p. 85.

5. Morton Beckner, *The Biological Way of Thought* (Berkeley: University of California Press, 1959).

6. See, for example, George C. Williams, *Adaptation and Natural Selection* (Princeton, NJ: Princeton University Press); Richard Lewontin, "Adaptation", *Scientific American* 239(3) (1978), pp. 156–69; and Stephen J. Gould and Richard C. Lewontin, "The Spandrels of San Marco and the Panglossian Paradigm: A Critique of the Adaptationist Programme", *Proceedings of the Royal Society, London* 205 (1978), pp. 581–98, these last two reprinted in Elliott Sober, ed., *Conceptual Issues in Evolutionary Biology* (Cambridge: Bradford/MIT Press, 1984, pp. 252–70).

that evolutionary theory is, in some non-trivial sense, "historical" is problematic. First, it does not mark off anything special about evolutionary theory. "Acceleration" in classical mechanics would count as an historical concept in just the way "adaptation" does.[7] In addition, as Hull remarks (p. 83), a great many evolutionary concepts are, in fact, ahistorical, and it seems that the process laws the theory provides can be formulated strictly in terms of these ahistorical concepts.

We believe that Darwinian evolutionary theory is *historical* for quite a different reason. In holding that the principal force of evolution is natural selection, Darwin built into the structure of his theory the idea of *direction*. Although Darwin was skeptical of the idea that there is some morphological, physiological or behavioral property that natural selection would always increase, he did think of selection as an improver. That is, he thought that natural selection in a reasonably constant environment would raise the average level of adaptedness or fitness found in a population. In this century, the quantitative theories of Fisher and Wright allow this intuitive idea to be made precise—and also vulnerable—in ways Darwin could not have anticipated.

Evolutionary theory is historical in the same way that thermodynamics is. Suppose you saw a movie in which a chamber is divided in half by a wall, with one side filled with oxygen gas, the other with hydrogen. The wall is then removed and the two gases mix together and become homogeneous. This sequence of events in the film allows you to say whether the film was being shown forwards or backwards. This conclusion is underwritten by the second law of thermodynamics, which implies that entropy is a quantity that (probably) increases in a (closed) system of this sort.

Fitness is to evolutionary theory as entropy is to thermodynamics. It is a quantity that the theory of natural selection predicts will increase under specifiable conditions. This is not to deny that natural selection may be confounded by other evolutionary forces (like drift or mutation), which may prevent this result from occurring. And even when selection is the only force at work, an increase in fitness cannot always be assumed.[8] Yet Fisher was right to call his result the "Fundamental Theorem of Natural Selection".[9] The conditions he describes are simple

---

7. Acceleration involves the comparison of an object's velocity at distinct times. An object's instantaneous acceleration, roughly, is a limit concept wherein the two times are made arbitrarily close together.

8. An increase in fitness is not inevitable if selection is frequency-dependent. See Elliott Sober, *The Nature of Selection: Evolutionary Theory in Philosophical Focus* (Cambridge: Bradford/MIT Press, 1984).

9. In R.A. Fisher, *The Genetical Theory of Natural Selection* (Oxford: Oxford University Press, 1930).

and general enough to show that the theory of natural selection, like the theory of thermodynamics, has a built-in temporal asymmetry. The theory enshrines a difference between the direction from present to future and the direction from present to past. The structure of the theory is *historical* in this non-trivial sense.

Historical Materialism

The principal objective of historical materialism is to discern the causal determinations that govern the structure and direction of historical change. In explaining by discerning causes, historical materialist explanations are unlike explanations proffered by traditional philosophies of history. However, like its predecessors, historical materialism does claim that the changes it aims to account for are developmental in character and have a determinate directionality. In orthodox historical materialism, as discussed in Chapter 2, directionality is an effect of the way economic structures are selected to maximize the rate of development of productive forces. Thus historical materialism is an optimizing theory.[10]

Optimizing theories are familiar in well-established scientific research agendas, including evolutionary theory in biology. Thus the theory of evolution by natural selection describes the process by which animals and plants best adapted to their environment tend to survive. However the fact that a particular trajectory would optimize the ability to adapt to certain conditions does not cause the system to follow that trajectory. Evolutionary theory, like "extremal" theories in physics, construes optimization as a consequence of a causal mechanism that also produces the changes in question. That a given change in gene frequencies increases the ability of living things to adapt does not explain why gene frequencies change. Rather, natural selection has two consequences: evolution—a change in gene frequencies—and, in addition, an increase in the quantity optimized. Thus evolutionary theory does not impute "foresight" to the systems it describes; nor does it maintain that future states of these systems determine present states. In short, it is not a teleological theory in a sense that would compete with standard ways of interpreting causality. Similarly, the fact that historical materialism depicts societies optimizing the rate of development of productive forces does not render

---

10. Cf. Chapter 4. An optimizing mechanism is sufficient for insuring directionality, but not necessary. The existence of "ratchet mechanisms" to prevent backsliding would suffice. Should historical materialism's optimizing claim prove indefensible, therefore, the theory could be modified without altering its distinctive conceptual structure—provided some direction-conferring mechanism is introduced to replace the optimizing mechanism the orthodox theory supposes.

the theory teleological. Historical materialism avoids teleology by deploying a conceptual structure similar, in pertinent respects, to Darwinian evolutionary theory and other well-established optimizing theories.[11]

Historical materialism provides an account of the processes that govern the structure and direction of human history. The theory purports to explain epochal historical divisions (modes of production) and the conditions for their emergence. Then it is claimed, in addition, that these modes of production explain legal and political "superstructures" and even "forms of consciousness" (ideologies). Since our concern is primarily with the dynamic processes the theory postulates, we shall focus on the explanations provided for epochal historical transformations, construed as changes in modes of production or economic structures. The relation of the "economic base" to superstructural and ideological components of social formations matters much less, we shall find, for the explication of what is specifically historical in Marx's theory of history.

As we have seen, Marx held that "forces of production" tend to develop continuously, bringing about discontinuous transformations of "social relations of production". Depending on the level of development of the forces of production, a given type of production relation facilitates or impedes ("fetters") the development of productive forces. When production relations fetter development, forces and relations of production are in a structurally unstable configuration. The structural instability is the material condition for epochal change—for the reorganization of social relations of production into new economic structures.

Orthodox historical materialism postulates a unique sequencing of discrete economic structures corresponding to different levels of development of productive forces—along which, it is claimed, history tends to

---

11. To say that, for historical materialism, societies tend to optimize a particular quantity is not to say that actual societies will in fact be optimal with respect to that quantity. Other forces may interfere. Thus many historical materialists acknowledge the possibility—and even the existence—of economic structures in which agents are prevented from transforming social relations of production, even while production relations fetter the development of productive forces. Within the Marxist tradition, the "Asiatic mode of production" is a case in point. In Chapter 2, this idea was noted as a possible counterexample to the Contradiction Thesis. But assuming the descriptive adequacy of the designation, it could be argued that in social formations where the Asiatic mode of production dominates, a complex of conjunctural features—including, among others, a highly centralized political administration, a characteristic pattern of town–countryside relations, technical requirements of agricultural production, and even religious ideology—combine to impede social transformations that would otherwise optimize the level of development of productive forces. Asiatic societies, according to this understanding, are materially ripe for epochal transformation, but incapable of organizing it. Unless overcome by external forces—for instance, by an expanding capitalism—these social formations are destined for permanent stagnation, not development.

move. Discrete economic structures give rise, moreover, to different forms of class domination, which in turn generate class struggles in and over social relations of production. In the orthodox view, these struggles are inexorable and their outcomes predictable. That class best suited, at a particular level of development of productive forces, for further developing productive forces will ultimately prevail. Thus there is *selection for* that set of production relations that is *optimal* for further developing productive forces.[12] For orthodox historical materialists, then, the *possibility* of change along the depicted trajectory is, in the long run, *sufficient* for the indicated change to occur. Where there is a transhistorical human interest in transforming economic structures to unfetter the forces of production, the requisite class capacities develop and social relations of production will be transformed accordingly. Thus, at the level of abstraction at which it is pitched—where the trajectory of historical epochs, not particular events, is the proper explanandum—orthodox historical materialism is a theory of historical inevitability, of an unavoidable sequence of epochal stages.[13]

As such, the theory is almost certainly untenable, as we have already maintained. But, as we shall see in Chapter 5, historical materialism can dispense with its commitment to historical inevitability, without becoming trivial or losing its distinctive character. For now, it will be convenient to keep the orthodox theory in mind the better to grasp the special characteristics of the kind of theory Marx developed. These features pertain to the more plausible, though less ambitious, historical materialisms we shall also go on to describe.

---

12. However, the orthodox theory does not specify the selection *mechanism*. That is, it has no analogue, strictly speaking, to the way evolutionary theory not only can compute the changes that will occur when selection and other forces act on a population, but also can explain why the ecological circumstances of the population generate a particular array of selection pressures. Historical materialism claims that history has a kind of optimizing property, but says little about the mechanism or mechanisms that make this true. On this issue, see the exchange between Cohen and Jon Elster in *Political Studies* xxviii, 1 (1980).

13. As discussed in Chapter 2, historical materialism construes the connection between forces and relations of production and also between base and superstructure as functional relations. In this way, the theory recognizes reciprocal interactions between the levels it describes. It is not a *unidirectional* causal theory. Nevertheless, it does appear to ascribe causal and also explanatory primacy to forces over relations of production; and also to the economic base over superstructural phenomena. We shall assess these primacy claims, among others, in Chapter 7. However, it should be noted here that even the most orthodox historical materialists acknowledge reciprocal interactions between forces and relations of production, and between base and superstructure. Thus historical materialists never treat the economic base as a mere epiphenomenon of the forces of production, having no causal efficacy in its own right; nor do they treat superstructural phenomena as epiphenomena of the economic base. In other words, according to one legitimate understanding of the often abused expression, historical materialists, even of the most orthodox kind, are not "vulgar Marxists".

The Explananda of Evolutionary Theory and Historical Materialism: Events vs. Trends

Evolutionary biologists and practicing historians usually aim to explain particular events, not major historical trends. Historical materialism, on the other hand, is a theory of trends and patterns of transformation. The explananda of evolutionary biologists and practicing historians are therefore relatively fine-grained. Historical materialists, on the other hand, attempt to explain the relatively coarse-grained properties of the epochal trajectory of social change.

The difference can be made clearer by reflecting again on the contrast between the conceptual apparatus of evolutionary theory and historical materialism, respectively. Contemporary population genetics allows the computation of the evolutionary trajectory of a population (or the probability distribution of possible trajectories) once the values of a specified set of parameters have been determined. Geneticists can then compute the changes in gene frequencies that will occur, given particular evolutionary forces. In this way changes of gene frequencies within populations, fine-grained changes, are explained. However, population genetics says nothing about large-scale changes in life's diversity. Major changes are understood as cumulative effects of small-scale changes. In principle, anything that can happen in evolution can be represented formally. Evolutionary biologists can therefore *describe* major transformations. But evolutionary theory provides no special insight into these changes, and gives no account of their structure or underlying dynamic.

It is easy to see why evolutionary theory has so little to contribute to the understanding of more coarse-grained events. If natural selection is indeed the pre-eminent evolutionary force, change is mainly the result of exogenous, often environmental, factors. Organisms change to track their environments. Selection will then produce small changes in gene frequencies on a timescale of relatively few generations. When this process continues throughout the millions of years during which life has and probably will exist on earth, the outcome is largely indeterminate. In as much as environmental change is itself highly variable in space and time, considerable diversity and very little overall pattern will result. Organisms will be assembled fortuitously and the collection of organisms, the totality of life, will be an accidental hodge-podge.

For standard evolutionary theory, then, the major epochs of natural history are "accidents". In principle, of course, these changes can be explained, given enough information about gene frequencies and the required parameter values. But evolutionary biologists have no distinct explanation for the trajectory of change itself. Darwinism construes epochs—the "Age of Dinosaurs", for example, or the "Age of Mammals"—in the same way that non-Marxian historians regard, say, the emergence of capitalism: as the fortuitous result of an accumulation of small-scale changes.

Practicing historians share the evolutionary biologist's focus on the particular. They too provide fine-grained explanations, depicting more general events or trends as accidental consequences of particular events. But there is a difference. Most historians would deny that any systematic general theory accounts for particular historical explanations. Historians have no analogue to natural selection. In this sense, mainstream historiography is essentially atheoretical in its treatment of patterns of change. Every change can be explained causally, at least in principle; but there is no general principle governing historical change and no systematic joining of particular explanations that bears explanatory interest.

For most historians "history", then, can designate anything in the past. There are no constraints on what counts as an historical event except that it has already occurred, and no constraints on the sorts of explanations historians may provide. Historical explanations and their explananda are irreducibly heterogeneous. To hold that history consists of a motley of past events, explained by any variety of causal or interpretive considerations, however, says nothing about historical materialism's prospects. It may be that there is no general theory of historical processes. But it may also be that the experienced complexity of the texture of history can give way to laws of its underlying dynamic. Neither claim is amenable to a priori proof or confutation. Whether or not history admits of a general theory is an issue to be discovered, not settled by fiat. Should historical materialism or some rival theory of comparable generality prove sustainable, the case against atheoreticism will be made. Meanwhile, the issue remains open.

In any case, the outcome should not matter much for particular historical explanations. Despite what many Marxists suppose, a general theory of history like historical materialism is too coarse-grained to affect explanations of most particular events significantly. Thus history itself might follow a technological imperative, while many particular events are explicable on quite different grounds. Practicing historians, like evolutionary biologists, are, in the main, theorists of fine-grained phenomena. Historical materialists, on the other hand, are only concerned with large-scale trends and epochal transformations. The principles that govern their explananda need not have explanatory resonance for more refined explananda.

These different ways of constructing their explanatory objects—epochal trajectories versus small-scale events—have important implications for the ways historical materialism and Darwinian evolutionary theory periodize history. Historical materialism periodizes history into discrete modes of production, which are conceived as real divisions derived, in principle, from the internal logic of the theory of the historical trajectory. It provides a list of "natural kinds" in much the way that chemistry provides a natural kind division of matter (into the elements represented by the periodic table). The theory of evolution, on the other hand, sees the divisions in the history of life as essentially contingent outcomes derived from an *ex post facto* analysis of the historical record.

Explanations in Evolutionary Theory and Historical Materialism: Endogenous and Exogenous Causal Processes

It is not particularly unusual to claim, as historical materialists do, that history admits of epochal divisions, or even that the periodization historical materialism proposes is explanatory. Concepts of feudalism, capitalism and socialism are widely held to have explanatory force and even to indicate real historical divisions. What is contentious is the claim that it is possible to construct a theory of the inherent tendency for societies to move from one of these forms to another along a predictable path. Unlike chemistry, therefore, historical materialism accounts for the list of forms in its "periodic table" by appeal to an inherent developmental dynamic.[14] Accordingly, historical materialism is a theory not just of possible variations, but of historical change. Historical materialism's distinctive historicity resides in its insistence on this very contentious point.

Historical materialism resembles teleological philosophies of history in conceiving the processes that move history along as endogenous. It is ever-changing relations (of correspondence and non-correspondence) between forces and relations of production that account, in the Marxian view, for modes of production and their sequencing. Historical materialist development is *internal* to systems constituted by forces and relations of production.[15]

---

14. Arguably, cosmology explains, in principle, the emergence—in cosmic history—of the elements the periodic table displays. However this may be, chemistry itself is not a dynamic theory in the sense that historical materialism is.

15. By *endogenous*, we mean internal to the system described. Whatever is not endogenous is, then, *exogenous*. Needless to say, the distinction is theory-relative in the sense that, for instance, it is (Marxian) social theory that tells us that, say, forces of production are endogenous to social systems while climate is not; or (Darwinian) evolutionary theory that tells us that mating systems are endogenous to populations, while, again, climatic change is not. In particular explanations, it may not always be immediately apparent whether or not a causal factor is endogenous to the system described. However, for the present purpose, the distinction is clear enough. In any case, our concern is not with the *identification* of particular factors as endogenous or exogenous, but with the character of the explanations provided by historical materialism and Darwinian evolutionary theory, respectively.

Mainstream historiography acknowledges few, if any, endogenous processes, and in any case assigns them no special explanatory importance. Evolutionary biology does recognize some causal factors internal to evolving populations, for example, random genetic drift and systems of mating. However, from a Darwinian perspective, it is natural selection, not endogenous processes, that determines the trajectory of organismic change. In the Darwinian world-picture, evolutionary change is not, for the most part, internally driven. In so far as natural selection governs biological evolution, evolution is a matter of fitting organisms to their environments.[16]

Historical materialism, in contrast, recognizes *only* endogenous causal factors. The theory provides no way to describe exogenous sources of change. It would therefore count against historical materialism if it turned out that the best explanation for some epochal historical transformation, say, the emergence of capitalism out of feudalism, appeals principally to exogenous causes. Historical materialism—or, more precisely, any historical materialism sufficiently general in scope to cover the transition from feudalism to capitalism—would be mistaken if feudalism turned out to be an inherently stable (though not immutable) economic structure that first became dislodged in Europe in consequence of causes distinct from the social structure of feudal societies— the special geographical situation of Europe, its particular forms of political administration, its characteristic pattern of town/countryside relations, its dominant religious ideology, its fortuitous "discovery" of the Americas, and so on. From an historical materialist point of view, exogenous factors, if actually instrumental in feudalism's demise, are effective only in virtue of feudalism's inherent structural contradictions.[17]

Historical materialism's distinctive historicity consists precisely in the role it accords endogenous processes. Admittedly, one could discern a

---

16. Of course, even the strictest Darwinians acknowledge, in principle, if not in practice, endogenous (biological) *constraints* on the changes that natural selection can produce; cf. Gould and Lewontin, "The Spandrels of San Marco and the Panglossian Paradigm".

17. Care must be taken, however, in determining what would count as contrary evidence to historical materialism. The theory is intended to explain not particular transformations within epochs, but the succession of epochs themselves. Within epochs, exogenous factors—particularly the impact of other societies—can be expected to alter the effects of endogenous development. Thus, in the Marxian view, capitalist societies are expected to extend capitalism by conquest (economic or political), since capitalist societies, in virtue of their "laws of motion", have a tendency to expand until rival, pre-capitalist social formations are brought into the capitalist orbit. Therefore, historical materialism would not predict capitalism to emerge endogenously *everywhere* as the solution to the contradictions of feudalism. In fact, it is unlikely, from a Marxian point of view, that capitalism would anywhere ever emerge endogenously again, once it has emerged endogenously somewhere once. Wherever there is the possibility of physical contact between capitalist and pre-capitalist political economies, the transition to capitalism will be assured through exogenous imposition, not endogenous development.

structure to historical change on the view that, as in evolutionary theory, what prompts transformations in human societies is mainly exogenous to historical systems. It might be, for example, that the direction of human history is explained by changes in climate, or by epidemiological factors, or by any number of other exogenous causes. These causes could effectively divide history into discrete natural kinds. It is even possible to imagine a theoretical warrant for sequencing these natural kind divisions into a determinate trajectory. We need only suppose that the exogenous causes are somehow joined in some kind of systematic temporal sequence. Thus we can imagine, say, a suitably general theory of trajectories of climatological change which could impart to history a predictable trajectory, but not an internally-driven direction in the sense of historical materialist development.

Thus an account of historical change that recognizes only exogenous causes would remain a theory of historical *variation* only, even if these exogenous causes are themselves amenable to the kind of general theory just indicated. For this reason, such an account would be less historical than historical materialism. The dynamic of change would be ascribed to factors *outside* history. Historical materialism, in contrast, though avoiding the objectionable teleology of earlier philosophies of history, conceives change propelled along by an internal necessity. In this respect, unlike accounts of historical change that consider exogenous variables decisive, historical materialism retains the radical historicity of the Hegelian view of history, while at the same time maintaining, unlike its Hegelian predecessor, the explanatory objectives characteristic of modern science.

The idea that evolution is internally driven, though alien to Darwin's outlook, has had its defenders. Lamarck, although he accorded some role to a "force of circumstance", wherein environmental factors could tinker with a species' morphology, physiology and behavior, nevertheless accorded primary importance to a progressive tendency for life to ascend from one stage of development to the next. The ladder of life was foreordained; lineages began by spontaneous generation and then begin the ascent. This developmental theory conceived of evolution as an "unfolding" of a pre-programmed sequence. Darwin's idea of natural selection transformed the way population change is theorized. For Lamarck, populations evolve because the organisms in them *change* in accordance with an internal dynamic. For Darwin, populations evolve because organisms *vary*, and an exogenous process then sifts and winnows. Indeed, natural selection can transform a population even when no organism changes at all.[18]

18. For discussion of Lamarck's theory, see Ernst Mayr's "Lamarck Revisited", in *Evolution and the Diversity of Life* (Cambridge, MA: Harvard University Press, 1975), pp. 444–535. For further analysis of the structural difference between developmental and variational theories of evolution, see Sober, *The Nature of Selection.*

Historical materialism thus not only provides a description of history's structure, accounts for that structure and orders the items of that structure chronologically; it also accounts for that ordering historically, by reference to processes that are endogenous to the very historical systems the theory identifies as its proper domain. In this regard, it is a radically historical theory, different in kind from evolutionary theory and also from rival accounts of historical change which, like evolutionary theory, conceive historical change as the effect of exogenous variables on historical communities.

Conclusion

Both historical materialism and Darwinian evolutionary theory advance two different kinds of hypotheses. First, each offers a general hypothesis about the *existence* of particular mechanisms that generate effects in the world—the "dialectic" of forces and relations of production in historical materialism, natural selection in evolutionary theory. Second, each theory also makes claims about the *primacy* of their respective mechanism for explaining the distinctive explanandum of the theory. These two kinds of hypothesis are often conflated, but they have a certain autonomy, since clearly an existence hypothesis can be valid and yet the associated claim to explanatory primacy may be false.

In evolutionary biology today, there is virtually no controversy over the existence of natural selection as a causally relevant mechanism. What is controversial is the traditional Darwinian claim that natural selection is the most important determinant of evolutionary change. It is uncontroversial that a body of theory provided in population genetics describes the consequences of various evolutionary forces, both singly and in combination. The equations require that one specify the values of relevant parameters like selection coefficients, mutation and migration rates, mating patterns and population size. Once these parameters are specified, the laws predict what the population will do. Debate in evolutionary theory concerns the relative importance these parameters have had in the actual history of life. Has natural selection been the preeminent force of evolution? Has random genetic drift played a significant role? Such controversies take the existence of Darwinian mechanisms for granted, but question their relative explanatory power in a particular empirical experiment: life on earth.

The situation is quite different in historical materialism. What is controversial in historical materialism is not just the hypotheses its proponents advance to explain actual history, but the very claim that historical materialism identifies a causally relevant process. Historical materialism asserts a (possibly counterfactual) claim about the effects on patterns of social change of the interactions of forces and relations of production (a) wherever the conditions under which it has application obtain, and (b) wherever there are no interferences of sufficient force to countervail the effects of historical materialist development. Historical materialists from Marx on, however, have not been content simply to postulate the existence of these endogenous mechanisms; they have also advanced the historical hypothesis that these mechanisms provide the primary explanation for the actual course of the history of human civilization. Of course, historical materialism does not deny that, as a matter of historical fact, exogenous factors—not recognized by the theory—have causal efficacy. But just as Darwinian theory hypothesizes that, as a matter of historical fact, natural selection is overwhelmingly the most important factor accounting for evolutionary change, so historical materialism supposes that, as a matter of fact, the dynamic processes the theory acknowledges actually account for (epochal) historical change. Thus historical materialism favors endogenous over exogenous causes twice over: its general laws acknowledge only endogenous processes, and its associated historical hypothesis asserts that these endogenous processes have played a crucially important role in determining the shape of human history.

Many critics of historical materialism challenge the claim that these mechanisms exist and impart any tendency at all to historical development. This challenge differs from the contention that these mechanisms, as a matter of fact, have not played the pre-eminent role the theory assigns them. What is denied is the claim that human history has any overall directionality, other than the trivial chronological directionality of the sequence of events. The transhistorical endogenous mechanisms postulated by historical materialism to determine the epochal trajectory of human history are not simply overwhelmed by other causal processes. On this view they don't exist and therefore cannot even generate a weak tendency for development.[19]

In the next chapter, we examine a particularly insightful example of this genre of criticism.

---

19. Typically, the evidence used against the existence hypothesis comes from the analysis of the empirical importance of other causes of historical change. Demonstrating the importance of other causes, however, is only evidence against the historical hypothesis that the forces and relations of production are sufficiently powerful causes to explain the overall contours of historical development by themselves. It does not constitute evidence against the existence hypothesis itself. To reject the existence hypothesis it is either necessary to show that some of the internal assumptions of the model are false (e.g. that human beings are not rational in the manner assumed by the hypothesis) or empirically to identify situations in which the conditions postulated by the theory hold, and yet the hypothesized effects are not produced.

Historical Trajectories

Criticisms of historical materialism tend to take two forms: either they are hostile attacks by anti-Marxists intent on demonstrating the falsity, perniciousness or theoretical irrelevance of Marxism, or they are reconstructive critiques from within the Marxist tradition attempting to overcome theoretical weaknesses in order to advance the Marxist project. In these terms, Anthony Giddens's two books, *A Contemporary Critique of Historical Materialism* and *The Nation State and Violence*, are rare works: appreciative critiques by a non-Marxist of the Marxist tradition in social theory.[1] While finding a great deal that is wrong with Marxist assumptions and theoretical claims, Giddens also argues that "Marx's analysis of the mechanisms of capitalist production ... remains the necessary core of any attempt to come to terms with the massive transformations that have swept the world since the eighteenth century."[2] Indeed, in his use of the labor theory of value and his analysis of the capitalist labor process, Giddens is closer than many contemporary Marxists to orthodox Marxism. These books are not wholesale rejections of Marxism, but attempts at a critique in the best sense of the word—a deciphering of the underlying limitations of a social theory in order to appropriate in an alternative framework what is valuable in it. While many of Giddens's arguments against historical materialism are unsatisfactory, his books represent a serious engagement with Marxism. They deserve a serious reading by Marxists and non-Marxists alike.

---

1. Anthony Giddens, *A Contemporary Critique of Historical Materialism* (Berkeley: University of California Press, 1981); and *The Nation State and Violence* (Berkeley: University of California Press, 1985).
2. *A Contemporary Critique*, p. 1.

An Overview of Giddens's Argument

The criticisms elaborated in these books are rooted in Giddens's general theory of social agency and action, or what he terms the theory of "social structuration". We shall not attempt a general assessment and summary of this broader framework. Instead we shall focus on a core theme, prominent in the first of the two books: Giddens's critique of the Marxist account of the forms and development of human societies and his elaboration of an alternative theory of history.

Giddens's argument revolves around three interconnected issues: (1) discovering the right methodological principles for analyzing the interconnectedness of different aspects of society within a social whole or "totality"; (2) determining a strategy for elaborating classificatory typologies of forms of societies; and (3) developing a theory of the movement of societies from one form to another within such a typology. Giddens criticizes what he takes to be the Marxist treatment of each of these issues: *functionalism* in the Marxist analyses of the social totality; economic or class *reductionism* in the typologies of societies rooted in the concept of mode of production; and *evolutionism* in the theory of the transformation of social forms. In place of these alleged errors, Giddens offers the rudiments of his general theory of social structuration: instead of functionalism, social totalities are analyzed as contingently reproduced social systems; instead of class and economic reductionism, forms of society are differentiated on the basis of a multi-dimensional concept of "space–time distanciation"; and instead of evolutionism, transformations of social forms are understood in terms of what Giddens calls "episodic transitions". These critiques and alternatives are summarized in Table 4.1.

Table 4.1 Summary of Giddens's Critique of Historical Materialism

	Central Marxist Concept	Giddens's Critique	Giddens's Alternative
1. Logic of interconnection of social whole	Functional totality	Functionalism	Contingently reproduced social system
2. Typology of social forms	Mode of production	Class and economic reductionism	Level of space–time distanciation
3. Logic of transformation	Dialectic of forces and relations of production	Evolutionism	Episodic transitions

Functionalism and the Social Totality

Giddens correctly observes that much Marxist social science relies expressly or covertly on functional explanations. He then criticizes functional explanations on a variety of grounds: for presupposing a false division between statics and dynamics; for suggesting that human actors are only agents of social relations and, most importantly, for falsely imputing "needs" to social systems. Giddens illustrates these points in a brief discussion of Marx's theory of the reserve army of labor:

> Marx's analysis can be interpreted, and often has been so interpreted, in a functionalist vein. Capitalism has its own "needs", which the system functions to fulfill. Since capitalism needs a "reserve army", one comes into being. The proposition is sometimes stated in reverse. Since the operation of capitalism leads to the formation of a reserve army, this must be because it needs one. But neither version explains anything about why a reserve army of unemployed workers exists. Not even the most deeply sedimented institutional features of societies come about, persist, or disappear, because those societies need them to do so. They come about *historically*, as a result of concrete conditions that have in every case to be analyzed; the same holds for their persistence or their dissolution.[3]

The only way that functional arguments can be legitimately employed in social science, according to Giddens, is when they are treated *counterfactually*: "we can quite legitimately pose conjectural questions such as 'What would have to be the case for social system X to come about, persist or be transformed?'"[4] But stating conditions of existence does not explain anything. Doing so merely indicates what needs to be explained.

Giddens is, we believe, substantially correct in his description of functionalist tendencies within Marxism and in his critique of these tendencies. Social reproduction, whenever it occurs, is not an automatically guaranteed process, but a phenomenon that calls for an explanation. While in some cases functional *descriptions* may be heuristically useful, they always raise questions of mechanism that must be addressed.

Nevertheless Giddens's critique of Marxian functionalism is in certain respects misleading. First, Giddens writes as if Marxists have ignored this problem. In fact, a number of debates among Marxists in the 1970s and 1980s focused precisely on functional explanations. It was a key issue in discussions of the work of Louis Althusser and other "structuralist" Marxists. As noted in Chapter 2, it has also played a central role

---

3. Ibid., p. 18.
4. Ibid., p. 19.

in "analytical" discussions of historical materialism.[5] Second, while Giddens is right to indict easy transitions from functional descriptions to functional explanations, he is wrong to dismiss functional explanations altogether. The functionality of a given institution or practice is never a complete explanation of that phenomenon, but it can surely constitute part of a proper explanation.

Consider the problem of racism. Marxists often attempt to explain racial domination in terms of its consequences for working-class disunity (divide and conquer). This is a functional explanation in the sense that the phenomenon, racism, is explained by its beneficial effects for capitalism. But it is clearly an incomplete explanation, if only because the fact that an effect would be beneficial does not guarantee that it will be produced. A docile and happy working class would be beneficial for capitalism too, but this fact hardly assures that workers will be happy and docile. Nevertheless, it could be argued that in the absence of its beneficial effects, racism would disappear *much more easily*. If this is the case, then the effects of racism would play a critical role in explaining racism's persistence. Giddens, we imagine, would accept this point, but still insist that it does not imply the legitimacy of functional explanations in social science. If the effects of racism are beneficial to capital*ism*, this helps explain its persistence only because the *actions* of capital*ists* support racism. The explanation, then, would be based on an analysis of the consciousness of actors and their associated strategies of action, not on the functional relation as such.

However, the fact that racism will actually have these beneficial effects is not a property of the consciousness of capitalists, but of the social system within which they form their beliefs. It is, to use Cohen's formulation, a "dispositional fact" of the social system. Similar situations pertain throughout biology. Thus, to use one of Cohen's examples, giraffes have long necks in consequence of natural selection for genes that produce long necks. But unless it had been a dispositional fact that longer necks would be beneficial for giraffes, natural selection would not have worked in the way it did. Similarly, unless it were a dispositional fact about a society that racism would produce the effects it does, what

---

5. It is striking that Giddens's books completely ignore *KMTH*, and the debate over the role of functional explanations in Marxism that it inspired. In this context, Jon Elster has been a particularly ardent critic of functional explanations. See, among others, "Cohen on Marx's Theory of History", *Political Studies* XXVIII:1 (March 1980), pp. 121–8, "Marxism, Functionalism and Game Theory", *Theory and Society* 11 (1982), pp. 453–82; and *Making Sense of Marx* (Cambridge: Cambridge University Press, 1985), Chapter 1. See also G.A. Cohen, "Functional Explanation, Consequence Explanation and Marxism", *Inquiry* 25 (1982), pp. 27–56; and "Reply to Elster, 'Marxism, Functionalism and Game Theory'", *Theory and Society* 11 (1982), pp. 483–96.

capitalists do, intentionally or not, to encourage racial divisions would produce different outcomes from their actual consequences.

This causal structure can be represented as follows:

(1) *Dispositional fact*: (Racism → divides workers)
(2) *Functional explanation*: (Racism → divides workers) → Racism

If elites *believed* that racism divides workers, this would constitute a crucial mechanism linking (1) and (2) that explains (in part) how racism becomes an institutional arrangement:

(3) *Functional explanation with intentional mechanism*: (Racism → divides workers) → Beliefs by elites that racism divides workers → Racism-enhancing practices → Racism

To be sure, the beliefs and practices of elites are important in this explanation. But the explanation of the outcome cannot be reduced to these beliefs and practices; the underlying functional relations are also important.

Dispositional facts are real properties of social systems. Thus they can legitimately figure in causal explanations of social processes and outcomes. It is, of course, difficult to defend claims about dispositional facts empirically. Arguments in support of such claims often rely on counterfactual analyses as Giddens suggests. But this does not imply that these analyses are only heuristic exercises, which point the way towards explanatory questions; claims about dispositional properties of social systems also figure in many answers.[6]

Some of Giddens's own arguments can be reconstructed as functional explanations based on dispositional facts about particular kinds of societies. Consider, for example, Giddens's account of the association between "nationalism" and the nation-state. How should we explain the fact that nationalism plays such a prominent role in modern states? Giddens argues as follows:

> With the coming of the nation-state, states have an administrative and territorially ordered unity which they did not possess before. This unity cannot remain *purely* administrative however, because the very coordination of activities involved presumes elements of cultural homogeneity. The extension of communication cannot occur without the "conceptual" involvement of the whole community of knowledgeable citizenry.... The sharing of a common

6. In Chapter 7, we shall develop an objection to Cohen's analysis of functional claims, but this will not undermine the present point.

language and a common symbolic historicity are the most thorough-going
ways of achieving this (and are seen to be so by those leaders who have
learned from the experience of the first "nations").[7]

According to Giddens, modern nation-states face a problem of social
reproduction. Nationalism, a common symbolic historicity, is the pre-
eminent solution. It is a dispositional fact about nation-states that
nationalism will contribute to social reproduction. Through a process of
historical learning, leaders come to understand this fact. Eventually, the
functional solution becomes generalized.

It is implausible that nationalism would become a general ideological
feature of nation-states if political actors did not recognize its cohesion-
producing effects, and encourage it deliberately. It might therefore be
argued that Giddens has not produced a functional explanation, after
all, because intentionality plays a role in the feedback mechanism that
establishes the functional outcome. Elster has stipulated this point in the
course of arguing that functional explanations seldom figure in sound
social scientific explanations.[8] For Elster, and perhaps for Giddens too,
if nationalism is intentionally encouraged, it is explained by the intentions of political actors, not by any supposed functional relation.
However, what is distinctive about this explanation is precisely its
dependence on a functional relation. If Giddens's analysis is right,
nationalism cannot *simply* be explained in terms of the intentions of
political leaders: those intentions are themselves formed within a set of
causal processes where particular functional effects are produced. The
fact that the actors recognize this causal relation and consciously take
steps to sustain the effects it produces does not imply that the causal
process is reducible to their intentions. We therefore reject Elster's
suggestion, implicit in Giddens's rejection of functionalism, that in a
proper functional explanation, the feedback mechanisms must remain
unknown to the human actors involved.

It is worth noting that even Elster would not banish functional
explanations altogether. Even if we adopt his very restrictive understanding of "functional explanation", and exclude accounts where
intentionality plays some role, there would remain situations in which
functional explanations would still be appropriate. Elster gives an
example in his discussion of the profit-maximizing strategies of capitalist
firms.[9] He argues that it is appropriate to answer the question, "why do

---

7. *The Nation State and Violence*, p. 219.
8. Cf. *Ulysses and the Sirens: Studies in Rationality and Irrationality* (Cambridge and
Paris: Cambridge University Press and Edition de la Maison des Sciences de l'Homme,
1979), Chapter 1.
9. Ibid., p. 31.

capitalist firms adopt on average profit-maximizing strategies?" with a functional explanation. The market acts as a selection mechanism that eliminates firms that adopt sub-optimal strategies. Therefore only firms that adopt profit-maximizing strategies will survive. Even if decision-making procedures within firms operate on "rough-and-ready rules of thumb", only those rules that happen to maximize profits will survive over time. The end-result, therefore, will be a distribution of strategies among firms that are generally functional for the reproduction of those firms, even though such a distribution was not intended by any actor within the system. Of course, it may happen that some capitalists consciously attempt to adopt profit-maximizing strategies. Elster's point is that we need not assume that they do in order to understand how the functional outcome is possible. Conscious profit-maximization may improve the efficiency of the selection mechanism, but the functional relationship is itself structurally ensured by the market.

To be sure, relatively few social processes have the properties of firms acting in competitive markets. Thus it is generally not the case that functional outcomes can result without any conscious intervention whatsoever. Functional explanations unconnected to intentional explanations are usually unsatisfactory precisely because no plausible mechanism for achieving functional outcomes can be found. Giddens is therefore justified in his suspicions of disembodied functional explanations. But his categorical rejection of functional arguments within social explanations is unwarranted.

Typologies of Social Forms

Marxists employ a distinctive strategy for classifying societies. They base their typologies of social forms on the concept of class structure. Class structure is itself based on the concept of the mode of production. While there are substantial disagreements over how the latter concept should be defined and precisely how class structures should be distinguished, there is general agreement among Marxists that these concepts provide the central principle both for differentiating types of societies and for providing a road map of the historical trajectory of societal transformations. Even where Marxists concede the autonomy of relations of domination distinct from class (e.g. ethnic, gender or national domination), they nevertheless characterize the overall form of society in terms of its class structure.

Much of *A Contemporary Critique* is devoted to challenging this principle of social typology. The accusation that historical materialism is an economic or class reductionist theory is, of course, a standard criticism. What is unusual about Giddens's position is that he rejects class-based typologies of societies without challenging the importance of class analysis in general.

Giddens raises the critique of reductionism in two contexts: first, he insists that only in capitalism can class be viewed as the central structural principle of the society as a whole. Therefore, in general, class structure provides an inadequate basis for specifying the differences between social forms. Second, he argues that societies are characterized by multiple forms of domination and exploitation which cannot be reduced to a single principle, class. The first of these claims serves as a basis for a critique of *inter*societal class reductionism, the second for a critique of *intra*societal class reductionism.

Intersocietal Class Reductionism

Societies should not be classified primarily in terms of their class structures, Giddens argues, because only in capitalism does class constitute society's basic structural principle. Only in capitalism does class permeate all aspects of social life. While non-capitalist societies may have had classes, class relations did not constitute their core principle of social organization. This argument forms the basis for a distinction Giddens makes between *class society* (a society within which class is the central structural principle) and *class-divided society* ("a society in which there are classes, but where class analysis does not serve as a basis for identifying the basic structural principle of organization of that society").[10]

Giddens's defense of this position revolves around his analysis of *power* and *domination*. Power, in Giddens's theory of "social structuration" is a subcategory of transformative capacity, in which "transformative capacity is *harnessed to actors' attempts to get others to comply with their wants.* Power, in this relational sense, concerns the capacity of actors to secure outcomes where the realization of these outcomes depends upon the agency of others."[11] This relational transformative capacity rests on resources used to get others to comply. In particular, Giddens distinguishes between *allocative* resources (resources involving control over nature) and *authoritative* resources (resources involving control over social interactions of various sorts). *Domination* is then defined as "structured asymmetries of resources drawn upon and reconstituted in such power relations".[12]

---

10. *A Contemporary Critique*, p. 108.
11. Giddens, *Central Problems in Social Theory* (Berkeley, University of California Press, 1979), p. 93. Italics in the original.
12. *A Contemporary Critique*, p. 50.

On the basis of these concepts of power and domination, societies can be classified along two principal dimensions:

(1) *The type of resource domination, allocative or authoritative, more important for sustaining power relations.* Giddens argues that it is only in capitalism that control over allocative resources *per se* is of prime importance. In all non-capitalist societies "authoritative resources were the main basis of both political and economic power".[13]

(2) *The magnitude of control over each of these resources in time and space.* This notion is the core of Giddens's complex concept of "space–time distanciation". The control over any resource can be specified in terms of its extension over time and space. This idea is easiest to understand if we focus on allocative resources. Hunting and gathering societies involve rather limited control over allocative resources in both time and space: food is acquired more or less continuously and with relatively short time-horizons, and trade over long distances (spatial extension of allocative resources) is very limited. On both of these counts, settled agriculture involves greater space–time "distanciation". Industrial capitalism, of course, extends such distanciation to historically unprecedented levels: production is organized globally and allocative time-horizons extend over decades in some cases. In terms of authoritative resources, the principal basis for the extension over time and space is the increasing capacity of a society for *surveillance*, i.e. for gathering and storing information and for supervising subordinate groups. The institutional sites for the extension of authoritative resources in time and space are initially the city and subsequently the state.

Taking these two dimensions together produces the general typology of societal forms in Table 4.2. This typology differs from the Marxist typology of modes of production. But are the two really incompatible? Giddens believes that they are. Nevertheless, the clash may be not as great as Giddens imagines.

The central qualitative break in Giddens's typology occurs between capitalism and all non-capitalist societies. Only in capitalism are allocative resources the central basis of power. Thus only in capitalism can class be viewed as the organizing principle of society. This claim appears to run counter to the Marxist thesis that class structures (or modes of production) are the basic structural principle of all societies. On closer inspection, however, the difference virtually disappears.

13. Ibid., p. 108.

Table 4.2 Giddens's Typology of Social Forms

		Type of resource which is the primary basis of power	
		Authoritative	Allocative
Level of space–time distanciation	Low	Pre-class societies	
	Medium	Class-divided societies	
	High	Socialist societies	Capitalist societies

First, we might ask: *why* is it that in non-capitalist societies authoritative resources are the basis of power, while in capitalist societies power is based on control of allocative resources? One could say that the question is illegitimate. The authoritative/allocative resource distinction could be viewed as a strictly taxonomic criterion for specifying different types of societies. Then there would be no meaningful answer to the question. Giddens, however, does not reject the question. In fact, when he attempts to explain the differences between the two types of societies, he emphasizes the causal importance of their respective economic structures: the role of agrarian production, the degree of economic autonomy of communities, the existence of free wage labor, the alienability of different forms of property, etc.[14]. While Giddens clearly emphasizes non-economic factors in his explanations of the *genesis* of capitalism (e.g. the specificity of the European state system), he argues that it is the distinctive property relations of capitalism that explain why class becomes such a central organizing principle of capitalist societies.[15] Such an explanation, however, is symmetrical: the distinctive property relations of feudal society (in contrast to capitalism) explain why in feudalism the control of authoritative resources is the central axis of power. To state our contention more generally: throughout Giddens's analysis, it is *variations* in the nature of property relations that explain *variations* in the relative centrality of control over allocative or authoritative resources in societies.

---

14. See, for example, ibid., pp. 114–15; *The Nation State and Violence*, pp. 70–1.

15. Classical Marxism, of course, sees class as central both to the problem of historical trajectories and to the problem of social structure. Thus, "class struggle is the motor of history" is as important a formula as "class structures constitute the base of society". Giddens consistently rejects the dynamic role attributed to class struggles in Marxism. But, contrary to his express declarations, it is not clear that he rejects Marxist claims for the centrality of class structures in the explanation of variations across societies.

Giddens's position actually resembles Marx's claim in *Capital* that the economy is "determinant" even if, in some pre-capitalist economic structures, other aspects of society are "dominant":

> My view is that each particular mode of production, and the social relations of production corresponding to it at each given moment, in short the economic structure of society ... conditions the general process of social, political and intellectual life. In the opinion of the German-American publication this is all very true for our own times, in which material interests are preponderant, but not for the Middle Ages, dominated by Catholicism, nor for Athens and Rome, dominated by politics.... One thing is clear: the Middle Ages could not live on Catholicism, nor could the ancient world on politics. On the contrary, it is the manner in which they gained their livelihood which explains why in one case politics, in the other Catholicism, played the chief part."[16]

This idea is also at the heart of Althusser's notion of society as a "structured totality" within which the economic structure determines which aspect ("instance" or "level") of the society is "dominant". To be sure, Giddens emphatically, and we think correctly, rejects the functionalist assumptions underlying Althusser's position. Nevertheless, when he tries to explain the differences in the relationship between allocative and authoritative resources in capitalist and non-capitalist societies, he adverts to just those considerations Marx and Althusser relied upon.

A second reason why Giddens's position is not as distant from Marxist formulations as he claims centers on the concept of class. Giddens narrowly ties class to "sectional forms of domination created by private ownership of property", where "ownership" means direct control over the use and disposition of means of production, and "private" designates legally guaranteed rights over those means of production. When a group of individuals appropriates surplus coercively, without actually owning the means of production privately, the appropriation is treated by Giddens as a consequence of control over authoritative resources, not allocative resources. Perhaps the appropriators control military personnel and are therefore able to extract a surplus. Class divisions still *result* from such appropriations, since the process produces differential access to allocative resources. The system of appropriation

---

16. *Capital*, vol. I (London: Penguin Books, 1976), pp. 175–6. Marx's reasoning is quite elliptical. The fact that feudal society could not "live on" Catholicism does not show why the mode of production has explanatory primacy. Giddens's analyses of how particular forms of social conflict and power relations are conditioned by particular forms of property relations provides a more refined analysis. His arguments, however, do not contravene Marx's point that it is fundamentally *differences* in property relations—class relations/ economic structures—which explain the broader structural *differences* between capitalist and feudal society.

divides individuals into social categories—perhaps even into groups of rich and poor. But the *basis* for the appropriation is not the class structure, but the structure of authoritative domination. Feudal exploiting classes, therefore, are not classes directly in virtue of property relations, but in virtue of the secondary effects of the redistributive mechanisms of feudal authoritative power. It is for this reason that Giddens maintains that feudal societies are class-divided but not strictly class societies.

This formulation depends, of course, on Giddens's definition of "class". Many Marxists define classes in terms of the mechanisms by which surplus products or surplus labor is appropriated, not by property relations as such.[17] But the appropriation of an economic surplus always involves combinations of economic and political mechanisms or, as Giddens would have it, relations to allocative and authoritative resources. In feudal societies this mechanism involves the direct use of extra economic coercion; in capitalist societies the political face of class relations is restricted to the guarantee of contracts, the protection of property rights and supervision of the labor process. In both kinds of societies, however, it is mechanisms of surplus extraction that specify the character of class relations.

Thus the disagreement between Giddens and Marxism is at least partly terminological. Many Marxists draw the same descriptive contrast that Giddens does between the economic mechanisms of class relations under capitalism, rooted in the labor contract and private property, and the extra-economic coercive mechanisms of non-capitalist class societies. Marxists agree with Giddens too that this qualitative distinction between capitalist and non-capitalist class societies represents a more fundamental break than any distinctions among pre-capitalist societies. Where they disagree is in how the term "class" is to be employed with respect to the use of authoritative and allocative resources in surplus appropriation.

Terminological disputes are seldom innocent. In general, drawing the boundary criteria for a concept opens up or closes off lines of inquiry. When Marxists treat the mechanism of appropriation, the exploitation of labor, as the principal basis for specifying class relations they do so, at least implicitly, because they hold: (1) that this mechanism determines tendencies towards struggle by supplying a set of social actors with opposing interests; (2) that typological distinctions based upon this mechanism constitute a sound basis for distinguishing societies with

---

17. For an important dissenting view in which a property relations definition of class is defended in Marxist terms, see John Roemer, *A General Theory of Exploitation and Class* (Cambridge, MA: Harvard University Press, 1982). The debate over the status of "private property" in the definition of class dissolves when "property" is extended to include a range of productive resources other than the means of production.

different dynamics, forms of social conflict and trajectories of development; and (3) that the elements of social forms so conceived do not operate independently, but instead form a kind of system. The last point is the most important. By combining the joint effect of control over allocative and authoritative resources in the specification of class relations, Marxists hold that these forms of resource control are not just contingently interconnected, but systematically linked in such a way that only certain kinds of variation can occur in their forms of combination. By excluding relations to authoritative resources from the concept of class, Giddens suggests, in contrast, that the social organization of authoritative resources and their development and transformation are independent of the social control of allocative resources. This is not to say that, for Giddens, the development of forms of control of authoritative resources has no effect on allocative resource control. It is only to maintain that their effects are contingent, not systematic.

Some implications of this difference will become clear when we consider Giddens's critique of "evolutionism". First, however, we turn to Giddens's complaints against Marxism's supposed intrasocietal class reductionism.

Intrasocietal Class Reductionism

Historical materialism is class reductionist, Giddens argues, not only in its treatment of the central differences between societies; it is reductionist in its treatment of the forms of domination within given societies. In addition to class exploitation Giddens argues that:

There are three axes of exploitative relationships ... which are not explained, though they may be significantly illuminated, either by the theory of exploitation of labor in general or by the theory of surplus value in particular. These are: (a) exploitative relations between states, where these are strongly influenced by military domination; (b) exploitative relations between ethnic groups, which may or may not converge with the first; and (c) exploitative relations between the sexes, sexual exploitation. None of these can be reduced exhaustively to class exploitation ...[18]

As Giddens points out, Marxists have often attempted to explain the existence and forms of these axes of domination as "expressions" of class, typically by recourse to functional explanations. If such reductionist accounts are illegitimate, interstate, ethnic and sexual relations of domination would have sources of variation not wholly explained by

---

18. *A Contemporary Critique*, p. 242.

class. Then the attempt to characterize the overall form of society exclusively in terms of modes of production and associated class structures would be plainly inadequate.

Many, perhaps most, contemporary Marxists accept much of this argument against class reductionism. In general there is a recognition that ethnic and sexual domination are not simply expressions of class domination. Some Marxists would add inter-state domination to this list as well. How much independence these relations have and how their articulation with the class system should be understood are, of course, matters of considerable disagreement. While tendencies towards functional reductionism continue in the Marxist tradition, it is nevertheless beyond dispute that the principal tendency of contemporary Marxist thinking opposes intrasocietal class reductionism.

Marxists would, however, disagree with Giddens where he suggests that the irreducibility of sex or ethnicity or nationality to class implies that these forms of domination/exploitation are of equal status in defining differences among societies. Most Marxists would continue to argue for a general primacy of class, even if other relations are not simple reflections of class. Thus it is often argued that class structure determines the limits of possible variation of other forms of domination, even if it does not determine the nature of these forms as such. If this position is correct, class relations do not simply "illuminate" the analysis of gender, ethnicity or nationality, as Giddens suggests; they determine the basic structural parameters within which these other relations develop.

This argument can, of course, be reversed. It can be argued, as some feminists have, that gender relations impose limits on forms of variation of class structure. It would certainly be plausible to hold too that the interstate system of political and military relations imposes limits on the possible forms of development of class relations. If the relations of limitation are symmetrical, then it is arbitrary to claim primacy for class relations.

Yet Marxists continue to argue for class primacy, though sometimes covertly or apologetically. Three kinds of argument are invoked to defend the primacy of class.[19] First, it is sometimes argued that, even if non-class forms of domination are irreducible to class, class systematically structures the subjectivity of actors. The point is not that individuals are always "class conscious" in the sense that they are aware of their class position and class interests, but only that their social

---

19. In Chapter 7 we shall examine some general issues involved in making claims for causal primacy. Here we are interested only in the kinds of substantive arguments that are made in favor of class primacy in theories of history.

consciousness is more shaped by class relations than by any other social relation. A second argument for class primacy shifts attention from the consciousness of actors to the constraints under which they act. The idea is that class relations, by structuring access to material resources, limit the capacities for action of different groups, including groups not reducible to class relations. For example, racial domination may be irreducible to class domination, and yet a condition for blacks struggling effectively against racial domination may be that they gain control over more of society's surplus product than they now enjoy. Thus, even if their interests or motivations for struggle are irreducible to class interests, the conditions for successful pursuit of these interests would be structured by class relations.[20]

Giddens effectively endorses these arguments, at least for capitalism. Thus he designates capitalism a class society, a social form in which class permeates all facets of social life, shaping forms of subjectivity and conditions of action. But he rejects the idea that all societies are class societies in this sense. We think Giddens is correct. We would add that, even under capitalism, arguments for the *centrality* of class in the formation of subjectivity and conditions for struggle are not necessarily arguments for the *primacy* of class. There almost certainly are situations in which racial or gender conditions more deeply stamp the subjectivity of actors and their conditions for struggle than class does. And while struggle for control over material resources is *an* essential condition for struggle against non-class forms of domination, there are other necessary conditions too—struggles over ideology and control of political institutions, for example, neither of which directly concerns material resources. Where multiple necessary conditions exist, it is arbitrary to assign to one of these necessary conditions the privilege of "causal primacy".[21]

There is, however, a third argument for the primacy of class. Marxists have argued for class primacy on the grounds that only class relations have an internal logic of development which generates a trajectory of transformations of the class structure. No other form of domination appears to have a similar developmental trajectory. Thus, while class

---

20. This argument rests on the distinction between the *interests* groups have and their *capacities* for realizing those interests (see Wright, *Class, Crisis and the State*, London, NLB: 1978, pp. 98–108). Functionalist attempts at reducing non-class relations to class relations typically involve a translation of non-class interests into class interests. The "interests" whites have in dominating blacks, for example, is explained in terms of the interests the bourgeoisie has in dominating workers: the former is functional for the latter. In this case, non-class *interests* are irreducible to class interests, but the *capacities* for realizing non-class interests are systematically constrained by the society's class structure.

21. Cf. Chapter 7.

structures cannot be accorded primacy with respect to other social relations in a *static* sense, they do enjoy *dynamic* primacy.[22] This argument assumes that class relations do indeed generate development endogenously. If they do not, Giddens's insistence on a pluralism of symmetrical forms of exploitation and domination would be difficult to fault. To assess this argument we therefore turn to the third complaint Giddens raises against historical materialism: its purported evolutionism.

Evolutionism

Throughout *A Contemporary Critique of Historical Materialism* Giddens attacks all forms of "evolutionary thinking" in social theory. He does so for both methodological and empirical reasons. Methodologically, he argues, evolutionary perspectives in social science are based on a notion of *adaptation*—typically, the adaptation of a society to its material environment. But, Giddens insists, it is a category mistake to talk about "societies" adapting: "the idea of adaptation falls in the same category as the functional 'needs' to which we have already objected. Societies have no need to 'adapt' to (master, conquer) their material environments."[23] Societies are not organisms and it is a mistake to see them evolving adaptively in the manner of organisms.

An alternative would be to reconstruct social evolution on the basis of a theory of individual human adaptation. Human beings adapt to their environment. Through such adaptations the societies they comprise are then pushed along an evolutionary path. But, according to Giddens, such a reconstruction fails empirically. While it no longer rests on a misleading reification of society, it is based on a false empirical generalization—that there is a transhistorical tendency for human beings to improve their material conditions of existence. In Giddens's view there simply are no transhistorical individual drives that can provide a basis for a general theory of social development.

The Marxist theory of history is thus doubly unsatisfactory. It is methodologically flawed in its presupposition that societies have transhistorical adaptive imperatives. And it is empirically false because, according to Giddens, there is no tendency for the forces of production to develop throughout history. Thus a "dialectic" of forces and relations of production cannot possibly serve as a basis for a general trajectory of historical change.

---

22. This argument too is examined and criticized in Chapter 7.
23. *A Contemporary Critique*, p. 21.

In place of evolutionary accounts, Giddens offers an explanation of social transformations in terms of what he calls "episodic transitions", "time–space edges" and "contingent historical development". "Episodes", Giddens writes, "refer to processes of social change that have definite direction and form, and in which definite structural transformations occur".[24] The directionality and dynamic of these changes are specific to each episode, each historically specific form of social transition. There is no general dynamic or direction to social change across episodes. "Time–space edges" refer to the "simultaneous existence of types of society in episodic transitions".[25] Giddens holds that evolutionary theories imply successions of societies in sequences of stages; while, in fact, different forms of society generally overlap. Finally, Giddens sees the overarching trajectory of historical development as radically contingent: "There are no 'inevitable trends' in social development that are either hastened or held back by specific historical processes. All general patterns of social organization and social change are compounded of contingent outcomes, intended and unintended …"[26] Instead of a theory of social evolution, Giddens thus envisions social change as a set of discontinuous, contingently determined, overlapping transitions that have no overall pattern or logic of development.

Our basic criticism of Giddens's argument is that it incorrectly assumes that the only way a theory of history can embody a principle of directionality is by treating the historical trajectory of social forms in a manner parallel to the life-cycle development of organisms. In contrast we shall argue that directionality implies neither an evolutionary model of society nor an organism-development model, and that both Giddens's own theory of space–time distanciation and historical materialism embody such principles of directionality. The challenge Giddens poses to Marxist theory is not that his theory is somehow *non-evolutionary* in contrast to historical materialism, but only that he has developed a substantively different account of history's structure and direction. Which theory, if either, is right can only be settled empirically. To this end, Giddens's strictures against evolutionism are misleading and diversionary.

---

24. Ibid., p. 23.
25. Ibid.
26. *The Nation State and Violence*, p. 235. Arguments of contingency play an especially important role in the analysis of *The Nation State and Violence*. Giddens argues, for example, that the universal scope of the nation state in the modern world is to be explained in part by "a series of contingent historical developments that cannot be derived from general traits attributed to nation-states, but which have nonetheless decisively influenced the trajectory of development of the modern world" (*The Nation State and Violence*, p. 256). Included in this list of contingencies is the long peace of the nineteenth century and the nature of the treaties following the First World War.

Directionality in Theories of History

Giddens is on firm ground when he rejects theories of epochal social change built on the idea that societies must develop along a unique path driven by increasing adaptation to environmental or material conditions. He is correct too in holding that one finds this image of social development in some Marxian accounts.

However, Giddens is wrong when he holds that "teleological" visions of historical development are automatically entailed by an *evolutionary* model. What Giddens rightly finds objectionable are "organism development" models of social change of an especially extreme and deterministic sort, not evolutionary models as such. The distinction is clearest in biology. Consider a theory of the development of an organism from conception to death that describes the genetic structure of the organism as effectively "programming" a process of development and decline.[27] Such a theory will claim that it is not at all accidental that organisms usually move through a particular sequence of stages, and that the reason for this sequence has a strongly endogenous character. In contrast, the now standard theory of biological evolution postulates neither an endogenous engine of change nor a programmed sequence of stages. There is no necessity for single-celled organisms to evolve into human beings or for any other actual evolutionary change to occur. Evolutionary theory allows for a retrospective explanation of the transitions that in fact took place. But the specific sequence of changes is a consequence of countless exogenous events. Thus Giddens is wrong to conflate evolutionary theories in general with theories of history that treat historical trajectories like deterministic theories of the life-cycle of organisms.[28]

However, the real issue in Giddens's critique of "evolutionary theory" is not his use of the term, but his views about the kind of theory a theory of history must be.[29] Giddens poses two basic alternatives: either a theory of history must be based on a strong organism develop-

---

27. We do not wish to endorse such a theory, partly because talk of "programming" often serves to de-emphasize the role of environmental contingencies. Clearly, some sequences of phenotypes (like the early process of zygotic division) are more plausibly treated by a stage theory than are others (like the order in which a human being learns facts of geography). The present point is that theories of this sort assign a pre-eminent, though not necessarily exclusive, role to endogenous causes of change that confer on the organism a definite trajectory of development.

28. See Chapter 3 for a more sustained comparison of historical materialism and Darwinian evolutionary theory.

29. In conflating organismic growth models of development with evolutionary theories Giddens is, after all, following the common usage of the term "evolution" in sociology. Most sociologists who refer to social evolution have in mind a model of development along a particular, determinate path.

ment model (i.e. his "evolutionary" theory) or it must treat epochal history as a matter of contingent connections between different social forms without any overall directionality across epochs. These are not, however, the only alternatives. Two other kinds of theories of epochal history are conceivable. As already suggested, one possibility is a genuinely evolutionary theory of the Darwinian kind. Such a theory would *not* postulate any overall directionality to history, but it would argue for a transhistorical mechanism that drives historical change—by analogy with natural selection. Or one could propose a theory that did acknowledge an overall directionality to historical change, but rejected the view that directionality implies a unique path and sequence of development. We call a theory of this sort a theory of *historical trajectories* (the plural ending marking the idea that such a theory rejects the deterministic implication of a uniquely possible trajectory). We think such a theory is plausible, and that both historical materialism and Giddens's own theory are examples.[30]

For a theory of history to embody a principle of directionality, it must propose a typology of social forms that can be ordered in a nonarbitrary way. Let us call these forms 0, 1, 2, etc. We can distinguish three conditions that suffice for directionality:

(1) The probability of staying at the same point is greater than the probability of regressing; $Pr(j \rightarrow j) > Pr(j \rightarrow i)$, for all $j > i$.
    In a proper theory of history, social forms must be "sticky downward".[31]
(2) There must be some probability of moving from a given level to the next higher level; $Pr(i \rightarrow i+1) > 0$, for all i.
(3) The probability of a "progressive" change is greater than the probability of "regression"; $Pr(i \rightarrow i+1) > Pr(i \rightarrow i-1)$, for all i.

There are several important things to note about these conditions. First, they do not imply that societies have "needs" or teleologically-driven tendencies. Inherent teleologies might be one way to satisfy these conditions, but they are not the only way. Second, these conditions do not entail that there is a sequence of stages through which all societies *must* move. They do not imply that the probability of skipping a stage is zero. Nor do they suggest that for any given stage there is only one

---

30. In the published essay on which this chapter is based, it was claimed that Giddens's and Marx's theories of history were both "evolutionary" in character. Given the understanding of evolutionary theory developed in Chapter 3, this clearly is not accurate, and thus we now describe these as theories of historical trajectory.

31. The notation Pr $(i \rightarrow j)$ means the probability of ending in state j if the system begins in state i.

possible future; there can be multiple alternatives. A theory of this sort merely claims that there is some positive impulse for movement and that movement is "biased" in a certain direction. It does not follow from these conditions that all societies must develop. Regression and stasis are compatible with our stipulated conditions. The theory can even describe circumstances in which regression and stasis are more probable than progress; this would be consistent with the theory describing other circumstances in which there is a bias towards progress. Thus, the theory can allow that in most societies, long-term steady states are more likely than epochal transformations. At the global level, there will be a tendency for movement in the specified direction.

Finally, this kind of theory need not postulate a universal mechanism of transition from one form of society to another. The mechanisms that explain movement between adjacent forms in the typology need not be the same at every stage. The theory provides a roadmap of history and specifies what kinds of movements are likely to be stable or unstable, reproducible or unreproducible. It does not postulate a universal process of transition. In this respect, theories of historical trajectories differ from theories modeled on Darwinism. But, as in biological evolution, there may be a high level of contingency involved in any particular transformation.

It is clearly non-trivial to affirm a theory of historical trajectories. Not every taxonomy of social forms satisfies the three conditions. Indeed, it could turn out that, in the final analysis, social forms cannot be conceived in the way a theory of historical trajectories requires.

The Marxist Theory of History

Historical materialism is a theory of historical trajectories. According to this theory, before capitalism there was no strong impulse for the development of the forces of production. Nevertheless there was some probability that the forces of production would develop, and the probability of regression was less than the probability of retaining previously achieved levels of productivity. In so far as the development of the forces of production renders certain forms of production relations more or less likely and stable, the cumulative character of the development of the forces of production would impart at least a weak directionality to the system.

To defend these claims, it is not necessary to rely on the idea that societies have needs or goals. All that is required is a defense of the claim that the development of the forces of production is "sticky downward". A number of arguments in support of this position can be advanced.

First, and perhaps least contentiously, there are no groups in society with fundamental interests in *reducing* the productivity of labour. There may be people whose interests have the unintended consequence of reducing labor productivity—for instance, their interests may lead to war and therefore to the destruction of productive capacities. Or, in some circumstances, workers might reduce productivity to protect their jobs. But in general no one has an interest in reducing labor productivity *per se.*

Second, the key aspect of the development of the forces of production is the development of knowledge of productive techniques, not the accumulation of hardware. With knowledge of productive technologies, levels of productivity can be restored even when physical means of production are destroyed. On the other hand, without the knowledge necessary for putting existing hardware to work, the means of production would be useless. Technical knowledge plainly has a sticky downward character; it *can* be lost, but it almost never is.[32]

Third, as Marx and Engels argued in *The German Ideology*, once a particular level of development is reached, people's "needs" come to depend on prevailing technologies. Thus there are individuals—and organized collectivities—with strong interests in retaining productive forces, at the same time that no groups have deep and abiding interest in reducing them.

Finally, there will always be individuals and groups with particular interests in enhancing labor productivity—and therefore in developing the forces of production. Whenever increases in labor productivity have the consequence of reducing the toil of direct producers, direct producers will generally want the forces of production to expand. This situation was nearly universal in pre-class societies. Direct producers may not have had any effective interest in increasing the surplus product, but they surely wanted to reduce unpleasant labor.[33] Thus in pre-class societies, direct producers had interests in increasing productivity. The vast majority may not have felt pressure to reduce toil; and they may not have had the capacity to innovate. But when innovations that reduced toil occurred—for whatever reason and however sporadically—they were generally adopted.

---

32. See *KMTH*, p. 41.
33. We do not mean to suggest that a transhistorical definition of "burdensome toil" can be provided. The content of the activities defined as toilsome undoubtedly changes with the development of the forces of production. But in the human encounter with nature, some activities are experienced as unpleasant and even painful. The weak impulse for technical innovation need not come from a transhistorical drive to "expand the surplus product" or even to "reduce scarcity" understood in terms of consumption, but simply to reduce toil. See *KMTH*, pp. 302–7, for an elaboration of this argument.

In societies with class exploitation, however, there is no longer a direct link between the development of the forces of production and the reduction of burdensome toil. On the contrary, in many cases the introduction of new technologies resulted in the intensification of the direct producers' burdens. Thus there no longer was a general interest in developing the forces of production. Ruling classes, however, did have at least a weak interest in adopting changes that increased labor productivity. This interest followed, in large part, from their class interest in maintaining or enhancing the level of surplus appropriation. To be sure, circumstances can be imagined in which an interest in enhancing exploitation conflicts with an interest in expanding productive capacities. But generally the former propels the latter. Thus, except in rare cases, exploiters had an interest in the development of productive forces. We do not mean to suggest that before capitalism ruling classes systematically encouraged technological innovation. But they generally accepted them when they occurred.

The pressure to develop was a relatively weak impulse throughout much of human history. It took hundreds of thousands of years of toilsome existence before some of the innovations that marked the transition from hunting and gathering to settled agriculture occurred. But, we maintain, that there was at least a weak impulse for development even throughout this period, and that whenever innovations did occur, they were not willingly relinquished.

The Marxist theory of history is not simply a technological typology of societal forms. At the heart of the theory is an account of the interconnection between forces and relations of production. As we have seen,[34] historical materialists hold: (1) that for a given level of development of the forces of production, only certain types of production relations are possible; and (2) that within a given form of production relations, there is a limit to the possible development of the forces of production. There is thus a relationship of reciprocal limitation between the forces and relations of production. However, we know that there is at least a weak impulse for the forces of production to develop. This impulse creates a dynamic asymmetry in their interconnection. Eventually the forces of production reach a point at which they are "fettered"—a point beyond which further development is substantially impeded in the absence of transformations of the economic structure.

As discussed in Chapter 2, Marxists have traditionally maintained that when fettering occurs, the relations will be transformed into a unique successor set of relations; and that societies will therefore move along a single path from one societal form to another. However, as we

---

34. Cf. Chapter 2.

have already argued, this claim presupposes that social actors with interests in "progressive" transformations will eventually acquire the capacities required to bring about the changes they want. The traditional account also supposes that only one form of social relations will unfetter the forces. We have suggested that neither supposition is likely. However, this conclusion does not impugn the claim that tendencies towards progress exist; nor does it challenge historical materialism's account of the directionality of the social forms it identifies. Thus a theory of history shorn of what is least defensible in orthodox historical materialism, but retaining the core structural aspects of the orthodox theory, would still count as a theory of historical trajectories. We shall suggest in Chapter 5 that a theory of this sort provides a good basis for reconstructing historical materialism.

Giddens's Theory of History

Marx's theory is not the only one that satisfies our three conditions for theories of historical trajectories; the framework elaborated by Giddens in *A Contemporary Critique of Historical Materialism* does too. Giddens formulates a typology of social forms which has a clear quantitative ordering along the dimension of space–time distanciation. How does this ordering meet our conditions for theories of historical trajectories? Giddens would deny that it does. He appears to reject any specification of tendencies towards movement through an ordered typology of social forms. In addition, he insists that the mechanisms of movement from one form to another are specific to each transition, and that there is no transhistorical impulse to move from tribal societies with low space–time distanciation to capitalist or socialist societies with high space–time distanciation.

On closer inspection, however, Giddens's own accounts seem to suggest a general progressive development. "Space–time distanciation" is a concept that captures the ability of people in a society to control allocative and authoritative resources in time and space for use in power relations. Expanding allocative space–time distanciation depends, in large part, on the development of the forces of production;[35] expanding authoritative space–time distanciation amounts to development of

---

35. Increasing allocative space–time distanciation is, in general, a by-product of the growth of productive forces. In most instances, therefore, the former is a good proxy for the latter. As we will discuss presently, the substitution is, in part, motivated by Giddens's *substantive* differences with Marxism. But, by focusing attention on a phenomenon less obviously associated with a plausible human interest (like the interest in expanding consumption and diminishing toil that motivates the Development Thesis), Giddens's move effectively dissociates historical change from a universal impulse to development. Our contention is that this implication of Giddens's theoretical framework is misleading.

means of surveillance. Increases in each dimension are human achievements: they enhance the capacities of at least some human beings to act.
Since the people whose capacities are enhanced by increasing distanciation will not willingly accept lower levels of distanciation once a given
level is achieved, there should be some tendency for this development to
be "sticky downward".

Of course, there may be *other* agents who would like to see the level
of distanciation reduced. But with regard to allocative resources, this
possibility is remote. As we have just argued, no one has a fundamental
interest in increasing burdensome toil or diminishing levels of consumption. Reductions in allocative space–time distanciation would,
typically, undermine the efficient use of available forces of production,
and thus in general there will be few, if any, organized interests for such
reduction. Giddens nowhere suggests otherwise.

The situation is different with respect to authoritative space–time
distanciation. There plainly are social actors, often with effective
capacities for struggle, with clear interests in reducing authoritative
space–time distanciation. Increasing capacities for surveillance can be a
real threat to certain categories of people. Thus territorial
centralization—an aspect of expansion of spatial authoritative distanciation—is frequently opposed by groups and communities unwilling to be
absorbed under a central authority. Such resistance could be described
as "authoritative-Luddism".[36] It should be noted that even Luddite
resistance is more often directed against the unequal distribution of
resources than against the resources themselves. In any case, Luddism
with respect to allocative resources, opposition to the introduction of
more productive technologies, is rare; resistance to increasing authoritative space–time distanciation is however a common occurrence in
history. Indeed, attempts at reducing overall authoritative space–time
distanciation have often been successful. It might appear, therefore, that
on this dimension, Giddens's approach does not imply a general directionality to social development.

Even here, however, we think Giddens's account retains the idea of
weak directionality in epochal historical development. While there will
often be contending social actors with interests in expanding, maintaining or reducing authoritative space–time distanciation, actors with
interests in expansion or maintenance will usually command more
authoritative resources already and will therefore generally prevail in
outright confrontations. Regressions may not be historical oddities. But,

---

36. "Luddism", named after the Luddite movement of the nineteenth century, refers to
the protest movements of workers directed against the introduction of labor-replacing or
skill-reducing machines. In this context it designates opposition to improvements in technical progress with respect to either authoritative or allocative resources.

at the very least, authoritative space–time distanciation will tend to be sticky downward.

Is there a significant probability of movement up? We think it is fair to answer affirmatively in light of Giddens's own analyses. At bottom, the impulse for expansion of space–time distanciation comes from conflict and competition. In class societies (capitalism), the process is impelled mainly by conflicts over allocative resources—by economic competition among capitalist firms. In class-divided societies (pre-capitalist societies with class divisions) it is rooted in conflicts over authoritative resources, primarily in military and territorial competition. What drives distanciation will therefore depend upon the kinds of resources that form the bases of social power. But because of the link between conflict, power, resources and distanciation, there will be at least a weak impulse for increasing distanciation throughout history. Again, this conclusion does not imply universal *progress.* Nor does it imply that all societies *will actually* increase space–time distanciation along both resource dimensions. It is simply a claim that there is a universal, if weak, impulse towards increasing distanciation, and thus a certain likelihood that increases will occur.

It appears, therefore, that what is novel in Giddens's account is not his rejection of the idea that historical change has an epochal directionality. It is the idea that the trajectory of history follows a dual logic, animated by the autonomous impulses of the expansion of space–time distanciation with respect to allocative and authoritative resources. Stated in more conventional terms (which Giddens would probably disavow), social development is the result of autonomous dynamics rooted simultaneously in political and economic structures. While in specific historical cases one may be justified in saying that one or the other of these dynamic processes constitutes the central locus of impulses for social change, there is no general priority of one over the other. In this sense, Giddens is a dualist and Marxists are monists.[37] Rhetorical stances aside, therein lies the difference.

Contending Theories of Historical Trajectories

What we have, then, are two contending accounts of history's trajectory, not a contest between an evolutionary theory (Marxism) and an anti-

---

37. Our use of the term "monism" is intended only to contrast with "dualism". As should be obvious from what we have already said, we do not mean to suggest that, for Marxists, there is only one (relevant) kind of social cause or that Marxism is in any other way "reductionist", as is sometimes implied by defenders of the so-called monist view of history.

evolutionary theory (Giddens).[38] Neither theory is "evolutionary", and both affirm a principle of directionality within historical trajectories rather than, as Giddens claims for his own theory, a random walk.

The debate over these alternatives is not methodological but substantive. On the one hand, Marxists attribute causal primacy to economic structures.[39] Giddens, on the other hand, insists that the developmental tendencies of political and economic structures are autonomous and that no general principles govern their interconnection. In different historically specific situations one or the other may be more important.[40]

It is not an easy task to adjudicate between these claims. Once a simple base–superstructure model is abandoned, it is difficult for Marxists to argue systematically for the structural unity of economic and political relations. It is therefore tempting to conclude that, in so far as real disagreements remain, Giddens's dualism is the more appropriate characterization. Many so-called "post-Marxist" theorists have succumbed to this temptation.[41] However, we believe that it is well not to take the dualist route. There are several compelling reasons for maintaining the core insights of the materialist account of historical trajectories.

First, as remarked, Marxists share Giddens's view that in pre-capitalist societies the appropriation of surplus labor (or products) relied on the use of extra-economic coercion (control over authoritative

---

38. To these, a third could be added, as elaborated in the work of Jürgen Habermas (see in particular, *Communication and the Evolution of Society*, Boston: Beacon Press, 1979): the claim that normative structures also have an autonomous logic of development producing a typology of societies based on their level of moral development (a kind of moral space–time distanciation, where "meaning" can be seen as an action-relevant resource).

39. In Chapter 7 a number of senses of causal primacy, some legitimate, some not, are investigated systematically.

40. The view that social relations and practices structured around allocative and authoritative resources have no intrinsic connections is also implicated in the difference between Giddens's concept of class and the concept adopted by most Marxists. The Marxist claim that the concept of class combines the relations of economic exploitation and authoritative domination within production is implicitly a rejection of the claim that these have genuinely autonomous logics of development; Giddens's restriction of class to relations of domination with respect to allocative resources affirms his view that allocative and authoritative domination are autonomous and contingently related processes. The adjudication of these contending class concepts and the typologies of social forms to which they are linked, therefore, ultimately hinges on these different substantive claims about the process of transformation of economic and political (allocative and authoritative) aspects of social relations.

41. See, for example, Barry Hindess, Paul Q. Hirst, Anthony Cutler and Athar Hussain, *Marx's Capital and Capitalism Today*, 2 vols (Routledge & Kegan Paul, 1978 and 1979), and Robin Hahnel and Michael Albert, *Unorthodox Marxism* (Boston: South End Press, 1980) and *Marxism and Socialist Theory* (Boston: South End Press, 1982).

resources). Thus it is not in dispute that the relationship between control over allocative and authoritative resources varies across social forms. Marxists, however, insist that the explanation for the primacy of authoritative resources in pre-capitalist societies—and for the primacy of allocative resources under capitalism—must be sought in the differences in the economic structures of these societies. Giddens provides no alternative explanation for this state of affairs, nor does he challenge the Marxist account. We consider the Marxist explanation sound. Thus we would conclude, with Marx, that the key to understanding changes in the relationship between allocative and authoritative resources lies in understanding the trajectory of development of economic structures. Political institutions may indeed enjoy considerable independence from economic structures. But the dynamics centered in property relations impose more fundamental limits on the overall process of social change than occurrences at the political ("superstructural") level.

Second, the motivational assumptions underlying claims for the development of productive forces are more plausible than parallel claims supporting the autonomous development of authoritative resources. Throughout most of human history, there has been a general interest in increasing the productivity of labor in order to reduce toil—and also often to increase the surplus product. This interest underwrites the sustained, if often weak, impulse towards expansion of the forces of production. We find no reason to think that there is a similarly universal interest in the expansion of social control over authoritative resources. Indeed, as already noted, such expansion is pervasively contested. There is therefore a less sustained impulse for development of allocative resources. There no doubt is a net developmental tendency for "space–time distanciation" with respect to authoritative resources. But this can be explained by the fact that the social actors supporting expansion have greater capacities (power) to accomplish their objectives. This greater capacity itself depends upon their control over allocative resources: the ability to pay troops and retainers, and to build the infrastructures of surveillance and communication. In other words, there is an asymmetry in the explanatory role of allocative and authoritative resources. The former provides a systematic basis for explaining developmental tendencies within epochal historical trajectories; the latter does not.

This conclusion is reinforced if we try to impute a rationale for expanding authoritative resources. The most obvious reason for seeking to expand along this dimension is precisely to enhance material well-being—by increasing consumption and/or reducing burdensome toil. Usually, the beneficiaries of increasing space–time distanciation of authoritative resources are individuals in ruling classes who use their augmented political power to increase their material welfare, directly or indirectly.[42] Perhaps this is why the impulse to develop authoritative resources appears less universal than the impulse to develop productive forces directly. In any case, in so far as the motive for expanding authoritative resources derives from the motive for improving material welfare, the development of authoritative resources is subordinate to motivations structured by allocative resources.[43] This is precisely what a Marxist analysis entails.

It is one thing to argue for the relative plausibility of a materialist theory of historical trajectories over Giddens's dualist theory. It is quite another to produce a substantive and compelling reconstruction of historical materialism. While we cannot elaborate such a theory, in the next chapter we will outline some of the directions in which this reconstruction might proceed.

---

42. It is interesting in this regard that many of the earliest historical advances in surveillance that Giddens identifies were concerned with the tallying of tribute. See for example his discussion of the early forms of writing in Sumer, *A Contemporary Critique*, p. 95.

43. It is, of course, conceivable that people want power for power's sake, not because it increases their material well-being. A desire for power could then provide the motivational basis for an autonomous development of authoritative resources. We are skeptical of this motivation, however; and, in any case, would caution against multiplying transhistorical human interests beyond necessity.

Towards a Reconstructed Historical Materialism

In the face of orthodox historical materialism's evident implausibility, many Marxists have abandoned the Marxist theory of history altogether. Both the Primacy Thesis and the Base/Superstructure Thesis are now almost universally rejected. Yet, as we have noted, Marxists continue to endorse the underlying intuition that historical materialism articulates— that history has a determinate structure—and continue to use concepts that derive their theoretical status from historical materialism. In our view, these intuitions are sound. What they suggest is that, at this point in the history of Marxian theory, historical materialism should not be abandoned, but reconstructed.

Orthodox historical materialism attempts to provide an explanation for the overall trajectory of historical development by linking together two pairs of concepts: forces and relations of production, and economic bases and superstructures. The interactions and contradictions between forces and relations of production explain the trajectory of economic structures; the interactions and contradictions between economic structures and superstructures explain the trajectory of superstructures. Accordingly, reconstructions of historical materialism involve rethinking each of these pairs of connections.

The Primacy Thesis

Orthodox historical materialism provides an account of:

(a) the necessary (material) conditions for change;
(b) the direction of change;

(c) the means through which change is achieved;

(d) sufficient conditions for change.

We have already argued that the least plausible of these claims is (d).[1] The orthodox theory claims that wherever there is an interest in epochal historical change, eventually the change will occur—subject only to the obvious proviso that conditions for sustaining human life remain in effect and that the initial conditions under which the theory applies continue to pertain. Where an interest in change exists, the capacities for change eventually follow. There is, however, no good reason to hold that an interest in change suffices to bring about the requisite material, organizational and intellectual capacities for change; and no reason, therefore, to propose an inevitable sequence of epochal historical stages. What we call *weak* historical materialism, claiming (a), (b) and (c), but not (d), thus suggests itself. Epochal transformation does not follow simply from an interest in bringing it about; the capacity for change is a non-redundant second ingredient, which must also be present. Epochal historical change is still rooted in material conditions (a); it still has a directionality (b), making changes "sticky downward", as described in Chapter 4; and changes are still actualized through class struggles (c); but there is no longer any claim to the inevitability of specific transitions.

Dropping (d) helps transform historical materialism from an "organism development" model of history into a theory of historical trajectories.[2] If agents capable of transforming relations of production are not *always* forthcoming when productive forces stagnate, it is obvious that production relations may not always develop *optimally.* The roadmap of historical development can thus have forks and detours, junctures in which more than one option is historically possible and in which suboptimal outcomes (with respect to the "unfettering" of the forces of production) can occur. The cumulative quality of the development of the forces of production still makes retreats on the map less likely than stasis or progression (thus the "sticky downward" directionality to historical trajectories), but eliminating the thesis of optimal selection of economic structures opens the possibility of multiple routes into the future.

Still, not everything is possible at every juncture, and throughout most stretches of history societies are not at junctures at all. Usually, there is sufficient compatibility between forces and relations of pro-

---

1. See Chapter 2.
2. See Chapter 4.

duction. Weak historical materialism is therefore not a trivial position. It provides an account of what is and is not on the historical agenda for different levels of development of productive forces. It depicts an historical map—an account of the patterns of correspondence or "contradiction" between forces and relations of production that open up and close off possibilities—and accounts as well for the direction of movement along the map. In addition, weak historical materialism makes claims about the means by which historical change (and stasis) is achieved. It is class struggle that, in the end, determines whether and how we move along the map the theory provides.

Weak historical materialism is thus the orthodox theory without the unlikely and unwarranted claim that what is necessary for epochal historical change is ultimately also sufficient. Yet, in spite of this difference, both orthodox and weak historical materialism hold that there is a lawlike tendency for relations of production to correspond to forces of production in ways that facilitate the continuous development of productive forces. Orthodox and weak historical materialism are therefore historical theories in the same way.[3]

The elaboration of weak historical materialism as a theory of historical trajectories is bound to provoke a reconstruction of the typology of economic structures Marxists have traditionally acknowledged. In Cohen's version of the traditional argument, there are only four kinds of economic structures: pre-class society, pre-capitalist class society, capitalism and post-class society (socialism/communism). If this list were exhaustive there would be little possibility of developing a nuanced theory of historical trajectories. One can hardly construct a "roadmap" with multiple routes when there are only four points on the map. Dropping the Optimality Thesis creates a theoretical opening that requires the development of a more differentiated typology of social forms.[4]

To this end, we think it is desirable to elaborate concepts of economic

---

3. The distinction drawn here between orthodox and weak historical materialism is different from the distinction sometimes drawn by evolutionary biologists between "strong" and "weak" selectionism. The latter distinction describes a disagreement over the power that natural selection exerts on evolution; it therefore concerns the relative causal importance of natural selection in the evolutionary trajectories of populations, not the cogency of natural selection itself.

4. If only four types of economic structure are possible, the Optimality Thesis would lose its bite. Even if it were true, it would not be informative to say that capitalism is the optimal economic structure at the point when feudalism is no longer viable (because feudal social relations fetter further development of the productive forces), if capitalism, post-capitalism and pre-class society ("primitive communism") are the only options. The thesis becomes interesting only after we identify a wider range of (possible) post-feudal economic structures.

structure at lower levels of abstraction than Marxists generally have. For example, capitalism is usually defined as a system within which the means of production are privately owned by one class (capitalists) which then hires (propertyless) direct producers (workers) in a labor market to set those means of production to work. Capitalists own the means of production; workers own their labor power. The property rights embodied in these forms of ownership, however, have many aspects; ownership is a bundle of rights. According to the received understanding, owners of means of production can use them as they please— sell them, destroy them, appropriate profits from their use, and hire and fire others to use them. However, in actually existing "capitalist" societies, some of these rights are effectively vested in other agents. Occupational safety requirements, pollution controls, capital export controls, job rights of workers and profit taxes all compromise capitalist property rights. The theoretical question, then, is whether transformations of capitalist property rights constitute the basis for qualitatively different relations of production. Philippe Van Parijs has argued that developed forms of "welfare state capitalism" constitute a distinct mode of production. If workers enjoy considerable property rights in jobs, and capitalists lose many of their rights over means of production and even over control over most of the social surplus, societies would no longer be capitalist in their "laws of motion", even if private property in means of production is still officially retained.[5] Many other differentiations among relations of production are conceivable—among pre-capitalist class societies and also among societies that orthodox historical materialists would regard as post-capitalist or socialist. If historical materialism is to be reconstructed into a useful and sustainable theory of historical trajectories, a richer elaboration of economic structures than those Marxists have traditionally acknowledged is an important priority.

Other kinds of reconstructions of historical materialism based on modifications of the Primacy Thesis are possible. An historical theory that advances only (a) and (b), which we might call quasi-historical materialism, is also conceivable. The resulting theory, in order to deny (c) plausibly, would have to propose an alternative—non-Marxian— account of the means through which the pattern and direction it shares with weak and orthodox historical materialism are achieved. One might argue, as does Richard Lachmann, that epochal transformations of systems of production are consequences of intra-ruling class conflicts rather than class struggles.[6] Lachmann argues that, in the transition from

---

5. Philippe Van Parijs, "A Revolution in Class Theory" 15, 4 (1986–87), reprinted in Erik Olin Wright et al., *The Debate on Classes* (London: Verso, 1990).

6. See Richard Lachmann, "An Elite Conflict Theory of the Transition to Capitalism", *American Sociological Review* 55, 3 (June 1990).

feudalism to capitalism, the central struggles revolved around conflicts between the crown, the nobility, and various categories of landlords and church elites; not between lords and serfs, or between emerging capitalists and feudal exploiting classes. To be sure, the outcomes of these conflicts are, in Lachmann's view, conditioned by the character of the existing economic structure and the level of development of the forces of production; but it is not class struggles as such that propel epochal transformations. A theory of this sort retains the first two elements of the orthodox theory, but drops the third and fourth. Needless to say, quasi-historical materialism diverges substantively from both the letter and spirit of Marx's theory of history. Yet it still retains the essential historicity of more traditional forms of historical materialism. The forces that push the system forward remain endogenous to the system, and the opening and closing of historical possibilities are still anchored to the level of development of the productive forces and their interconnection with relations of production.

A third mitigation of historical materialism maintains (a), but at least partially abandons (b). Weak, like orthodox, historical materialism purports to account for the large-scale features of history's overarching structure and trajectory from the earliest times to the present and into the future. *Limited* historical materialism might hold that the theory pertains not to all of human history, nor even just to the history of class societies, as *The Communist Manifesto* suggests, but only to the history of certain kinds of class societies. The most natural way to construe a claim of this sort is as a claim about the relative causal importance of the historical materialist dynamic. Limited historical materialism would then claim that historical materialist development is, as a matter of fact, overwhelmed by rival causes—perhaps of an exogenous character—for some, but not all of human history. Marx plainly did accord considerable generality to the theory he proposed; it would remain to provide an alternative rationale, distinct from the indications Marx provided, for limiting historical materialism's generality as a theory. Still, a limited historical materialism—satisfying (a) and (c), but applying to less of human history than historical materialists commonly suppose in (b)—is conceivable. Such a theory would be no less historical than historical materialisms of a more general ambition.

The Base/Superstructure Thesis

G.A. Cohen has suggested that for historical materialism to be plausible it should be restricted to a theory of economic structures and of other social practices only in so far as they affect these economic structures.[7] Thus there *could* exist endogenous, dynamic historical processes even at the level of abstraction at which historical materialism is pitched that are distinct from the one the Primacy Thesis identifies so long as they do not interfere with the historical materialist dynamic. On this basis Cohen draws a distinction between "inclusive" and "restricted" historical materialism. This distinction has important ramifications for the Base/Superstructure Thesis.

On the traditional "inclusivist" view, the "superstructure" consists of all non-economic social phenomena. To claim that the base explains the superstructure, therefore, is equivalent to saying that the economic structure explains all non-economic properties of society. This claim is preposterous if it is taken to mean that the economy explains every fine-grained aspect of non-economic institutions; and no Marxist, however committed to the orthodox theory, has ever supposed otherwise. Inclusive historical materialism, therefore, implies that only "important" or "basic" or "general" properties of superstructures are explained by the economic base.

The problem with this formulation, as Cohen points out, is that there is no good way to distinguish important from unimportant properties of superstructures. Thus there is no basis for understanding the explanatory scope of the Base/Superstructure Thesis. To solve these problems, Cohen argues that historical materialism should be reconstructed in a more restricted way. What Cohen suggests is that historical materialists need only hold that economic structures explain functionally those aspects of non-economic phenomena that have effects on the social relations of production. He thus identifies the "superstructure" with those non-economic institutions and practices that serve to stabilize the economic base. It is only these phenomena that historical materialism purports to explain functionally. Thus, for restricted historical materialists, many erstwhile "superstructural" explananda with little or no relevance to the reproduction of relations of production fall outside the scope of the theory.

Inclusive historical materialism was a theory of general history—that is, of virtually everything historical. Restricted historical materialism, in contrast, would hardly count as a theory of general history. To suggest that Marxists ought to endorse restricted, not inclusive, historical materialism, is therefore to diminish the theory's explanatory pretensions substantially, while enhancing its plausibility.

---

7. G.A. Cohen, "Restricted and Inclusive Historical Materialism", *Irish Philosophical Journal* 1 (1984), pp. 3–31; reprinted (with modifications) in G.A. Cohen, *History, Labour and Freedom: Themes from Marx* (Oxford: Clarendon Press, 1988), Chapter 9.

However, restricted historical materialism is still an ambitious theory. It explains many aspects of non-economic phenomena functionally. To be sure, it need not imply that superstructures invariably reproduce class relations. But it does maintain that there will be a systematic *tendency* for functional arrangements to emerge and persist. The underlying claim is that *dys*functional arrangements—political institutions, for example, that undermine the dominant property relations—will be unstable and will therefore tend to be transformed. The situation is analogous to incompatibilities between forces and relations of production. Certain combinations of base and superstructure are incompatible in the sense that they generate systematic instabilities. When such incompatibilities arise, something has to give—the relations have to change or the super-structures must. The general Marxist assumption is that the power of ruling classes is such that, in general, they will be able to prevent funda-mental changes in the production relations. Thus there will be a stronger tendency for political institutions and policies to be transformed to restore compatibility with economic structures than vice versa.

A further retreat from the Base/Superstructure Thesis would involve a rejection of even this restricted form of the functional argument. Thus instead of claiming that state policies are functionally explained by relations of production (in so far as they affect these relations), one could regard them simply as consequences of the balance of power of classes engaged in struggles over the state. Different class actors command different resources and have different capacities to impose sanctions on their opponents and generally to make their will prevail. The trajectory of state policies could be viewed as the outcome of conflict among these forces. On this understanding, no endogenous mechanisms, geared towards selecting functional outcomes, would play any explanatory role.

Arguably, this kind of account would remain Marxist in the sense that its explanatory apparatus is still rooted in class analysis. However, by dropping the functional explanation of the superstructure, which restricted historical materialism upholds, the linkage between a society's base and its superstructure becomes less determinate. This in turn would have considerable ramifications for the kinds of explanations Marxists might provide. If the functionalist Base/Superstructure Thesis were dropped altogether, it would be easy to allow for the persistence of suboptimal and contradictory "superstructural" forms, contingent upon the power and intentions of social actors. On this view, for example, a myopic but powerful bourgeoisie might sustain policies or institutions that undermine its class interests.

We believe that the degree of determinacy implied by restricted historical materialism is helpful in making sense of the social world.

However, in the end, the viability of restricted historical materialism—
and, indeed, of historical materialisms generally—can only be settled
empirically. Our belief is therefore speculative. At this stage in the
reconstruction of historical materialism, it is not yet clear—beyond the
most general indications—even how to formulate hypotheses that the
evidence can then corroborate or infirm.

Historical Materialisms

We have considered a number of modifications of the orthodox theory
that retain its essentially historical character, while diminishing its
explanatory pretensions but enhancing its plausibility. In sum, we have
distinguished four types of historical materialism, as illustrated in Table
5.1. These types vary in their account of the linkage between forces and
relations of production, on the one hand, and the linkage between sets
of production relations or economic structures and noneconomic structures, on the other.

In *strong historical materialism*, the level of development of the
forces of production functionally determines a unique economic structure. In *weak historical materialism*, the forces of production only determine a range of possible sets of relations of production; selections within
this range are determined by historically contingent causes that bear
particularly on the capacities of class actors to transform the relations.
Inclusive historical materialism holds that economic structures determine all important properties of non-economic institutions (at appropriate levels of abstraction). On this view, the historical trajectory of
economic structures determines the basic contours of human civilization
overall. *Restricted historical materialism*, finally, holds that economic
structures explain only those non-economic institutions that bear on the
reproduction of the economic structures themselves.

Marx himself, and most Marxists after him, endorsed a strong, inclusive historical materialism. For reasons already discussed, today this

Table 5.1 A Typology of Historical Materialisms

		Relation of Base to Superstructure	
		Inclusive	*Restricted*
Relation of forces of production to relations of production	*Strong*	1	2
	Weak	3	4

ambition seems indefensible. Weak, restricted historical materialism is a far more plausible version of the core insight all historical materialisms articulate. We would venture that, if a defensible Marxist theory of history can be maintained, it will have to be along such lines. We have already suggested that the jury is still out and is likely to remain out for some time.

From Historical Materialism to Sociological Materialism?

We have only gestured towards defending weak restricted historical materialism. We have spoken of a roadmap of historical trajectories, but the actual routes still remain only vaguely understood. We have endorsed the classical argument that the level of development of the forces of production imposes limits on possible relations of production, but we have not pushed that argument beyond the very abstract idea of compatibility proposed by Cohen. Neither have we elaborated it in a way that puts substance behind the idea of multiple possibilities and alternative trajectories. We have, in other words, provided only a few brief indications of what a full-fledged reconstruction of historical materialism would involve.

Because of the uncertainties that cloud even the most plausible versions of historical materialism, it is tempting to retreat even further from the core elements of the Marxist theory, perhaps all the way towards sociological materialism. It is in this spirit, though undoubtedly for different reasons, that Etienne Balibar advanced a view of historical materialism as a theory of social forms, but not of *transitions* between social forms.[8] In doing so, he continued to use the term "historical materialism". But what he suggested is only a materialist sociology—a sociology that explains by means of materialist categories.[9] Balibar's "historical materialism" is, at most, only vestigially historical. In so far as it appears otherwise, it is because he assumed the typology of modes of production that genuine historical materialisms propose. But a materialist sociology is not a materialist theory of history. Purported historical materialisms that do not theorize transitions—that fail to postulate any direction of change between epochal structures—are not

---

8. See, for example, his "The Fundamental Concepts of Historical Materialism", in L. Althusser and E. Balibar, *Reading Capital* (London: New Left Books, 1971).

9. "Materialism" in this context is a view about the nature of social causality. For a materialist, the pertinent social causes are material—that is technological or economic, as opposed to ideas or other "ideal" factors (like values or norms). A materialist sociology, then, is a sociology that explains by reference to material causes.

historical materialisms in our sense. They are not even historical theories in the sense that Darwinian evolutionary theory is historical.

It may be necessary, however, to go Balibar's route. Eventually, even weak restricted historical materialism may prove indefensible. A materialist sociology could, however, remain distinctively Marxist in its conceptualization of class and in its focus on the effects of class structures and class struggles. We shall argue in Chapter 8 that there is a sense in which Marxism can be identified with class analysis. Thus, arguably, the Marxist agenda could sustain even the abandonment of historical materialism. Some consequences of such an outcome will be examined in Chapter 8 as well.

The Politics of Historical Materialism

From an orthodox perspective, individuals in advanced societies confront only two epochal alternatives: capitalism and socialism. If, as we have suggested, the actual choices are more complex—if there are alternatives to capitalism and socialism, as traditionally conceived—a simple, bipolar politics would be profoundly ill-informed. Historical events have shown that the consequences of being ill-informed in this regard can be devastating. A flawed roadmap has led many anti-capitalists to support despotic state socialisms, arguably setting the socialist project back for decades. Weak historical materialism, reconstructed and elaborated, can help rectify this potentially damaging situation.

However, we should be careful not to exaggerate the political implications of moving from strong to weak historical materialism and from inclusive to restricted historical materialism. It is easy to be misled because of the role historical materialism has played, not always with good reason, in some historically important intra-Marxist political debates. Two examples, important mainly in the historical period in which historical materialist orthodoxy held sway, illustrate these points.

Reform vs. Revolution

For Marxists of the Second International, and then in a different way after the Bolshevik Revolution, the principal political division on the left was between revolutionaries and reformers. In this dispute, historical materialism seemed to weigh in on the revolutionaries' side. In depicting economic structures as discrete *sets* of production relations that change discontinuously (to accommodate to ever increasing levels of development), historical materialism suggested, even if it did not strictly imply, that history advances in revolutionary leaps. Reformers, on the other hand, appeared to endorse a model of change that denied radical discontinuities. It might therefore appear that acknowledging a variety of possible economic structures in addition to capitalism and socialism would mitigate the revolutionary implications of the orthodox theory. A series of small leaps can look increasingly like continuous motion.

However we would suggest that weak historical materialism is equally compatible with the views of reformers and revolutionaries. The reform vs. revolution debate, properly understood, concerns the extent to which political superstructures can withstand attempts at small-scale transformations in social relations of production. Very generally, reformers hold that structural changes can take place gradually, without the superstructure inevitably undoing their effects. Revolutionaries, on the other hand, hold that superstructures are so powerful that production relations can only be transformed abruptly and totally. Seen in this light, it is evident that the reform vs. revolution debate is orthogonal to disputes between strong and weak historical materialists. The former debate can be engaged, in principle, no matter how many discrete economic structures historical materialists acknowledge. Indeed, it is worth noting that, even as the reform vs. revolution debate raged, reformers never challenged the idea that socialism and capitalism are distinct modes of production, and that ostensible alternatives to one or the other are only hybrid and generally transitional forms. They adhered to the orthodox account of historical possibilities as steadfastly as the revolutionaries did. What reformers and revolutionaries disputed had to do with how to go from one place to another on the same impoverished roadmap; not with where there was to go.

Normative Judgments vs. Material Interests

Within the Second International and thereafter many Marxists have disparaged the role of moral denunciation and normative argumentation in the struggle for socialism. By asserting an *inevitable* sequence of epochal historical stages, orthodox historical materialism seemed to make normative assessments of alternative economic structures superfluous. According to the received view, moral arguments might, in some cases, stir class actors to mobilize against existing arrangements. They might therefore help facilitate epochal transformations. But in the end, transformations occur, in the orthodox view, because insurgent social classes have a material interest in their occurrence. For classical Marxism, therefore, it is strictly unnecessary, even if it can be marginally helpful, to fault capitalism on normative grounds.

Strictly speaking, however, the traditional Marxist distaste for normative argumentation is not a consequence of strong historical materialism *per se*, of a commitment to a theory that provides an account of necessary *and sufficient* conditions for insurgent social classes bringing about epochal historical transformations. It follows instead from the *additional* conviction that it is workers' material interests, not their moral judgments, that propel them to overthrow capitalism. Around the turn of the century, this idea was sustained by the conviction that "the laws of motion" of capitalist societies would lead to stagnation and ultimately to breakdown. In Cohen's strong historical materialism, a different material interest—in diminishing burdensome toil—plays a similar role. Thus Marxists, following Marx's own lead, have generally argued that moral revulsion is not historically efficacious, except marginally. But they could have thought otherwise and remained strong historical materialists nevertheless. Strong historical materialists could have argued, for instance, that workers inevitably become socialist revolutionaries in part because they inevitably come to be moved by capitalism's injustice. That they did not so argue is perhaps a consequence of the fact that they were embroiled in polemical controversies with "utopian socialists", or because they were inclusive historical materialists who thought morality part of a society's superstructure—and therefore tendentially supportive of existing social and political arrangements. It was not because they thought that contradictions between forces and relations of production suffice to account for the actual trajectory of epochal historical change.

But even if the move from strong to weak historical materialism and from inclusive to restricted historical materialism does not by itself move normative considerations to center-stage, it plainly suggests this shift in focus. If nothing else, it moves the question of the development of class capacities into the foreground. More importantly, if a restructured historical materialism presents a more complex roadmap than was traditionally conceived, the need for normative argumentation becomes all the more urgent. For it then becomes crucial to reflect normatively on post-capitalist social and political arrangements. It is now clear that the reluctance of traditional Marxism to do so was naive and even pernicious.

However, it is one thing to motivate class actors; and something else to defend socialism normatively. For weak historical materialists, historical materialism only reveals what is *materially* possible. But to hold that socialism is materially possible is not automatically to imply that it is also desirable. That case must be made. Thus weak historical materialism, joined with the political convictions all Marxists share, makes the normative defense of Marxist political objectives unavoidable. To defend Marxist political commitments, and also to mobilize individuals in their behalf, weak historical materialists, unlike their orthodox forbearers, cannot be silent or derisive in moral debates.

PART II

Explanation

Introduction

Research programs, Marxism's included, can be characterized in terms of their methods and their results. They are not monolithic enterprises; nor do they always possess their own unique cluster of methodologies and putative successes. Often there is variation within programs and more or less continuous gradations between them. But for all that, there remains the fact that different research programs exhibit different central tendencies.

In Part I, we concentrated on one of Marxism's major theoretical results: historical materialism. While we argued that substantial portions of orthodox historical materialism cannot withstand scrutiny, its core does seem viable.

In Part II, we turn our attention to a number of methodological issues implicated in the project of reconstructing Marxism. By "methodology" we refer to views about how to develop social theory and conduct research: how to construct explanations, what it means to claim that some causes are more important than others, how to form and transform concepts, and how to gather and evaluate data in research. Typically, methodological doctrines are supported by philosophical arguments, but they can also be practical heuristics not grounded in any philosophical defense.

One of the hallmarks of the Marxian tradition in social theory has been the claim that Marxism embodies distinctive methodological doctrines that sharply distinguish it from "bourgeois" social theory. While the substance of such claims has varied considerably, there has been virtual unanimity among Marxists that Marxism and its rivals are separated by a deep, and philosophically irreconcilable, methodological fissure. At times, as in Lukács's famous pronouncements in his essay "What is Orthodox Marxism?", methodological doctrines are held to be the only thing that differentiates Marxism from its rivals.[1] All of the substantive propositions of Marxism could be rejected, Lukács wrote, and yet Marxism would remain valid because of its distinctive method. While most defenders of the claim to methodological distinctiveness have not taken such an extreme position, there has been a virtual consensus within the Marxist tradition that Marxist and bourgeois methodologies are radically opposed.

As we remarked in Chapter 1, this consensus no longer exists. Analytical Marxists reject claims for Marxism's methodological distinctiveness, insisting that what is valuable in Marxism is its substantive claims about the world, not its methodology.

In Chapter 6 we explore a longstanding problem in the philosophy of social science: the opposition between methodological holism and methodological individualism. Marxists have often prided themselves on their holistic treatment of social life. One of the great flaws in "bourgeois" social science, it has often been claimed, is its individualism, its tendency to treat individuals as disconnected atoms, shorn of their crucial relational properties. The historical alignment of Marxism with holism has not prevented some instances of "crossing over"—of non-Marxists who espouse holistic approaches and of Marxists who see some virtue in methodological individualism. Still, a strong historical case could be made for the claim that Marxism has possessed a distinctive central tendency that eschews individualism and embraces holism. The historical record also shows that some have seen this inclination as a virtue of Marxist theorizing, while others have viewed it as a debilitating vice. In Chapter 6, we try to clarify precisely what is at issue in the holism/individualism debate. We propose a way of acknowledging the importance of micro-foundational accounts that does not require the reduction of macro-level phenomena to their micro-foundational bases.

Chapter 7 examines two related issues, which have figured prominently in debates between Marxists and theorists working in "post-Marxist" radical theory: what it means to consider one cause more important than another, and in what senses causes can be thought to enter explanations in qualitatively asymmetrical ways. Base and superstructure are said to be asymmetrically related to each other in historical materialism. This conceptual ingredient within Marxist theorizing is also deployed when Marxists compare their own proposals with models constructed within other research traditions. For example, Marxists and feminists often disagree about the different contributions that class and gender make in structuring the oppression of women. Marxists and neo-

---

1. See Georg Lukács, *History and Class Consciousness* (London: Merlin Press, 1971), pp. 1–26.

Weberians disagree about the roles played by class conflict, on the one hand, and autonomous tendencies in state bureaucracies, on the other, in shaping state policies. Both in describing what is true within Marxist theories and in describing relations that obtain between Marxist and other theories, the concept of causal priority looms large. Clarifying the meanings that have been assigned to this idea is the principal task of Chapter 7.

The theses we develop in these chapters are more often deflationary than constructive. Our approach to the issues of holism and individualism involves identifying several senses that may be given to reductionist and anti-reductionist pronouncements. Some versions of both positions are palpably implausible. With respect to the ones that remain, we argue that there should be considerable agreement among social scientists, and that when there is not, the problems are to be resolved empirically, not by formulating a priori methodological maxims. Thus we think that much, though not quite all, of the venerable debate between methodological individualists and methodological holists is much ado about nothing. Likewise, in the case of causal asymmetries, we clarify a number of distinct meanings that may attach to the claim that one cause is "more important" than another. We then show that many apparently substantive disputes in the social sciences rest on misunderstandings of what such claims assert. Once clarified, many of these disputes turn out to lose their substance.

In general, then, our message is that it is important to clarify methodological issues in order to clear the decks for substantive analysis. Too often, radical theorists imply that their opponents are adequately discredited simply by showing that their arguments violate some foundational methodological precept: they are reductionist, or economistic, or undialectical, or individualistic. Our hope is that in clarifying the issues around a number of these methodological problems we will show that, in general, there is much less to these positions than meets the eye.

===============6===============

Marxism and Methodological Individualism

Perhaps the most striking example of the rejection of claims to Marxian methodological distinctiveness comes from those analytical Marxists who explicitly declare themselves proponents of "methodological individualism", thereby endorsing a methodological position they attribute to sound social science, but one that virtually all Marxists have traditionally rejected.[1] As is well known, Marx inveighed against the "individualism" of the classical economists and contractarian philosophers, heaping scorn on efforts to conceive individuals abstracted from social relations and on theories based upon the imputed choices of these "abstracted individuals". And nearly all Marxists, whatever their differences, have accorded explanatory relevance to social "totalities", in apparent opposition to the strictures of individualist forms of analysis. Furthermore, until quite recently, proponents of methodological individualism have been equally scornful of Marxism. Some methodological individualists—Hayek and Popper, among others—have even promoted methodological individualism expressly as an alternative to Marxian explanatory practices. It is therefore ironic, to say the least, to maintain that what is worth taking seriously in Marx's thought can be reconstructed in methodological individualist fashion; and that only by recasting Marxian explanations in this way can we save the "rational kernel" (as Marx might have put it) of Marx's thought from the indefensibility of so many of his own formulations and from the obscurantism that afflicts much of what has come to be identified as Marxism.

---

1. Of course, not all Marxists working in an analytical style would follow Elster in this regard, but the position has been advanced by a number of influential figures. See, for instance, Adam Przeworski, "The Challenge of Methodological Individualism to Marxist Analysis", *Politics & Society* (forthcoming); and John Roemer, *A General Theory of Exploitation and Class* (Cambridge, MA: Harvard University Press, 1982).

We are sympathetic to the idea that what is distinctive in Marxian theory is substantive, not methodological, and that the methodology adopted by Marxists ought to be just good scientific methodology. But methodological individualism is *not* good scientific methodology, even if, as we shall show, some of the intuitions that motivate it are sound.

The plausibility of Marxian methodological individualism depends, of course, on what methodological individualism is thought to be. Unfortunately, at the current stage of discussion, many of the obscurities that have always pervaded debates about methodological individualism are effectively reproduced in the Marxian context. One objective of this essay is to try to reduce this confusion by clarifying the stakes in claims for and against methodological individualism, both as these apply to the specific context of Marxian explanations and to social scientific explanations generally.

In the next section, we characterize methodological individualism by contrasting it with three other methodological stances towards explanation in social science. This will be followed by a more intensive discussion of methodological individualism itself. We shall argue that the reductionist ambitions of methodological individualism cannot be fulfilled. Nevertheless we shall argue, in the final section of this essay, that a practical implication of methodological individualism—that the micro-foundations for macro-level theory should be elaborated—is timely and important, even if methodological individualism itself is not.

Throughout this discussion, Jon Elster's book, *Making Sense of Marx*, will be a central point of reference.[2] Elster is among the most insightful of Marxian methodological individualists, and his book represents the most sustained attempt by anyone within the Marxian tradition to defend methodological individualism. It is therefore a useful point of departure for an examination of the doctrine's strengths, as well as its flaws.

A Typology of Methodological Positions on Explanation

Methodological individualism is a claim about *explanation*. It is the view that all social phenomena are best explained by the properties of the individuals who comprise the phenomena; or, equivalently, that any explanation involving macro-level social concepts should in principle be reduced to micro-level explanations involving only individuals and their properties.

---

2. Jon Elster, *Making Sense of Marx* (Cambridge: Cambridge University Press, 1985).

In order to give methodological individualism a precise definition, it will be helpful to contrast it with three other possible views: *atomism, radical holism* and *anti-reductionism.*[3] The first two positions, at least in their pure form, probably have no actual defenders. However they are implicit tendencies within social theory. Indeed, in debates over methodological individualism, disputants sometimes appear to confuse their opponents' views with one or the other of these positions. Thus defenders of methodological individualism depict anti-reductionists as radical holists, and defenders of anti-reductionist positions sometimes regard methodological individualists as atomists. Therefore, in order to clarify the issues at stake in the controversy over methodological individualism, it will be useful to map out all four possibilities.

These methodological stances towards social scientific explanation differ in what they regard as explanatory. They can be distinguished on two dimensions: whether or not they regard the properties of and relations among aggregate social entities as *irreducibly* explanatory; and whether or not they regard relations among individuals as explanatory.[4] Aggregate social entities include such things as societies, groups, classes, organizations, nations, communities. Such entities have properties (e.g. inflation rates, institutional forms, distributions of income) and exist in a variety of relations to each other (e.g. relations between unions and corporations, between nations, between collectively organized classes). Individuals also have both properties (e.g. beliefs, abilities, resources) and exist in a variety of relations with other individuals (e.g. sibling relations, employer–employee relations, etc.). Taking these two dimensions together, we get the following typology of principles of explanation of social phenomena.

Atomism

Atomism is a methodological stance that denies that relations are ever genuinely explanatory, whether those relations are between individuals or between social entities. Consider any social phenomenon—for example, the transformation from feudalism to capitalism. An atomist would say that this transition can in principle be fully explained by causal processes operating strictly internal to individuals in the society in

---

3. Each of these positions, properly understood, register claims about the (social) world. Thus anti-reductionists do not oppose reductionism on methodological grounds; indeed, they favor theoretical reductions whenever they are possible. The name "anti-reductionism" reflects a considered view of what is known about successful social scientific explanations—as does atomism, radical holism *and also methodological individualism.*

4. These dimensions are not strictly symmetrical since "properties of individuals" are not included in the second dimension. The reason for this is that atomism accepts the explanatory relevance of properties of individuals but not relations among individuals.

question. While *interactions* among these individuals matter for explaining the emergence of feudalism, the causal processes that govern the outcomes of such interactions are entirely intraindividual.[5] The atomist would insist, in other words, that only entities that are fully constituted non-relationally are explanatory.

On the face of it, atomism seems plainly unsustainable. In our everyday lives we exist within a network of relations to other people—as parents, siblings, employers, customers, etc. And these relations appear to be explanatory, and also, it would seem, irreducible: being a parent, for instance, necessarily involves another individual, the child. But atomism is not quite so implausible as it may at first appear. The atomist might argue that everything that seems explanatory about irreducible relations between individuals actually is explanatory only because of the corresponding (non-relational) psychological states of these individuals; that what matters explanatorily in, say, power relations between individuals is not an irreducible relation between these individuals, but their beliefs and desires, considered atomistically. If I believe you will punish me if I do X and you believe that I have these beliefs, then we will each act in particular ways. The apparent power "relation" between individuals, the argument would go, is really no more than a set of reciprocal beliefs and it is these beliefs, rather than any "objective relation", that explains actions.

Although we grant that beliefs and desires explain actions, it seems to us that the world outside the mind helps explain why agents think and want what they do. One plausible explanation for such things as beliefs about power is the objective power relations between people. Beliefs about power are formed, in part at least, by the *practices* of the powerful and the powerless. The enduring interconnection among these practices is precisely what is meant by the "power relation" between the powerful and the powerless. If such relations help explain beliefs and beliefs help explain action then (assuming transitivity) such relational facts help explain agents' actions. Atomism *might* be right in claiming that relational facts affect actions only by virtue of their affecting (atomistic) mental states. But it is a *non sequitur* to conclude from this that irreducibly relational facts are explanatorily impotent.

It is for this reason that theorists who insist on the reducibility of social explanations to individual explanations generally defend the

---

5. If the concept of "relation" is equated with "interaction", then, plainly, no theorist could deny the explanatory relevance of relations. Even a radical atomist would acknowledge that the interactions of a parent with a child is consequential for the child. What is being claimed by atomists, therefore, is not that interactions have no consequences, but that interactions are governed entirely by mechanisms located within the atomistically constituted entities engaged in the interactions.

explanatory importance of genuinely relational properties of individuals. This combination of methodological commitments—a belief in the reducibility of social explanations to individual explanations and a belief in the explanatory importance of relations among individuals—defines what is generally called methodological individualism.

Methodological Individualism

Methodological individualism shares with atomism the view that social explanations are ultimately reducible to individual level explanations. Elster states this claim explicitly at the beginning of *Making Sense of Marx*. He defines methodological individualism as "the doctrine that all social phenomena—their structure and their change—are in principle explicable in ways that only involve individuals—their properties, their goals, their beliefs and their actions. To go from social institutions and aggregate patterns of behavior to individuals is the same kind of operation as going from cells to molecules."[6]

Elster, however, is not an atomist in that he does not proscribe irreducible relational properties of individuals from social scientific explanations. Indeed, Elster argues that the inventory of individual properties that is the basis for explaining social phenomena extends far beyond the beliefs, desires and other psychological properties of individuals. He concedes that "many properties of individuals, such as 'powerful', are inherently relational, so that an accurate description of one individual may involve reference to others".[7] "Relational properties" would also include being a sibling or a parent or an employer. Nowhere does Elster (or any other Marxist defender of methodological individualism) claim that these relational properties are reducible to atomistic properties.

It is sometimes thought that methodological individualism implies a rejection of the holistic claim that "the whole is more than the sum of the parts". While atomism unequivocally regards wholes as no more than collections of parts, the fact that methodological individualism accepts the explanatory relevance of relational properties implies that, unlike atomism, it can accept this central tenet of its putative rival.

The issue hinges on what is meant by "sum" and "parts". One way of reading the holistic claim is the following: the parts of society are individuals with *atomistic* properties, i.e. properties that can be defined for each individual independently of all other individuals. The whole, then, is "greater" than the "sum" of these parts in the sense that the properties

---

6. *Making Sense of Marx*, p. 5.
7. Ibid., p. 6.

of the whole come from the systematic relational patterns of *interaction* among these individuals—the relations that bind them together—and not simply from the aggregation of their atomistic (i.e. non-relational) properties. On the other hand, if *relational* properties are included in the descriptions of the parts themselves, then it is no longer true that the whole is more than the sum of its parts. Everything that was included in the word "greater" in the holistic formulation has now been packed into the redescription of the "parts".[8]

This point can be illustrated formally. Let us say that we have a system with two "parts", X and Y. If the whole, Z, is equal to the sum of the parts, we would say that:

$$Z = b_1X + b_2Y$$

That is, the relevant magnitude of Z is completely determined by the sum of effects b_1 from part X and b_2 from part Y. If there are interactions between X and Y of the form XY, then:

$$Z = b_1X + b_2Y + b_3XY$$

and thus the whole is greater than the sum of its parts (i.e. the interaction of X and Y has effect b_3 on Z in addition to their additive effects). Now, let us redescribe the parts in the following way:

$$X^* = X(1 + b_3Y/2b_1) \quad Y^* = Y(1 + b_3X/2_b2)$$

In these new descriptions of the parts, the interactions of the parts-within-the-whole are represented as relational properties of the parts themselves. With these new descriptions, it is no longer the case that the whole, Z, is greater than the sum of its newly described parts, for now:

$$Z = b_1X^* + b_2Y^*$$

It is important to note that these redescriptions are only possible *post facto*, after the parts are inserted into the whole (i.e. after all of the interactions with other parts are determined). This reparameterization can make atomism look more plausible than it deserves. But such appearances should not mislead us into thinking that relational properties are eliminable, not just nominally, but in fact.[9]

---

8. This familiar deflation of the holism/individualism debate is elaborated, for example, in Ernest Nagel, *The Structure of Science* (London: Routledge & Kegan Paul, 1961).

9. This algebraic reformulation is closely analogous to the way some evolutionists defend the idea that the single gene is the unit of selection. See Elliott Sober, *The Nature of Selection: Evolutionary Theory in Philosophical Focus* (Cambridge, MA: Bradford Books, 1984), Chapter 7.

Methodological individualism remains distinct from both radical holism and anti-reductionism in its insistence that only relations among individuals can be irreducibly explanatory. Methodological individualists deny that aggregate social categories are ever irreducibly explanatory. If a social property is explanatory, this is because it is reducible to relational properties of particular individuals. The property of a society "being in a revolutionary situation", for example, is not irreducibly explanatory in the methodological individualist view. This property possesses whatever explanatory force it has in virtue of the properties of and relations among the individuals in the society. The aggregate social property "revolutionary situation" is no more than an aggregation of all of these particular individual properties and relations. It is only a *convenient* expression. Thus any explanation in which the expression "revolutionary situation" appears can be reduced in principle to an explanation (no doubt of considerable complexity) involving only properties of and relations among individuals.

Radical Holism

Radical holism stands in sharp contrast to methodological individualism. For radical holists, relations among individuals are essentially epiphenomenal with respect to social explanations. They are generated by the operation of the whole, and in their own right they explain nothing. It is not simply that "the whole is more than the sum of its parts". Rather, the whole is the sole genuine cause and the parts (even when constituted relationally) are mere artifacts. Macro-social categories—capitalism, the state, class relations—are not merely irreducible to micro-level processes. They are unaffected by these processes.

It is difficult to find explicit defenses of radical holism in its pure form, but there are certain explanatory tendencies in social science that reflect this kind of thinking. The Marxist tradition, because of its stress on the "totality", has perhaps been particularly susceptible to such ideas. Three examples are worth mentioning: teleological reasoning in the theory of history, extreme formulations in arguments for structural causality, and what can be termed "collective agency" arguments.

Holistic teleologies figure in accounts of history that see the trajectory of social change as objectively directed towards an ultimate goal that exists independently of the subjective goals of human actors. In these cases, explanatory force is ascribed to this "end" of history. Individuals, then, are only agents of goal-achieving impersonal social forces; and what they do or choose is explained by—but does not explain—social phenomena. Their actions and choices are not mechanisms but consequences of the immanent principle whose career social science is supposed to trace. In putative explanations of this sort, social facts explain social facts directly without individual-level mechanisms playing any explanatory role.

A parallel tendency towards radical holism, of considerable importance in recent Western Marxism, is suggested by some of the more extravagant declarations of Louis Althusser and his followers.[10] Despite their express opposition to vestiges of Hegelian teleological thinking, Althusserians effectively reproduced some of its more dubious features. Thus Althusser proposed the obscure notion of "structural causality", according to which structures cause structures and individuals are only "supports" of social relations.[11] While such claims may simply reflect Althusser's rhetorical style, some Althusserian explanations appear to dispense with individual level mechanisms in principle.

Collectivist-agency arguments are embodied in statements of the form: "the bourgeoisie was unwilling to make compromises" or "the proletariat took advantage of the crisis" or, to take a famous quote from Marx, "mankind always sets itself only such tasks as it can solve".[12] In most cases, such expressions are simply elliptical or at worst express a certain expository sloppiness rather than deep methodological error. The real referents in the statements could be, for example, organizations (parties, unions) which are viewed as representatives of the classes in question, or the statements could be claims about the distribution of beliefs in the relevant populations. There are times, however, when such expressions seem to imply a belief in collective consciousness and collective agency, where a class or even humanity as such thinks, chooses and acts. Generally, such non-elliptical treatments of collective subjects are linked to holistic teleologies of history: the objective purpose of history in the teleology is represented as the goal of a genuinely Collective Subject. But even when collective subjects are not linked to teleologies of history, positing such entities tends to marginalize the explanatory relevance of individual-level relations within a holistic argument.

---

10. Cf. *For Marx* (London: New Left Books, 1969); and *Reading Capital* (London: New Left Books, 1970).

11. There are places in Althusser's work in which the treatment of individuals as "bearers" and "supports" of the structure can be interpreted as consistent with micro-foundational reasoning. Thus, for example, in his analysis of ideology, Althusser discusses the process through which individuals are formed as subjects. This analysis of "interpellation" could be considered an account of how social structural causes shape micro-individual states, which in turn have effects on the social structural relations themselves. See Louis Althusser, "Ideology and Ideological State Apparatuses", in *Lenin and Philosophy* (London: New Left Books, 1971). For a much more systematic development of these relatively primitive arguments of Althusser's which makes the micro-mechanisms of subject-formation much more explicit, see Goran Therborn, *The Power of Ideology and the Ideology of Power* (London: NLB/Verso, 1982).

12. Karl Marx, Preface to *A Contribution to the Critique of Political Economy* (1859).

Elster vehemently attacks all of these forms of radical holism—or what he calls "methodological collectivism"—in Marx's work and the Marxist tradition. He has been particularly intent on attacking functional explanations within Marxism—explanations of the existence and persistence of particular social institutions because of their beneficial effects for ruling classes—on the grounds that such explanations generally reflect teleological thinking about the nature of society and history and typically ignore the importance of specifying micro-level mechanisms.

These errors, Elster argues, are derived from the methodological doctrines Marx inherited from Hegel. We believe instead that sloppiness and rhetorical excess are more nearly the culprit than considered, radical holist convictions. Few, if any, Marxists have ever imagined that functional relations could be established in the absence of micro-level mechanisms or that collective agents could ever be more than aggregations of individual actors. But Marxists (including Marx) have indeed failed rather frequently to trace out the implications of these (eminently sensible) beliefs. Elster has done well to identify instances, even if he has misrepresented their source and character.

In any case, Elster is right in so far as he inveighs against radical holism. The plain fact that if there were no people there would be no societies underwrites the methodological assumption that causal mechanisms involving individuals must always be implicated in social explanations. The issue is not whether the individual level of analysis can be eliminated, but how it should be linked to macro-level social analysis. Methodological individualism maintains that macro-level phenomena can always be reduced to their micro-level realizations, at least in principle. Anti-reductionism rejects this thesis.

Anti-reductionism

Anti-reductionism acknowledges the importance of micro-level accounts in explaining social phenomena, while allowing for the irreducibility of macro-level accounts to these micro-level explanations. Methodological individualism insists that an important goal of science is to reduce explanations to ever more micro-levels of analysis. For a methodological individualist, to explain a phenomenon is just to provide an account of the micro-mechanisms that produce it. Aggregate, supra-individual social categories are therefore admissible only *faute de mieux*, in consequence of our cognitive limitations or the inadequate state of our knowledge. In contrast, anti-reductionists do not prejudge in any given problem whether macro-level (social) explanations are finally reducible to micro-level (individualist) accounts.

This may seem like a paradoxical stance: how can one be simultaneously committed to the irreducibility of social explanations to individual-level explanations and to the importance of elaborating micro-foundations? The resolution of this apparent paradox is discussed in the next section.

Anti-reductionism v. Methodological Individualism

Methodological individualists insist that in principle it is desirable not simply to *add* an account of micro-causes to macro-explanations, but to *replace* macro-explanations with micro-explanations. Were we able, methodological individualists would have us ban aggregate social concepts or else tolerate them strictly as expository conveniences.[13]

The issue of reductionism of the macro to the micro in social explanations parallels issues familiar in the philosophy of mind.[14] Any particular distribution of properties among individuals constitutes a particular social state. Similarly, any particular configuration of neurophysiological states of human brains constitutes a particular mental state. It would therefore seem that a complete account of individual properties (or neurophysiological configurations) would constitute a full and adequate explanation of social phenomena (or mental states) and their effects. Thus it would seem reasonable to conclude that we should be able, at least in principle, to reduce macro-phenomena to micro-phenomena.

To understand why this is not so, it will be helpful to introduce the familiar distinction in the philosophy of science between *tokens* and *types*.[15] "Tokens" are particular instances: for example, a particular strike by a group of workers in a particular factory or an idea in the head of a particular individual. "Types" are characteristics that tokens may have in common. Thus a particular strike—a token event—can be subsumed under a variety of possible "types": *strikes, class struggles, social conflicts*, etc. Similarly, being rich is a type of which Rockefeller is one token. Types are general categories that subsume particular events or instances.

---

13. A thorough methodological individualist reductionist would also argue that, in principle, individual-level explanations should be reduced to neurophysiological explanations, and neurophysiological explanations ultimately to explanations only involving atomic particles and their interrelations. The ultimate ambition of science is to reduce all phenomena to the operation of physical laws.

14. See, for example, the development of these ideas in Jerry Fodor, *The Language of Thought* (New York: Thomas Crowell, 1975), Chapter 1.

15. For a general discussion of the type/token distinction as it applies to the problem of reductionism, see R. Boyd, "Materialism without Reductionism", in N. Block, ed., *Readings in Philosophy of Psychology* (Harvard University Press, 1980).

Reductionism raises different issues for tokens and types. Most Marxists, because they are materialists, probably would endorse *token*-reductionism.[16] Thus, if current views about the relation between human beings' minds and brains are correct, Marxists (and most non-Marxists too) would concede that a particular mental state in a particular individual can be explained by describing the brain state of that individual at that moment in time. Similarly, for social phenomena, particular instances can be explained by appeal to the activities, properties and relations of the particular individuals who collectively comprise the phenomenon.[17]

The real debate, then, concerns the reducibility of macro-social types to micro-individual types. The distinction between tokens and types can be applied both to social entities and to individuals. Thus, we can define capitalism as a type of society and the United States in 1987 as a token instance of that type. And we can define the capitalist–worker relation as a type of relation among individuals, while the relation between the owner of a particular firm and the employees of that firm would constitute a token instance of such a relation.[18]

Both methodological individualists and anti-reductionists admit the explanatory power of type-concepts referring to individuals. Where they

---

16. "Materialism", in this context, is the claim that all tokens are "made" of matter. To oppose materialism would be to accord ontological status to (putatively) non-material entities (like disembodied minds or *élans vitals*).

17. A number of philosophers have defended the idea that a person's brain state at a given time does not uniquely determine what the person believes at that time. The point is that the content of a belief also depends on the person's physical environment and on the social environment as well. The former thesis has been defended by Hilary Putnam in "The Meaning of 'Meaning'", in *Mind, Language, and Reality* (Cambridge: Cambridge University Press, 1975), the latter by Tyler Burge in "Individualism and Psychology" *Philosophical Review*, 95 1986, pp. 3–43. We do not take a stand on the plausibility of either of these positions here, and the latter idea is best laid to one side for the purposes of grasping the analogy we see between the problem posed by methodological individualism and the mind/body problem.

18. Discussions about "social relations" often ignore the distinction between type concepts that refer to relations among individuals and type concepts that are irreducibly social. The "capital–labor relation" is a type concept that identifies the theoretically salient properties that all of the particular instances of relations between capitalists and workers have in common. In this sense it is a micro-level type concept. While this concept may be irreducibly relational—that is, it cannot be represented in atomistic terms—it does not contravene the strictures of methodological individualism, since the relations it describes are among individuals. Ironically, perhaps, those "fundamentalist Marxists" (as they are sometimes called), who emphasize the supreme explanatory importance of the capital-labor relation for understanding capitalism and who most categorically assert the methodological distinctiveness of Marxism may be closer to methodological individualism than those Marxists who emphasize the importance of various kinds of aggregate social entities such as class formations, state apparatuses, etc. Explanations based on the capital–labor relation may be very *abstract*, but they are still fundamentally rooted in a micro-logic. An abstract analysis in terms of micro-type concepts is not equivalent to a macro-level analysis.

differ is in their view of the explanatory status of type concepts referring
to aggregate social entities: methodological individualists insist that such
type concepts can be reduced to type concepts referring only to individuals; anti-reductionists argue that, in general, this is not possible.

The type/token distinction allows us to see that a science will have at
least two sorts of explanatory projects: it will seek to explain why *token*
events occur and also to explain the nature of the *types* that fall within
its domain. Thus we would want to explain why specific instances of
capitalism emerged when and where they did, but also explain what
capitalism is. The methodological individualist would be committed to
the micro-reducibility of both the token social event *and* the social type.
Our quarrel is not with the first of these claims, but with the second.

Our objection can be clarified by an example in which type-reductionism is justified. Consider "water" (that is, a kind of substance, not a
particular sample of water). When we say that water is reducible to H_2O,
we mean that whatever effects water has can be reduced to effects of
H_2O. In any explanation in which water plays an explanatory role, the
effects of water come from the effects of aggregates of H_2O molecules.

This reduction is possible for water because there is a single micro-
property corresponding to the macro-property in question. Something is
water if and only if it is an *ensemble of H_2O molecules*. However in the
case of social phenomena (and mental states), there is, in fact, no
similarly unique correspondence between *types*. Consider mental states.
For any kind of mental state—for example, the belief that snow is white,
the intention to buy a chocolate bar, the feeling of pain—there are in
principle many, perhaps infinitely many, physical states that could
realize the mental state in question. This relationship is referred to as
one of *multiple realizability*: mental states can be *multiply realized* by
many different brain states. Similarly for social phenomena: many
distributions of properties of individuals—their beliefs, desires,
resources, interrelationships—can realize the same social type. In
the case of multiply realized properties and relations, type–type
reductionism will not be possible.

The reason why reductionism is not possible in such cases is well illustrated by an example from evolutionary biology. The property of "fitness" figures in many explanations in evolutionary theory. To every
token instance of fitness (i.e. the fitness of a particular organism in a
particular environment), there corresponds a particular configuration of
physical facts about the organism in question. In each of these instances,
we can say that the physical facts explain why this particular organism
has the degree of fitness it does. There is no reason to believe, however,
that any single physical property corresponds to the general category
"fitness", that the same mechanisms explain the fitness of, say, a frog

and a giraffe. In all likelihood, fit organisms share no physical properties in virtue of which they are all fit. The *only* explanatorily relevant property they share is that they are instances of a single (multiply realized) type. Thus, while a token reduction of individual instances of fitness to physical mechanisms is possible, a type reduction is not. Fitness is supervenient on its micro-realizations.[19]

Methodological individualists are type-reductionists with respect to social phenomena. But to insist on type-reductions as an a priori methodological requirement is plainly unwarranted. The feasibility of type-reductions is an empirical question. It *could* be the case that type-reductions actually are possible in this domain. But they almost certainly are not. Type-reductions would be possible if the relation between social phenomena and individual properties were like the relation between water and H_2O. But in so far as the relation of social facts to their micro-realizations is like the relation of mental states to brain states or like the relation of fitness to physical properties of morphology and physiology, type-reductionism will prove to be a fruitless quest.[20]

Consider the fact that capitalist societies have strong tendencies towards economic growth. This property is explicable, in part, as a consequence of the competitive character of capitalist markets, which generate innovations and continual investments that, cumulatively, produce growth. This process, in turn, is explained by the survival of those firms which most effectively make profits in the market. Survival and profit-making, in this explanation, are similar to "fitness" in evolutionary biology. For each token instance of economic survival, we can identify a set of decisions made by individuals with particular beliefs, preferences, information and resources that explains why a particular firm survives. However, there need not be anything in common *at the micro-level* between the mechanisms that enable firm X to survive and the mechanisms that enable firms Y or Z to survive. X may survive because of the passivity of workers (enabling capitalists to introduce innovations without resistance); Y because of the ruthlessness of the owner; Z because of the scientific/technical rationality of the manage-

---

19. Cf. A. Rosenberg, "The Supervenience of Biological Concepts", in E. Sober, ed., *Conceptual Issues in Evolutionary Biology* (Cambridge, MA: MIT Press, 1984); and E. Sober, *The Nature of Selection*, (Cambridge, MA: MIT Press, 1984), Chapter 1.

20. The argument that social type concepts cannot be reduced to individual-level type concepts is very similar to the frequent claim of holists in social science that macro-phenomena have "emergent properties". An emergent property is a property that can only be described at the macro-level. If, however, such properties were not multiply realized, then any explanation in which they figured could be reduced to the corresponding micro-level explanation. The claim, therefore, that emergent properties are irreducibly *explanatory* depends upon the supervenience of the macro on the micro.

ment team, and so on.[21] The social-level explanation of growth in terms of the macro-processes of competitive market relations, therefore, can be realized by a vast array of possible micro-mechanisms. Accordingly, token reductionism is possible in this case, but type reductionism is not.

In short, the reductionist program of methodological individualism fails because science has explanatory projects beyond the explanation of token events. Besides asking why this organism or that firm survived, we also want to explain what various objects and processes have in common. When the properties cited in answer to such questions have multiple realizations at the micro-level, the explanations provided by the macro-theory will not, even in principle, be reducible to a micro-account.[22]

The Relevance of Micro-foundational Analysis for Macro-theory

It might be thought that anti-reductionism implies that micro-level analyses are either unimportant or, worse, irrelevant to macro-theory. But this impression is unfounded; anti-reductionism is not radical holism. Indeed, far from rejecting micro-levels of analysis, the form of

---

21. If a common property or process among these firms, specifiable at the micro-level, were discovered, a type-reduction of the macro- to the micro-level would be possible in this case. Our point is that this would be an *empirical discovery*, comparable to discovering in evolutionary biology, contrary to current theory, that all instances of fitness reflect a single micro-level mechanism.

22. Graham Macdonald and Philip Pettit, in their book *Semantics and Social Science* (London, Routledge & Kegan Paul, 1981), pp. 144–9, consider the idea we develop here, but reach a different verdict on its plausibility. Suppose that A and B are social properties and that there is a non-accidental regularity such that whenever A obtains, so does B. "In that case", they say, "while each particular A–B succession might be explicable just by reference to individuals, there would be no individualistic explanation of the succession taken as a nomic regularity; this, because there would be no unified individualistic way of characterizing the regularity, each A–B succession being liable to bear any of an indefinite number of individualistic descriptions" (p. 145). They concede that such irreducibly social regularities would be a problem for methodological individualism; however, they argue that no such lawful regularities could be well supported empirically or theoretically motivated, and that social scientists would be countenancing "anomalies and miracles" to recognize such laws (even were they probabilistic in form). We are not convinced by Macdonald and Pettit's arguments for this conclusion; moreover, we doubt that the purely philosophical reasons they adduce could settle this matter. For example, there could be many different individual level explanations for individuals' being unemployed and thus many individual-level explanations for the rate of unemployment. Nevertheless, a change in the rate of unemployment could be lawfully related to a change in the rate of inflation. This "nomic connection" would then be irreducible to the individualistic explanations of unemployment. It is worth noting that Macdonald and Pettit believe that their argument refutes sociological functionalism. Our view is that functionalism stands or falls on whether it is empirically adequate; there is no purely conceptual argument that defeats it from the start.

anti-reductionism we have described attaches great importance to the "micro-foundations" of macro-explanations.

By "micro-foundations" we mean the following. There are four possible explanatory connections between social phenomena and individuals' properties: first, individuals' properties can explain social phenomena; second, social phenomena can explain individuals' properties; third, individuals' properties can explain individuals' properties; and fourth, social phenomena can explain social phenomena. The critique of radical holism implies that the fourth of these explanatory connections is legitimate only when the causal chain in the explanation involves combinations of the first two. That is, social phenomena explain social phenomena only in so far as there are linkages—causal mechanisms—that work through the micro-individual level. Social structures explain social structures via the ways they determine the properties and actions of individuals which in turn determine social structural outcomes.[23] The investigation of such micro-pathways through which macro-structures have their effects is the study of micro-foundations.

In defending methodological individualism, Elster advances two reasons why a concern with micro-foundations is important in social science. His reasons are sound, even if the reductionist ambition of Elster's overall methodological position is not.

First, as a practical matter, the specification of micro-mechanisms is often indispensable for establishing the credibility of macro-level explanations. Because it is so difficult empirically to distinguish spurious correlations from genuine causal relations, and because so many causes may obscure the relationships posited in a theory, the elaboration of microfoundations is necessary for rendering a social theory credible. Thus Elster writes:

> If the goal of science is to *explain by means of laws*, there is a need to reduce the time-span between *explanans* and *explanandum*—between cause and effect—as much as possible, in order to avoid spurious explanations. The latter arise in two main ways: by the confusion of explanation and correlation and by the confusion of explanation and necessitation.... Both of these risks are reduced when we approach the ideal of a continuous chain of cause and effect, that is, when we reduce the time-lag between *explanans* and *explanandum*. This, again, is closely related to going from the aggregate to the less

---

23. It must be emphasized that the necessity of micro-mediations does not imply that the macro-explanation is reducible to those micro-mechanisms. The theory of fitness in evolutionary biology implies the existence of innumerable micro-mediations, of micro-mechanisms through which different instances of fitness are realized. Yet the theory of evolution is not reducible to any causal law operating at the level of these micro-mechanisms.

aggregate level of phenomena. In this perspective, reductionism is not an end in itself, only a concomitant of another desideratum.[24]

Of course, there is no reason to believe in general that there will be a single micro-foundation for any given macro-social phenomenon. As we argued above, the fact that there are many micro-states for a given macro-state is precisely what makes individualist reductionism impossible. Nevertheless, since every macro-process must have micro-realizations, the elaboration of the possible micro-foundations adds credibility to macro-arguments.

In addition, Elster offers a less heuristic reason for seeking micro-foundations:

> It is not only our confidence in the explanation, but our understanding of it that is enhanced when we go from macro to micro, from longer to shorter time-lags. To explain is to provide a *mechanism*, to open up the black box and show the nuts and bolts, the cogs and wheels, the desires and beliefs that generate the aggregate outcomes.[25]

Elaborating the micro-foundations of macro-social explanations not only improves confidence in theories; it also deepens them. Provided that we allow for the possibility of multiple micro-foundations for a given macro-explanation (and thus for the non-reducibility of the macro-phenomenon to the micro-foundations), the discovery of the micro-level processes through which macro-level phenomena are realized enriches theoretical understanding.

The relevance of micro-foundational analysis for macro-structural theory can be illustrated by Elster's discussion of class formation in *Making Sense of Marx*. Class formation is the process by which classes are constituted as collective actors in class struggles. Marxists have been interested in sorting out the relationship between different kinds of social structural conditions and different kinds of class formations. Certain conditions, for example, may be particularly conducive to the formation of revolutionary class organizations; others may give rise to reformist organizations.

Elster holds that the key to understanding class formation is understanding the mechanisms that facilitate or hinder the development of class consciousness in individuals. To explore these mechanisms, Elster deploys a range of concepts derived from the theory of rational strategic interaction (or "game theory"). Specifically, he urges that the process of

---

24. *Making Sense of Marx*, p. 5.
25. Ibid.

class formation be understood in terms of ways of solving the familiar "freerider" problem, the problem of motivating individuals to contribute towards some "public good" that redounds to everyone's advantage, regardless of contribution. Elster describes this problem as follows:

> Clearly, whatever anyone else does, it is in my interest to abstain. If all others engage in collective action, I can get the freerider benefit by abstaining, and if everyone else abstains I can avoid the loss from unilateralism by abstaining too. Since the reasoning applies to each agent ... all will decide to abstain and no collective action will be forthcoming.[26]

If workers are rational egoists, they will prefer to be freeriders on the sacrifices of others rather than to make these sacrifices themselves. The theoretical issue, then, is to understand how the freerider problem can be overcome. If micro-level solutions are properly specified, we then can inquire into the social structural conditions conducive to creating these solutions.

Many "solutions" to the freerider problem have been discussed in the literature on collective action: individuals may act out of habit rather than rational calculation; side-payments and sanctions of various sorts may be used by the leadership of an organization to encourage participation; individuals may irrationally exaggerate the importance of their individual participation for the success of the collective action and thus believe that the benefits of the struggle in fact depend on their involvement when in fact this is not the case; the "game" may be repeated indefinitely so that actors take into consideration possible sanctions in the future for present behavior; preference orderings of individuals may change in ways which make them more altruistic. Some or all of these may be present in any given empirical context.

Elster's proposal is to understand class solidarity as a transformation of the preference orderings characteristic of a freerider problem (the prisoner's dilemma pay-off matrix) to an assurance game. Whereas in a prisoner's dilemma, each individual prefers to sponge off the sacrifices of others, in an assurance game each individual's highest preference is to cooperate with others (to join in common sacrifices) so long as each person feels assured that others will cooperate as well. In an assurance game people are unwilling to be unilateral altruists—to make sacrifices even if no one else is willing to do so. They do not want to be "suckers". But they prefer cooperation over freeriding. Elster designates this preference ordering "conditional altruism".

Elster's account of possible micro-foundations for overcoming the

---

26. Ibid., p. 360.

freerider problem suggests a particular research agenda: that we explore the social conditions which enhance or undermine conditional altruistic preference orderings and which facilitate or hinder the translation of individuals' preferences into solidaristic practices. Elster holds that many of Marx's own analyses of working-class formation can be interpreted in this light. For example, Marx ascribed considerable importance to the concentration and interdependence of workers in large factories. These factors are important in part because of the way they increase the level of information among workers about the likely preferences and behavior of fellow workers. Such shared information is crucial for conditional altruistic *preferences* to lead to solidaristic *practices*. Similarly, Marxists have always emphasized the importance of leadership and organization in class formation. Elster argues that leaders may play a particularly important role in struggles in which conditional altruist motivations are present:

> Obviously, leaders are always necessary, regardless of the motivation of individuals to coordinate collective action. If the motivations are also such that individuals must be assured of each other before they act, leadership takes on the additional function of providing such assurance. If one individual knows and is trusted by one hundred people, he can create the information conditions by two hundred transactions—first asking each of them about their willingness to join the collective action and then telling each about the willingness of everyone else. By contrast, bilateral communication between the hundred will require about five thousand acts of communication. The information gains from leadership can be quite substantial.[27]

Organization and leadership thus provide potential participants with an indirect communication network essential to convincing them that they will not be "suckers" in collective struggles.

Table 6.1 What is Explanatory of Social Phenomena?

		Properties of and relations among aggregate social entities are irreducibly explanatory	
		Yes	No
Relations among individuals are explanatory	Yes	Anti-reductionism	Methodological Individualism
	No	Radical Holism	Atomism

---

27. Ibid., pp. 366–7. Everything that Elster says about "leaders" as individual persons would also apply to organizations.

While these kinds of social determinants of class formation—concentration and interdependence of workers in large factories, the emergence of effective organization and leadership, etc.—have long been recognized as important, it is unlikely that the role of these factors in enhancing the information requirements for solidarity would be recognized in the absence of an elaboration of micro-foundations. Specifying micro-foundations, then, can help to elaborate the range of different social structural conditions capable of satisfying the same micro-level requirement (in this case, providing the information conditions for translating conditional altruistic preferences into solidaristic actions). Ethnic homogeneity, for example, may help to compensate for the disadvantages of small factories; or, in a complimentary manner, ethnic heterogeneity may counteract the favorable information conditions of large factories.

The elaboration of micro-foundations, therefore, helps provide theoretical order to the categories used in the macro-explanations of social theory. This, in turn, can facilitate the task of resolving empirical anomalies in research. Consider, again, the micro-foundations of conditional altruism in class formation. The theory predicts that ethnic homogeneity will increase the likelihood of class formation because of the ways it facilitates the information requirements of class solidarity. We then observe cases of ethnically homogeneous working-class communities or workplaces within which the level of manifest class solidarity is low. The elaboration of micro-foundations helps to guide research towards explaining the failure of the prediction. Is solidarity low because some other social factor has undermined the information conditions, counteracting the effects of ethnic homogeneity? Or is it low because the preference orderings of the workers is not in fact conditionally altruist? Or, in spite of favorable information conditions and conditional altruism, is solidaristic struggle low because some social condition has raised the costs of collective action to the point that workers are afraid to struggle? Or, finally, is it because some alternative set of micro-foundations needs to be specified for the process of class formation itself? Without a focus on micro-foundations, it is difficult to know what questions to ask in the face of such anomalies.

It is one thing to call for the elaboration of micro-foundations of macro-theory and another to specify the form such micro-foundational analyses should take. Methodological individualists, Marxist or not, have generally emphasized rational strategic action models. These models assume rationality in that actors are held to choose actions that maximize the probability of achieving some goal. The models are strategic in that they assume actors make choices knowing that other actors also make choices in pursuit of their goals (thus, in making choices everyone must take everyone else's choices into account). Because of the emphasis on this kind of model, the work of writers like Elster, Przeworski, Roemer and others has sometimes been designated "rational choice Marxism".[28]

Many Marxists have been suspicious of the call for micro-foundational analyses by analytical Marxists because of the use of these models. Rational actor models are closely identified with methodological individualism and even neoclassical economics. But, as we have argued, belief in the importance of micro-foundational analysis does not require commitment to methodological individualism. In addition, there is no need to equate micro-foundational analyses with rational strategic actor models. There are many other possible kinds of micro-foundations of social phenomena. Theories of socialization which emphasize the inculcation of norms, habits and rituals, or even psychoanalytic theories of the unconscious can be used. The Marxist theory of ideology, understood as a theory of the process of forming social subjects, can also provide a basis for elaborating micro-foundations.[29] One therefore can reject formal rational strategic action models and still acknowledge the importance of micro-foundational analyses.

In any event, those analytical Marxists who have deployed rational actor models have done so because they feel they are heuristically useful, not because they believe that actors are in fact universally rational and selfish. Elster emphasizes this point. Understanding the kinds of behaviors which would be predicted on assumptions of selfish rational strategic action, Elster argues, can be a useful foil for specifying the ways in which non-selfish preferences and non-rational cognitive processes shape individual action. Precisely what the mix is in any given problem between rationality and irrationality, selfishness and altruism, intentionality and habit is, in Elster's view and in ours, an empirical question.

Conclusion

Marxist defenders of methodological individualism like Elster have been particularly concerned to attack what they see as tendencies towards radical holism in the Marxist tradition. The antidote they prescribe is placing the elaboration of micro-foundations at the center of the agenda of Marxist theory and research. We believe that tendencies towards radical holism are better ascribed to intellectual sloppiness than to

---

28. See, especially, Alan Carling, "Rational Choice Marxism", *New Left Review* 160 (1986).

29. See Goran Therborn, *The Power of Ideology*.

considered philosophical commitment. Nevertheless, these tendencies *are* evident among Marxian writers (and others too); and the prescription Elster and his co-thinkers propose is reasonable.

But it is neither necessary nor helpful to frame the call for microfoundations as a call for methodological individualism. To ban social types as objects of investigation is to impoverish the explanatory objectives of social science, and to contravene reasonable practices in the social sciences. Micro-foundations are important for macro-social theory because of the ways they help focus our questions and because of the ways they enrich our answers. But there is much more to science than their elaboration. If social types, as we suspect, are multiply realized, then micro-foundational accounts, important though they may be, cannot suffice to capture the explanatory power of macro-level theories.

We share the general view of analytical Marxists that what are most valuable and distinctive in the Marxist tradition are its substantive theses about the world. Marxian claims to methodological distinctiveness, generally, are misleading at best and harmful at worst. But so are assertions by methodological individualists concerning the proper way of understanding explanation in social science. Social science ought to be methodologically anti-reductionist if the properties and relations it investigates are multiply realized. This, we stress, is an empirical question, not one to be settled by methodological fiat.

7

Causal Asymmetries

Many debates in the social sciences revolve around issues of causal primacy and other asymmetries.[1] Often, proponents of contending positions agree that certain causes are relevant for explaining some phenomenon, but differ in their assessments of the relative importance of these causes (*quantitative asymmetry*) or in their understanding of the qualitatively different ways in which they enter into particular causal processes (*qualitative asymmetry*). Our aim in this chapter is to clarify the meaning of both quantitative and qualitative causal asymmetries and analyze their interconnection. We shall argue that sustainable causal primacy claims amount to assertions of one or another kind of *quantitative* asymmetry; claims for causal primacy that appeal to *qualitative* asymmetries either reduce to quantitative asymmetry claims or else are confused in ways that elude successful reconstruction.

These issues have been particularly salient in debates between Marxists and their critics. Marxists have generally argued that class (or the closely associated concepts of economic structure or forces of production) is the most important cause of many phenomena—from large-scale social changes to forms of the state, ideology and the oppression of women.[2] Critics of Marxism, including many "post-Marxists", have

---

1. In the philosophical literature on causation, the expression "causal asymmetry" typically designates asymmetries between causes and their effects. We shall use the expression differently—to designate asymmetries among causes in multicausal systems.

2. There are contemporary Marxists who reject claims for the causal primacy of class or, perhaps more precisely, reject the very legitimacy of making such claims. In somewhat different ways, the idea that it is meaningless to assign weights to different causes has been advanced by Richard Wolfe and Stephen Resnick in *Knowledge and Class* (Chicago: University of Chicago Press, 1988), and by Barry Hindess and Paul Q. Hirst, *Marx's Capital and Capitalism Today* (London: Routledge & Kegan Paul, 1977).

argued that other causal processes, irreducible to class, are at least as important. Two examples illustrate the issues in contention.

Both Marxists and neo-Weberians agree that class structure and the institutional rules of the political game are causes of state policies in contemporary capitalist societies. They differ, however, in their claims about the role these causes play. Marxists generally hold that class structure is the most fundamental cause of state policies, while neo-Weberians claim either that political factors are more important, or that the relative importance of particular causes depends on historical circumstances. Typically, Marxists also argue that there is a qualitative asymmetry between class and political institutions in the shaping of state policies: class structure determines the *limits* of possible variations in state policies, while political institutions and practices only *select* policy outcomes within these limits. A parallel claim is usually absent from neo-Weberian accounts of state policies: class and political factors are simply treated as two relevant causes.[3]

Another example arises in debates between Marxists and feminists over explanations of the oppression of women. Feminists and Marxists generally agree that specific forms of oppression of women—from wife battering and sexual harassment to job discrimination, unequal divisions of housework and political exclusion—are affected both by causes rooted in class relations and by causes rooted in gender relations. However, most Marxists, following Engels, have insisted that class domination is the most important cause of the oppression of women, and even that the system of property relations determines the ways in which other causes operate. Thus, while many Marxists acknowledge the importance of patriarchal ideology in explaining the oppression of women, they argue that the consequences of these cultural factors depend upon the class structural context within which they operate.[4] Thus they argue for the causal primacy of class and for the qualitative asymmetry of class and gender. Non-Marxist feminists have usually insisted, in opposition, that gender-based mechanisms, distinct from and

---

3. A Marxist perspective on these problems is provided by Goran Therborn in *What Does the Ruling Class Do When It Rules?* (London: NLB, 1978). A neo-Weberian perspective can be found in Theda Skocpol, "Bringing the State Back in: False Leads and Promising Starts in Current Theories and Research", in Peter Evans, Dietich Rueschemeyer and Theda Skocpol, eds, *Bringing the State Back In* (Cambridge: Cambridge University Press, 1985), pp. 3–37; and "Political Response to Capitalist Crisis: Neo-Marxist Theories of the State and the Case of the New Deal", *Politics & Society* 10:2 (1980). For a comparison of Marxist and neo-Weberian approaches which attempts to forge a Marxian synthesis, see Robert Alford and Roger Friedland, *The Powers of Theory* (Cambridge: Cambridge University Press, 1985).

4. See Johanna Brenner and Maria Ramas, "Rethinking Women's Oppression", *New Left Review* 144 (1984).

irreducible to class factors, are more important than class in explaining forms of women's oppression, and also that these mechanisms have effects that are independent of class structure.[5]

Remarkably, causal asymmetries have received little attention from philosophers of science. While there is a vast literature on the metaphysics of causation and the status of causes within scientific explanations, there has been hardly any discussion of what it means to assign differential importance to causes in multicausal systems or of the qualitatively different ways in which causes enter into causal processes.[6] If the intuitions that practicing social scientists had about these issues were clear and consistent, the dearth of philosophical analysis would be understandable. But of course, there is no consensus among social scientists. Throughout the social sciences, causal primacy claims abound—amidst general confusion about what causal primacy and other causal asymmetries involve. Such confusion is an impediment to theoretical advance.

Preliminary Considerations

Before launching into an analysis of causal asymmetries, it will be useful to lay out some of the assumptions we shall make and to indicate the boundaries of our discussion.

Causes and Explanations

We take it for granted that it is legitimate to attempt to construct causal explanations of particular phenomena by identifying the underlying

---

5. The purported mechanisms may be psychosexual (e.g. Nancy Chodorow, *Mothering*, Berkeley: University of California Press, 1978); biological (Mary O'Brien, *The Politics of Reproduction*, London: Routledge & Kegan Paul, 1983); cultural (Michèle Barrett, *Women's Oppression Today*, revised edition, London: Verso, 1989); or economic (Heidi Hartman, "The Unhappy Marriage of Marxism and Feminism", in Lydia Sargent, ed, *Women and Revolution*, Boston: South End Press, 1981).

6. For some discussion of causal primacy, see Richard Lewontin, "The Analysis of Variance and the Analysis of Causes", *American Journal of Human Genetics* 26 (1974) pp 400–11, Elliott Sober, "Apportioning Causal Responsibility", *Journal of Philosophy* 85 (1988), pp. 303–18, Richard Miller, *Fact and Method* (Princeton, NJ: Princeton University Press, 1987); and Clark Glymour *et al.*, *Discovering Causal Models in the Social Sciences* (Orlando: Academic Press, 1987). There is an extensive literature that attempts to partition the causal factors contributing to an event, for example, by distinguishing triggering causes and causal background conditions. See, for example, the essays in Tom Beauchamp, ed., *Philosophical Problems of Causation* (Encino and Belmont: Dickenson Publishing Co., 1974). This body of work, however, is not focused on the main subject of our analysis since it is not concerned to explicate a quantitative or comparative notion of "greater causal importance".

mechanisms that generate them. We thus adopt a "realist" view of scientific explanation. In our view, these mechanisms exist independently of our theories of them. As realists, we reject the stance, emblematic of "post-modernist" discourse theory, that science is simply one linguistic practice among others, in which the validity of claims is settled entirely within its own discursive practices.[7] We assume, in other words, that causes are real and that science aims at their discovery. Our task is to sort out the senses in which, in particular explanatory contexts, some (real) causes are more important than others, and the different ways in which these causes enter into causal processes.

We shall sometimes use *cause* and *explanation* interchangeably. Some readers may find this usage tendentious. But it is not. We are agnostic here in the continuing debate on the relationship between causality and explanation. Some philosophers have insisted that scientific explanations must always be causal; others have denied this view.[8] We sympathize with the former position, but the analysis that follows does not depend on its truth. It is enough, for our purpose, if it is conceded that *some* explanations are causal. These are the only explanations that concern us. When we talk about explanations of events, we mean *causal* explanations. Whether these are the only explanations proper to science, it is causal explanations that generate problems about causal primacy and causal asymmetries.

Genuine vs. Spurious Causes

Distinguishing genuine causal relations from spurious correlations is a persistent problem throughout science. This problem is particularly acute in the social sciences, where reliable techniques for testing hypotheses are frequently unavailable. However, it will not be necessary for us to address this problem here. Our aim is only to make sense of the claim that one (genuine) cause is more important than another and that different (genuine) causes enter into causal processes in qualitatively distinct ways. Accordingly, we shall not attempt to defend the causal explanations we use as illustrations, but shall assume that real causal relations, not spurious correlations, are involved. If our examples are incorrect, others could be substituted.

---

7. For an influential discussion on the left of the view that causal relevance is constructed within discourse, see Ernesto Laclau and Chantal Mouffe in *Hegemony and Socialist Strategy: towards a radical democratic politics* (London: Verso, 1985).

8. For example, compare Wesley Salmon's *Scientific Explanation and the Causal Structure of the World* (Princeton, NJ: Princeton University Press, 1984) with Carl Hempel's *Aspects of Scientific Explanation* (New York: Free Press, 1965).

Pragmatic vs. Explanatory Importance of Causes

It is sometimes suggested that primacy claims are only pragmatic. Thus, from a political point of view, the "most important cause" of poverty might be the cause that is most susceptible to political manipulation. Attributions of relative importance, therefore, could simply be designations by investigators of those causes that, for one reason or another, interest them more. We do not doubt that there is, in fact, an important pragmatic component to many actual primacy claims, nor even that some primacy claims are only expressions of investigators' interests. However, we do deny that causal primacy is *only* a pragmatic notion. In what follows, we shall not be concerned with the pragmatics of explanation at all. Our aim is to provide an account of primacy claims that represent or purport to represent objective asymmetries among real causal processes.

Epistemological Primacy

In many empirical problems, information about some causes is more important than information about others in affecting the ability to predict outcomes. In this sense, some causes are more important epistemologically than others. If, for example, there are two separately necessary and jointly sufficient conditions for an outcome, and one of these conditions is almost always present while the other is present only half of the time, it is more useful—for predictive purposes—to find out whether the second condition obtains than whether the first condition does. Thus suppose that the necessary and sufficient conditions for the election of a socialist candidate are (a) the presence of a working-class majority in the electorate, and (b) the presence of a well-organized socialist party. Imagine too that the working class is a majority in 90 per cent of all constituencies but that socialist parties are well organized in only 50 per cent of elections. In this case, knowledge of the party variable would increase the ability to predict the outcome of the election more than knowledge of the class variable.

However, like pragmatic considerations generally, epistemological primacy is not causal primacy in the sense that interests us. The relative importance of a cause for producing outcomes is not the same thing as the relative importance of *knowledge* of that cause for predicting outcomes. In a causal process in which two necessary conditions are jointly sufficient, there is no sense in saying that one condition is causally more important than another.

Individuating Causes and their Effects

A problem that constantly befuddles debates about the importance of different causes in multicausal processes is the correct designation of the object of explanation (the explanandum) and of the causes that explain it (the explanans).

Consider, first, the object of explanation. For disputes about causal primacy and other asymmetries to be resolvable, the disputants must of course agree about what they are trying to explain. In practice, however, many debates over causal primacy are confounded by subtle—or not so subtle—shifts in the explanatory problem. For example, in the debate between Marxists and neo-Weberians over the explanation of state policies in capitalist societies, the issues are frequently put in apparently opposed, abstract ways. However, when we turn to the empirical arguments offered on one or the other side, it often turns out that the neo-Weberians are trying to explain relatively fine-grained details of the timing and provisions of state policies, whereas the Marxists are trying to explain relatively coarse-grained properties that involve the consistency of the policies with the reproduction of capitalism.[9] Both parties could be correct about their respective explananda. There may still be disagreements about which of these explananda is more important to study—because of pragmatic considerations, reflecting the interests of investigators, or because certain explananda may themselves be important as causes in other explanations. But debates over what questions to ask should not be conflated with debates over the relative importance of causes in explanations of the same phenomena. While many causal primacy disputes only arise in consequence of confusions or unclarities in specifying explananda, the issues we shall explore occur in contexts where the explanandum is fixed.

Problems of demarcating the categories used in explanations are not

---

9. In their analysis of the origins of the modern welfare state, for example, Ann Orloff and Theda Skocpol ("Why Not Equal Protection? Explaining the Politics of Public Social Spending in Britain, 1900–1911, and the United States, 1880s–1920", *American Sociological Review*, 49:6 (1984), pp. 726–50) argue that Marxist accounts are unsatisfactory since class-centered causes do not explain the specific timing of the introduction of key pieces of welfare state policy. In explaining the introduction of national old age insurance programs in the United States, Britain and Canada, for example, they demonstrate that the timing across the three countries is heavily shaped by the specific institutional properties of the state. A Marxist reply to this analysis could be that while class factors may not explain why these policies were introduced in Britain before the First World War, in Canada in the 1920s and in the United States in the 1930s, class-centered mechanisms do explain why no capitalist state had such policies in the mid-nineteenth century while all developed capitalist societies had such programs by the mid-twentieth century. This reply, of course, constitutes a shift in explananda—from explaining variations across countries in the introduction of social programs to explaining the common temporal pattern among these countries.

restricted to the definition of the "dependent variable"; they are equally important, and difficult, in specifying "independent variables". The importance of a cause in the explanation of some phenomenon plainly depends, at least in part, on how the contributing causes are described.

Consider the explanation of fatal automobile accidents. It might be concluded that driver dysfunction is a more important cause of automobile accidents than are driving conditions (weather, road quality, etc.), according to some plausible understanding of "most important cause". But if "driver dysfunction" is decomposed into, say, drunkenness from beer consumption, drunkenness from hard liquor consumption, drunkenness from wine, incompetence, drowsiness caused by medications, etc., we might then find that something else—perhaps weather or road conditions—becomes the "most important" cause of fatal automobile accidents within this expanded, disaggregated list. Thus, it might be held that conclusions about causal primacy are artifacts of an essentially arbitrary decision about how to aggregate different causes under more abstract systems of classification.

One way out of this difficulty is to advance the claim that certain causes can be grouped together in non-arbitrary ways. One might argue, for instance, that the intoxicants that lead to drunkenness should all be grouped together since they all cause accidents through the same proximate accident-producing mechanism. Then drunkenness in its various forms would constitute a "natural kind" in the inventory of causes of accidents. To the extent that such natural kind groupings can be elaborated, claims about causal primacy become less vulnerable to arbitrary redescriptions of the explanatory problem.[10]

In the social sciences, the problem of describing causes and effects "correctly"—in a way that enhances understanding of the causal structure of the world—is pervasive. Frequently, there are no solid, theoretical foundations for classifying concrete causes into more abstract, natural kind categories. Thus, social scientists often are forced to rely on common-sense determinations and ordinary intuitions to categorize causes and the phenomena they purport to explain. There is little else they could do.[11] However, there is no a priori reason why such common-sense descriptions should correspond to real causal structures; investigators might someday *discover* that some (or all) of their intuitions about natural kind divisions are wrong. Arguably, some extant work in social

---

10. When no unique set of natural kinds is available, it may be useful to see whether a claim of causal primacy is robust over changes in the underlying taxonomy. Invariance of this sort is one sign that the asymmetry is not an artifact of one's mode of description.

11. In the physical and biological sciences, well-confirmed theories provide investigators with a better purchase on natural kinds, but even here puzzles about how to individuate explanans and explananda can arise.

science, Marxist or otherwise, already points in this direction. Until such theoretical advances are firmly established, substantive debates about causal asymmetries will always be vulnerable to redescription of the categories deployed in debates.

While the problem of describing causes and their effects may plague many actual debates over causal asymmetry, we do not believe that this difficulty diminishes the relevance of trying to refine our understanding of the logic of these asymmetries. Getting the right descriptions is an aspect of the general problem of discerning real causal relations; understanding how those causes are quantitatively and qualitatively interconnected remains a distinct problem. It is to that problem that we now turn.

Quantitative Asymmetry

We shall identify two kinds of quantitative asymmetry, each tantamount to a sense of *causal primacy: distribution-dependent causal primacy* and *causal potency*. The first asymmetry expresses the idea that some causes are "more important" than others in explaining particular phenomena; the second expresses the idea that some causes are "more powerful" than others in producing particular effects.

Distribution-dependent Causal Primacy

It is commonplace to identify relative causal importance with the *relative frequency* of a given cause. Thus it would be natural to say that smoking is a more important cause of lung cancer than plutonium exposure, if more instances of lung cancer are caused by smoking than by exposure to plutonium. This claim does not imply that smoking is a more powerful carcinogenic agent than plutonium. It is compatible with the distribution-dependent primacy of smoking over plutonium exposure that plutonium is, in some intuitive sense, more "dangerous" than smoking. Thus, we might think that a "small amount" of plutonium poses a greater risk than does a "small amount" of smoking and still insist that smoking is a more important cause of lung cancer.

The distribution-dependent importance of a cause is a function of two relations: its distribution in the population and its potency. Two carcinogens could be equally frequent causes of cancer (and thus equally important in the distribution-dependent sense) despite very different distributions, if the rarer property is sufficiently more carcinogenic. This idea can be represented using the following definitions:

$F(s_i)$ = the percentage of the population that smokes at exposure level i

$F(p_j)$ = the percentage of the population that is exposed to plutonium at level j

$P(s_i)$ = the probability of an individual getting cancer *because* of exposure to smoking at level i

$P(p_j)$ = the probability of an individual getting cancer *because* of exposure to plutonium at level j[12]

The levels "i" and "j" in these expressions are specified in whatever units are chosen for the factor in question—say, cigarettes per day or grains of plutonium, or whatever.

The percentage of the population that will, on average, in fact get cancer due to a given causal property at a given level of exposure is given by:

$C(s_i)$ = $F(s_i) \times P(s_i)$ = the percentage of the population that will get cancer due to smoking at exposure level i

$C(p_j)$ = $F(p_j) \times P(p_j)$ = the percentage of the population that will get cancer due to plutonium at exposure level j

The total incidence of cancer due to a given causal factor in a given population, then, is:

$$C(s) = \Sigma_i C(s_i) = \Sigma_i [F(s_i) \times P(s_i)]$$
$$C(p) = \Sigma_j C(p_j) = \Sigma_j [F(p_j) \times P(p_j)],$$

---

12. The probability of a person getting cancer *because of exposure* at a given level is not the same as the conditional probability of getting cancer for people who are exposed at that level. Suppose that 10 per cent of people with no exposure to any known carcinogen get cancer and 25 per cent of people who are exposed to smoking at level i get cancer. Under these conditions one could argue that smoking at level i increases the probability of getting cancer by 15 per cent (relative to the probability of getting cancer without smoking). The relevant probability here is therefore the *difference* in *conditional* probabilities of getting cancer for people at given exposure levels compared to some baseline. We are thus assuming in this example that the increase in conditional probability of an individual getting cancer from exposure at a given level compared to not smoking at all is an appropriate way of measuring the *causal potency* of that level of exposure. This may not always be the case. In focusing on potency, we want to know *how much of a difference* a cause makes towards its effects. If in real situations exposure to a given carcinogenic agent is itself empirically associated with some cancer-suppressing cause—if, for example, people who smoked also happened to be less prone genetically to cancer than non-smokers—then the empirical differences in conditional probabilities would not effectively identify the causal potency of the specific exposure levels. We shall ignore such complications in this analysis. For a discussion of these issues see, Nancy Cartwright, "Causal Laws and Effective Strategies", *Nous* 13 (1979), pp. 419–37.

where in each case the summations are carried out over all the exposure levels for each cause.

The claim that smoking is a more important frequency-dependent cause of lung cancer than exposure to plutonium then means just that $C(s) > C(p)$.[13] In this case, the lower cancer-inducing levels of smoking affect a sufficiently greater proportion of the population than do the higher cancer-inducing levels of plutonium exposure—to a degree such that the greater potency of plutonium is offset. Smoking is a more important cause of cancer than plutonium in consequence of the actual frequencies and potencies of these causal factors.

The object of explanation in this case is the *distribution* of lung cancer within a population, not the contraction of the disease by specific individuals. For any given individual with lung cancer, exposure to plutonium could be the most important cause of his or her illness. To determine the importance of causes in this sense, it would be necessary to assess the potency of each of the causes that actually affected the person's history.[14] However, our concern here is not with particular events, but with the distribution of events in populations. To claim primacy for smoking in this sense is to maintain that, given the relative potency and distribution of the carcinogenic agents in contention, smoking is the most important cause of lung cancer within the population.

Frequency and potency are distinct properties of causal mechanisms. What explains the frequency of a cause will generally not explain its potency. To explain the frequency of smoking in a population, it might be necessary to appeal to theories of cultural mores or to invoke the political power of the tobacco industry. The extent of plutonium exposure can perhaps be explained by the growth of nuclear energy production. Causal potency, on the other hand, would, in all likelihood, be explained by biochemical or physiological accounts of the role exposure to these agents plays in producing cancers of the lung and other organs.

---

13. If some people were exposed to both plutonium and smoking, the equations would become more complex, but so long as the effects of exposure from each carcinogen are independent of the other—so long as the effects are strictly additive, not multiplicative—then the simultaneous exposure to two carcinogens in no way changes the meaning of distribution-dependent causal primacy discussed here. If, on the other hand, the two carcinogens interact in ways such that their conjoined effects are greater than their additive effects, attempts at attributing causal primacy in a distribution-dependent sense could well break down.

14. Explaining how an individual contracted lung cancer is similar to assessing situations of "temporal asymmetry" among a set of causes (see p. 160). The central issue is to identify which, among a variety of causes that intersect the biographical trajectory of the individual, had the biggest effect on the probability of that person's getting cancer. This is a problem of relative causal potency, not distribution-dependent primacy.

In this example, the explanandum, lung cancer, is dichotomous; a person either has it or does not have it. In such dichotomous cases, claims about distribution-dependent causal primacy, therefore, concern the relative importance of different causes in affecting the conditional probabilities of the outcome. Nothing of importance hinges on this fact. Our account would not be substantially changed had the explanandum been a continuous variable. The only difference is that, with continuous variables, we would have to compare correlations, not probabilities.

For example, in sociological studies of income inequality, two factors widely deemed causally efficacious are education and "occupational status" (roughly a measure of the social standing of an occupation). Which is the "more important" cause of personal income?[15] As posed, this question is unanswerable because a unit of education and a unit of status are incommensurable. A one-year difference in education may make a bigger difference in income than, say, a one-point difference on some scale of occupational status; but so far we have no more reason to compare one year with one status point than with, say, 365.

To overcome this problem, sociologists typically compare correlations among variables rather than effects measured in terms of fixed units. The correlation between education and income reflects how much deviation from the average amount of education is associated with deviations from the overall average income. The resulting units are "standard deviations", measures of deviations from the mean within a particular distribution relative to the total dispersion of values in that distribution.[16] A correlation of education and income of 0.5 means that an individual who moves up one standard deviation from the mean on education (which in a typical "normal distribution" would mean having an education at about the 67th percentile of the distribution), would have on average 0.5 standard deviations more income.

---

15. In the present context we shall ignore complications arising from the fact that, in the real world, these causes are not strictly independent since education is itself a cause of occupational status.

16. More technically, a standard deviation is defined in the following way:

$$s = \sqrt{\dfrac{\sum_{i=1}^{N} (X_i - X)^2}{N}}$$

The expression within parentheses is the deviation of each individual observation, X_i, from the mean of X for all observations. The standard deviation, then, is calculated by squaring each of these individual deviations, adding up these squared terms over all observations and then dividing by the total number of observations, N. The greater the dispersion of the distribution around the mean value of X, the greater will be the standard deviation.

Suppose that the correlation of status and income is 0.6 and the correlation of education and income is 0.4. What the correlations in this case show is that variation in income is more closely tied to variation in status than to variation in education.

Does this difference in correlations justify the claim that status is a "more important" cause of income than is education? Correlation is not causation. This truism might suggest that, among real causes, different *degrees* of correlation need not indicate different *degrees* of causal *importance*. However, this inference is incorrect: if a causal problem is properly specified, then in the same sense that one is justified in seeing some causes as more important than others because they are more frequent, one is justified in seeing differences in correlations as differences in causal importance.

The formula for a correlation coefficient is given by the following equation:

$$r_{xz} = b_{zx}(s_x/s_z)$$

Where:

r_{xz} = the correlation of x and z

b_{zx} = the unstandardized slope relating z to x (i.e. b_{zx} tell you how many units of z increase for each unit of x, when both are measured in their "natural" units)

s_x = the standard deviation of the distribution of x

s_z = the standard deviation of the distribution of z

Now suppose we have two correlations with z, r_{xz} and r_{yz} (the former could be the correlation of education and income, the latter status and income). To hold that $r_{xz} > r_{yz}$ is to say that:

$$b_{zx}(s_x/s_z) > b_{zy}(s_y/s_z)$$

which reduces to:

$$b_{zx} \cdot s_x > b_{zy} \cdot s_y.$$

The claim that a cause with a higher correlation constitutes a "more important cause" than one with a lower correlation rests on the linkage between the distribution of this cause in the population and the strength of its effects on Z. As with causal frequency, the comparison of correlations depends on one term (b_{zx} and b_{zy}) that reflects the strengths of the effects of X and of Y on Z, and one term (s_x and s_y) that is strictly a function of the distributional properties of the two variables.[17]

One might object to the idea that a greater correlation implies a more important cause on the grounds that b_{zx} could be greater in some meaningful sense than b_{zy} while the associated correlation is smaller. This situation would resemble the case where plutonium is held to be a more potent cause of cancer than smoking, at the same time that it is a less important cause of the actual distribution of cancer in a particular population. To say that "X is more important than Y as a cause of Z because X has a higher correlation coefficient" means that the *distribution* of X is a more important cause of the *distribution* of Z, *given* the linkage between the distribution and causal potency of X.[18]

Causal Potency

Causal potency plays a role in distribution-dependent causal primacy, since the relative importance of different causes depends upon the linkage between their prevalence and the strength of their effects. However, in making distribution-dependent causal primacy claims, it is not necessary actually to compare the potency of two causes. Causal potency can therefore be considered a distinct kind of causal primacy.

The problem of assessing the relative potency of different causes is, of course, that causes come in radically heterogeneous units. There is, as noted, a powerful intuition that plutonium is a more potent cause of lung cancer than smoking. A tiny grain of plutonium lodged in the lungs will almost certainly produce cancer, whereas steady smoking for years

---

17. Note that while the standard deviation of Z—s_z,—affects the actual correlations, it does not enter into the comparison of the two correlations.

18. This account of correlation coefficients has no direct implications for the relative explanatory importance of *changes* in the distributions of X or Y for *changes* in the distribution of Z—because the causal potencies of X and Y may itself be caused in part by the distributions of X and Y. Thus, for education, the income-generating effect of, say, a high school degree almost certainly depends in part on the distribution of educational levels in the population: if the proportion of high school graduates increases, the causal efficacy of a high school degree would likely decline. Moreover, it is partly because of the income-producing power of education that people seek it. In this (dynamic) sense, the distribution of educational levels is in part explained by the causal potency of education on income. Wherever there is reason to suspect some dynamic interdependence of the causal potency of X and Y with their respective distributions, it is illegitimate to draw conclusions about the consequences of changes in the distributions of X and Y for changes in the distribution of Z from facts about the correlations of X and Y with Z.

This kind of problem, in the guise of frequency-dependent selection, is important in evolutionary biology. It occurs when the fitnesses of traits in a population depend on their frequencies. For example, the advantage an organism receives from protective coloration might be enhanced by the trait's rarity. Another example is studied in the theory of the evolution of sex ratios. In many instances a parent maximizes fitness by producing offspring of the minority sex. See Elliott Sober, *Nature of Selection* (Cambridge, MA: MIT Press, 1984) for discussion of these issues.

Figure 7.1 Contrasting Functional Forms Linking a Cause and its Effect

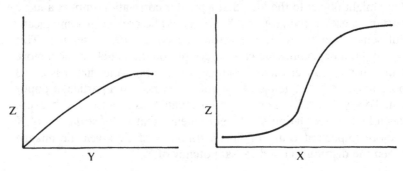

merely makes lung cancer more likely. Still, there seems to be no theoretically well-motivated way to regard a "tiny" amount of plutonium as a comparable unit to "years" of smoking. Unless the units of two causes can be made commensurable, it is meaningless to compare their relative causal power.

The situation, however, is not quite hopeless. Whenever it is possible to map out the magnitude of effects for all relevant values of a cause—by establishing the overall functional relation between a cause and its effects—there are a variety of strategies that allow investigators to standardize the "units" of the cause for purposes of comparing causal potencies. Suppose that we want to compare the potency of two causes, X and Y, on Z, where these have the functional forms represented in Figure 7.1.[19] Each of these graphs is expressed in the natural units of each cause. Cause X has an S-shaped relation to Z: as values of X increase, Z increases quite slowly at first, then very rapidly, asymptotically reaching some maximum value. Cause Y has a more linear relation to Z over most values of Z. With these two functional forms, there are various ways one could compare the potency of the two causes. One could compare the maximum effects of the two causes—i.e. the magnitudes of Z at the point where further increases in the causes produce no change in Z. In this case, X would be maximally more potent than Y. Or, one could pick a midpoint in the function and ask whether around that point a 10 per cent increase in X produces a larger effect on Z than does a 10 per cent increase in Y. In that region of the values of the two causes, X appears to be more potent.[20] Such comparisons do not stan-

---

19. Again, we shall not explore the issue of possible interactions between X and Y in producing Z; for simplicity we shall only discuss the additive case. In many contexts, of course, the functional form of the relationship of X to Z will itself vary over values of Y.

20. As these functions illustrate, if the causal relationship between X and Z is non-linear, then the verdict about the causal potency of X compared to some other variable may depend upon the point at which such comparisons are made.

Table 7.1 Hypothetical Relation between Race, Gender and Annual Earnings

		Men	Women	Row means
Race	White	$20,000	$12,000	$16,000
	Black	$16,000	$8,000	$12,000
	Column means	$18,000	$10,000	$14,000

Cell entries are mean incomes for race by gender categories (fictional data).

dardize the effects of the causes in terms of the factual distributions of these variables, but in terms of the causal structure that links them to their effects.[21]

There is one common kind of cause for which these functional relations can be straightforwardly mapped out—causes that assume an essentially binary (on/off) form. For example, if we wanted to know whether the racial division between blacks and whites or the gender division between men and women has a more powerful impact on individuals' earnings in the United States, we can directly compare the causal potency of the two causes. Consider the hypothetical example presented in Table 7.1. In this table, the difference in income between men and women is $8,000 while the difference between whites and blacks is $4,000.[22] A straightforward interpretation of these results is that the gender dichotomy has greater causal potency for earnings than does the race dichotomy.

This conclusion depends upon the assumption that these dichotomies

---

21. In the example just discussed, it could be the case, for example, that in the real world the values of X are all located at the lower part of the possible values, so the steep part of the curve is never encountered, whereas the values of Y are located at all values.

22. In this concocted example, the difference between men and women is exactly the same among blacks as it is among whites (and equivalently, the racial differences are identical within each gender). In technical terms this means that there are no "interactive" effects between the two factors being considered; the effects are strictly additive. That is, the difference in income between white men and black women is equal to the simple sum of the gender difference and the race difference. It should also be noted that this table can be represented as a multiple regression equation using "dummy" variables (0–1 variables) to represent gender and race in which:

Income = constant + B_1RACE + B_2GENDER

where RACE = 1 for whites, and 0 for blacks, and GENDER = 1 for men, and 0 for women. In this example, the constant = $8,000, B_1 = $4,000, and B_2 = $8,000. If there had been an interactive effect of race and gender—i.e. if the effects of gender were different in the two races—then this would appear as a multiplicative term in this equation (Gender × Race).

adequately represent the metric for the two causes under investigation. Treating the two causes as dichotomies, in effect, implies that a "one unit" change in sex is equivalent to a "one unit" change in race. At first glance, the assumption that these causes can be adequately represented in binary form seems acceptable, particularly for sex, in so far as sexes are biologically dichotomous. The situation is less clear for race, to the extent that it is a social construction, not a biological given, that racial distinctions are binary. One can imagine a world in which what is causally important about "race" is skin color, and in which skin color is finely graded into different shades. Then the proper metric of race-causes would not be the simple dichotomy black/white. In consequence, questions could be raised about the legitimacy of comparing a "unit" of race (however understood) with a unit of sex.

On further scrutiny, similar considerations apply even to sex. Sex is biologically dichotomous, and this fact, in virtue of its salience, affects its socially efficacious causal properties. But "gender" (sex as a social category) need not mimic sex as a biological category. It is conceivable, for instance, that sex-causes operate through a relatively continuous metric—from highly masculine to highly feminine. The biological dichotomy might still be a good empirical *indicator* of these causal determinations. But, again, a "unit" of sex would no longer be commensurable with a "unit" of race.[23]

Whether it is appropriate to treat sex or race as dichotomous variables depends on how these causes operate in the world. If biological sex is causally efficacious for earnings only because of its link to masculinity/femininity or if race is causally efficacious by virtue of its linkage to gradations of skin color, it would misrepresent the causal powers of these variables to treat them as if they were dichotomous. This is not an issue that can be decided a priori, but only after evaluation of the relevant evidence.

The requirements for establishing either of the kinds of quantitative causal asymmetries we have identified—distribution-dependent causal primacy or causal potency—are arduous. To demonstrate distribution-dependent causal primacy it is necessary to know the distribution of the various causes in the relevant population, and to have a way to measure the magnitudes of their effects. To demonstrate relative causal potency it is necessary to be able to specify the functional form that links causes to their effects.

---

23. If race and/or gender were really continuous variables, then there would still be ways to render their units comparable. One could, for example, compare the effects for the extreme values for each variable. This strategy should not be confused with an analysis based on a simple dichotomy.

In practice, these requirements are often impossible to satisfy for many of the issues that have animated debates in the social sciences, especially among radical scholars. Generally, it is impossible to define the distribution of causes or their relative potency in explanations of such phenomena as large-scale social change, revolutions, the contradictions of state policies, and the transformation of gender relations.

There is a variety of ways that social scientists react to this situation. One response is to restrict investigations to those for which properly specified quantitative answers can be provided. Doing so effectively diminishes social science, forcing a focus only on easily measurable phenomena distributed in well-defined populations. This response is characteristic of much contemporary American sociology.[24] A second response is to continue to ask the broad, classical questions, but to avoid making primacy claims. The explanatory objective of social science would then be just to identify causes, without trying to specify their relative importance. Many radical social theorists today embrace this objective.

A third alternative is to shift attention away from quantitative to qualitative asymmetries. Often, qualitative asymmetries are taken as providing the basis for causal primacy claims. We shall argue, however, that differences in the way causes enter into multi-causal processes have nothing directly to do with relative causal importance. It is often of great explanatory interest to discern qualitative asymmetries. But it is a mistake to regard these differences as distinctions in causal importance.

Qualitative Asymmetry

In the simplest causal structure in which several causes operate together to produce some outcome, each cause generates its effects independently of the others. The result is the "sum" of the effects of each separate cause. This simple additive model is represented in Figure 7.2. When the outcome is an "event", the effects of each cause can be interpreted as its impact on the probability of the occurrence of the event. Each cause, then, contributes to this probability independently of the others.[25] When the outcome is a "variable", each cause contributes to

---

24. The narrowing of questions motivated by the requirements of measurement also tends to direct analysis towards data tagged to individuals. In general, it is easier to define the relevant populations and observe the relevant distributions of attributes when the variables attach to individuals rather than institutions, structures, societies or states.

25. The sum of the effect-probabilities of a set of additive causes can be greater than 100 per cent. This is particularly the case when there are multiple sufficient causes present for some event to occur.

Figure 7.2 Underlying Causal Model without Qualitative Causal Asymmetries

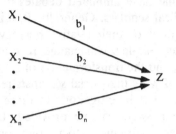

the magnitude of the variable. For most real-world processes, additive models are obviously implausible. Nevertheless, most empirical research in the social sciences assumes this kind of model. While this assumption may be useful in some contexts, many of the debates that animate social science, particularly in its more radical traditions, involve issues raised by more realistic accounts that countenance qualitative asymmetries.

The asymmetries we shall explore vary along two dimensions: first, whether they are *systemic* or *contingent*; and second, whether they are *synchronic* (involving the simultaneous operation of several causes) or *diachronic* (involving the temporal ordering of causes). Putting these dimensions together yields four general categories, as represented in Figure 7.3: contextual asymmetry, functional asymmetry, temporal asymmetry and dynamic asymmetry. We shall discuss each of these asymmetries in turn.

Contextual Asymmetry

In many instances, some causes—which we shall term "contextual causes"—determine the conditions under which other causes generate their effects. Such contextual causes need not be integrated into any general system; contextual asymmetries, as in the examples that follow, can exist among contingent assemblages of causes. In addition, since both contextual causes and the causes they structure operate simultaneously, contextual asymmetry claims are synchronic.

We shall examine two putative types of contextual asymmetry. The first, based on the contrast between causal limits and selections, does represent a genuine qualitative asymmetry. However, this type of asymmetry has often been misconstrued as a kind of causal primacy. The second case we shall investigate focuses on interactive effects of two or more causes operating simultaneously. Contrary to first appearances, such interactions do not constitute an instance of even qualitative causal asymmetry, or so we shall argue.

Figure 7.3 Forms of Qualitative Causal Asymmetry

	Synchronic	Diachronic
Contingent	Contextual asymmetry	Temporal asymmetry
Systemic	Functional asymmetry	Dynamic asymmetry

Limits and Selections

The concept of "structural limitation" has played an important role in contemporary Marxism. The idea is that in some explanatory problems it is possible to partition causes into two general categories: those that explain the *range of possible outcomes*, and those that explain *what actually occurs* within that range of possibilities. The first set of causes is said to impose "limits" on the outcome, whereas the second "selects" an outcome from within those limits. Thus in rational choice theory, it is common to distinguish the feasible set of alternatives individuals face from the choices they make from within that set. The former is explained by, among other things, the distribution of resources, the institutional rules of the game, and the relative power of actors; the latter by such subjective factors as individuals' preferences. The causes implicated in setting limits are often said to be "more fundamental" than those that select outcomes from within those limits in so far as the former establish the conditions of possibility under which the latter operate.

This kind of explanatory configuration has played an important role in on-going debates about politics—for instance, in discussions of "non-decision-making" and in the analysis of "non-events".[26] The theory of non-decision-making focuses on mechanisms that exclude potential alternatives from the political agenda. It purports to explain why certain alternatives are never raised in the public arena, or, if they are raised,

---

26. For early discussions of these issues see Peter Bachrach and Morton Baratz, "The Two Faces of Power", *American Political Science Review*, 51 (December 1962), pp. 947–52. Stephen Lukes popularized these issues in his analysis of the three faces of power in *Power: a Radical View* (London: Macmillan, 1974) in which he distinguishes between the power to directly affect a person's behavior (face 1) and the power to define the range of alternatives or set the agenda (face 2). Claus Offe has presented a particularly pointed discussion of these issues as they apply to the problem of the capitalist state in his influential essay, "Structural Problems of the Capitalist State: class rule and the political system. On the selectiveness of political institutions", in Klaus von Beyme, ed., *German Political Studies*, vol. I (Beverley Hills and London: Sage, 1974).

why they tend to be marginalized. The mechanisms that explain these "non-events" are usually quite distinct from the mechanisms that explain how decisions are made from among alternatives actually in contention.

Marxists argue that capitalist property relations impose limits on state policies. Exceptional circumstances apart, only policies that are broadly compatible with private capital accumulation are possible. The range of allowable policies may be more or less extensive, but the feasible set is limited, in the final analysis, by the functional requirement of reproducing capitalism. Within the range of possible policies, specific choices will generally depend on causal processes distinct from those that reproduce capitalist property relations as such—the rules that govern elections, patterns of regional conflict, the strength of unions, private interest associations, political parties and other collective actors on the political stage, cultural and ideological resources of political actors, and so on. These factors may themselves be shaped by the functional requirements of the capitalist mode of production, but they also enjoy a certain degree of causal autonomy. Thus it could be argued that under conditions in which capital accumulation is heavily based on industrial production, environmental pollution policy is limited by the requirement that it not so threaten profits as to precipitate massive disinvestment and capital flight. However, within this constraint, a wide range of environmental policies may still be feasible, and there is no reason to believe that the policies actually adopted will always be those most favored by capitalists. The mobilizing capacity of environmental movements and the rules of electoral politics as they intersect the geographical distribution of environmental issues might explain which policy is adopted from within the allowable set.[27]

Where a distinction can be drawn between limits and selections, an exclusive focus on the selection process will result in incomplete explanations. A more profound explanation will investigate both limits and selections. However, it is also tempting to maintain that causes that generate limits are *ipso facto* "more fundamental" or "more important" than are causes that select specific outcomes from within those limits. Thus Marxists often argue that since class structural factors impose limits on possible state policies, they are the most important causes of state activity. This conclusion, we believe, is not warranted.

Examples abound in which selections are more "important" than limits, according to any likely understanding of "important". Imagine the following case: an individual chooses a pear from a basket of fruit.

---

27. For a discussion of the social forces which impose limits on the agenda of pollution control, see Matthew A. Crenson, *The Unpolitics of Air Pollution: a study of non-decision-making in the cities* (Baltimore: Johns Hopkins University Press, 1971).

Two causes are involved: the range of fruits available in the basket and the person's preferences for different kinds of fruit. Suppose that there are thirty kinds of fruit in the world and that twenty-five of them are included in the basket. Which is the more important cause of the individual's choice of a pear—the composition of the fruit basket or the individual's tastes in fruit? The answer is indeterminate given the information so far specified. It might be that, even if all thirty kinds of fruit had been available, the individual would still have chosen a pear. In this case, the structural limitation on the individual's choice is irrelevant. On the other hand, if the individual would have preferred one of the five excluded kinds of fruit, the limiting process would provide an important part of the explanation of the final outcome.

In general, there is no simple way to determine whether the reduction of possibilities represented by "limits" is larger or smaller than the reduction represented by "selections", and unless we can compare this narrowing of options, claims about the relative importance of limits and selections are ill founded. More generally, to make the claim that a process of limitation is a more important cause of an outcome than is a process of selection is to argue, in the senses we have already discussed, either for the relative causal potency of limits and selections or for the relative distribution-dependent causal importance of the two kinds of causes. Unless units can be assigned so that the effects of limits and selections can be compared, determinate answers are likely to be unavailable.[28]

Nevertheless, there is a powerful intuitive sense on the part of political radicals that the Marxist claim (or something very close to it) is correct: that the limits imposed by the nature of the property relations in a society more powerfully explain the policies of the state than the mechanisms that select particular policies from within those limits. What explains this intuition, we believe, is imprecision in specifying explananda. What Marxists want to account for are not quite state policies as such, but certain *excluded* state policies—namely, radical, pro-working-class policies. The claim, then, is that the central mechanisms that

---

28. While it will, in general, be problematic to compare the magnitudes of a process of limitation and a nested process of selection (i.e. one that occurs within a given set of limits), it may be possible to compare two processes of limitation. That is, suppose X_1 and X_2 both impose limits on possible values of Z, without one of these constituting a selection within the other. Then, if all of the values of Z permitted by X_2 are included in the set permitted by X_1, but not vice versa, we could unambiguously say that X_1 more powerfully limits Z than does X_2. However, in real-world explanatory contexts in which multiple causal limits operate, it is generally not the case that one causal limit strictly subsumes another.

explain why the state does *not* systematically empower and mobilize the working class are causes that shape the agenda of politics—the limits—not causes that select options within the given political agenda.

It would be difficult to exaggerate the importance in this context of specifying explananda precisely. The vulnerability of structural limits asymmetry arguments to the specification of the object of explanation is illustrated well in a recent analysis by Ann Orloff and Theda Skocpol of the emergence of social insurance policies in capitalist democracies.[29] They chose as their "dependent variable" the timing of the introduction of social insurance in Britain, Canada and the United States—1904 in Britain, 1922 in Canada and 1933 in the United States. How should this timing be explained? Why this order? Why was the United States such a laggard, not introducing social security until the massive disruption of the Depression? Why was social security introduced in Britain so early? To answer these questions, they examine the kinds of explanation they feel would be advanced by Marxists (class conflict would explain the timing), by industrialization theorists (the level of development would explain timing) and by social democratic political theorists (the strength of socialist parties and labor movements would explain the timing). After showing that none of these explanations is satisfactory, they offer their own explanation, which revolves around the particular institutional capacities of these three states and the historical legacies of prior policies with which political forces in these societies had to contend. For example, they argue that the experience of pervasive corruption associated with Civil War pensions in the United States contributed significantly to the long delay in the introduction of social security there.

This analysis appears to conflict with Marxist interpretations, but we think the conflict is illusory. Very generally, the Marxist analysis of capitalist development explains why no capitalist country had a social security program in 1850 and why all developed capitalist countries had some form of social security by 1950. The structure of capitalist property relations and the conditions for the reproduction of capital accumulation explain the basic limits of possibility on such redistributive state policies. Within those limits, however, a wide variety of historically contingent factors—contingent with respect to theories of capitalist development—explain specific types of variation, such as the timing of the initial introduction of social insurance programs. By choosing a relatively fine-grained aspect of social policy—the timing of its introduction rather than the fact that it was introduced within, say, a 100-year period—the structural limits on the process fall into the background, and

---

29. Ann Orloff and Theda Skocpol, "Why Not Equal Protection?"

state-centered political mechanisms become more important.[30] Once alternative explananda are clearly distinguished from each other, and once it is granted that a two-stage process is incompletely analyzed by an exclusive focus on the second stage, it turns out that no issue of substance divides the opposing parties.

Interactive Causality

There is a second kind of causal structure, which we shall call "interactive causality", that appears to be a type of contextual asymmetry. As illustrated in Figure 7.4, cause X affects the causal relation between Y and Z. Of course, X may also directly affect Z in the simple additive way. The purported asymmetry derives from the fact that, in addition to its direct effects, X shapes the effects of Y on Z, while Y does not, symmetrically, shape the effects of X on Z. We shall argue that interactive causalities of this sort are not genuine contextual asymmetries.

Interactive causality arguments often appear in explanations of specific historical events, for example, when "precipitating events" are distinguished from "fundamental causes". Thus in Figure 7.4, X might stand for the underlying social conditions that comprise the "fundamental cause" of some event; and Y could be viewed as a precipitating cause in the sense that it would not have the consequences that it in fact has, but for the presence of the fundamental causes with which it interacts. In explanations of the First World War, for example, the assassination of Archduke Ferdinand is often treated as a precipitating event

Figure 7.4 Interactive Asymmetry

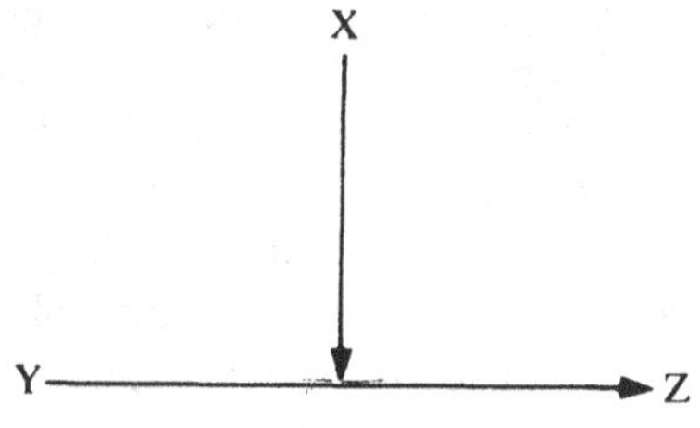

30. This reconstruction of the argument by Orloff and Skocpol suggests a more general proposition: whenever one makes an argument about structural limits on some social process, it will be true that the more fine-grained the form of variation is that one is trying to explain within that process, the more likely it is that relatively contingent factors will play an important explanatory role. Imagine that instead of trying to explain the order of introduction of social insurance for these three countries, we found two countries that introduced their reforms in the same year, but in different months. Explaining the relative timing of introduction for those two countries, one would suspect, would be even less systemically determined than the timing explored in the Orloff–Skocpol research.

because it had the consequences it did only against the background of
the geopolitical tensions generated by inter-imperialist rivalries in
Europe. It is conceivable that, had the Archduke not been assassinated,
the First World War might not have occurred. However, most explanations of the origins of the war assume that some other precipitating
event would have occurred anyway, making the war virtually inevitable
around the time it actually began. Most historians would therefore
contend that the occurrence of *some precipitating event or other*, if not
the actual assassination of Archduke Ferdinand, was a necessary condition for the outbreak of the First World War. Then the argument
would be that the efficacy of this precipitating event, whatever it is, is
asymmetrically related to the prevailing social and political conditions.

Marxists sometimes advance similar claims, especially when they
inveigh against their critics. Thus Marxists frequently hold that the
effects of many causal processes depend upon, say, the dominant mode
of production or the structure of class relations or the balance of class
forces. These claims depend upon the existence of interactive causal
structures—linking distinctively Marxist explanatory factors with other
causal mechanisms. An example of this kind of argument can be found
in what has come to be known as the "Brenner Debate".[31] Since the
publication in 1976 of Robert Brenner's article "Agrarian Class Structure and Economic Development in Pre-Industrial Europe", the venerable Marxist debate over the transition from feudalism to capitalism has
been joined by historians with a variety of theoretical orientations.[32] At
the core of the debate are competing explanations for the differing
trajectories of economic growth and, eventually, the emergence of capitalist development, among the different societies in early modern
Europe. To explain these phenomena, Brenner argued that "economic
rationality", as it has been understood since Adam Smith, became
possible and even inevitable in consequence of outcomes of historically
specific class struggles, themselves consequent upon particular characteristics of the class structure of late feudalism in England and, in miti-
gated fashion, elsewhere in the West. Brenner also argued that now
orthodox demographic and commercial explanations for economic

---

31. See T.H. Aston and C.H.E. Philpin, eds, *The Brenner Debate: Agrarian Class
Structure and Economic Development in Pre-Industrial Europe* (Cambridge: Cambridge
University Press, 1985).

32. The article that launched the Brenner debate appeared in *Past and Present* 70
(February 1976). The earlier version of this debate was waged in expressly Marxian terms
in the pages of *Science and Society*, in a series of articles sparked by Paul Sweezy's criticisms of Maurice Dobb's *Studies in the Development of Capitalism* (London: 1946, repr.
1963, 1972). The *Science and Society* debate has been republished, with additional
material, as *The Transition from Feudalism to Capitalism* (New York and London: Verso,
1978).

growth are flawed in so far as they fail to acknowledge the centrality of class structure and conflict.

While historians may disagree about the facts of the matter, it is plain that the principal issues in contention in the Brenner Debate are of a conceptual character, and have to do with claims about causal interactions. From the outset, Brenner formulated his thesis in these terms:

> It is the purpose of this article, to argue that ... attempts at economic model-building are necessarily doomed from the start precisely because, most crudely stated, it is the structure of class relations, of class power, which will determine the manner and degree to which particular demographic and commercial changes will affect long-term trends in the distribution of income and economic growth—and not vice versa.[33]

In this statement, X in Figure 7.4 represents the "structure of class relations", Y stands for "demographic and commercial changes", and Z represents "long-term trends in the distribution of income and economic growth". Brenner's claim is that X determines the effects of Y on Z while Y does not determine the effects of X on Z.

We believe that the translation of these kinds of causal interactions into claims about qualitative asymmetries among causes is illegitimate. In the case of precipitating causes, one could as well say that the precipitating cause explains why the underlying conditions produced the effects they did when they did, as vice versa. Without that precipitating cause, the underlying conditions would not have had the consequences they did. If the underlying conditions appear more fundamental, it is because what they address is important to most investigators' interests, while the explananda for which the precipitating event is indispensable are usually of little concern. Thus, in almost any imaginable explanatory program, it is more important to know, say, why a war of global dimensions broke out roughly when it did than to know why hostilities began precisely on August 14, 1914. Similarly, in the Brenner debate, one could argue that the endemic demographic cycles of feudal society explain why variations in class structure affected long-term growth the way they did. In both cases, the arrows in Figure 7.4 can be switched, with Y intersecting the arrow between X and Z, *without indicating any change in how these causes actually work.*

The essential symmetry in an interactive causal process is reflected in the mathematical equation generally used to represent such interactions.

---

33. "Agrarian Class Structure and Economic Development in Pre-Industrial Europe", *Past and Present* 70 (February 1976), p. 11.

Take the Brenner theory of long-term economic growth in the transition from feudalism to capitalism. Very roughly, this process can be represented by the following equation:

$$\text{Growth} = B_1(\text{CLASS}) + B_2(\text{DEMOGRAPHY}) + B_3(\text{CLASS} \times \text{DEMOGRAPHY})$$

The coefficients B_1, B_2 and B_3 designate the effects on growth of the factors contained in the parentheses. The interactive effect is represented by the multiplicative term. In Brenner's formulation of his thesis, quoted above, this expression is rewritten as follows:

$$\text{Growth} = B_1(\text{CLASS}) + [B_2 + B_3(\text{CLASS})](\text{DEMOGRAPHY})$$

The total effect of demography on growth—$[B_2 + B_3(\text{CLASS})]$—thus embodies a term reflecting the class structure; or, as Brenner would have it, the manner in which demography affects growth is determined by class. The problem, of course, is that the equation can be rewritten symmetrically as:

$$\text{Growth} = [B_1 + B_3(\text{DEMOGRAPHY})](\text{CLASS}) + B_2(\text{DEMOGRAPHY})$$

In other words, there is nothing in the formal structure of the interaction that supports a claim for qualitative asymmetry.

Nevertheless, in both the mainstream historian's account of the origins of the First World War and in Brenner's analysis of the emergence of capitalism, there do seem to be real asymmetries among causes. In each instance, however, the asymmetry is quantitative, not qualitative.

To describe a cause as a precipitating event is to say that the probability of the outcome it helped produce was already very high before the precipitating cause occurred. The general social conditions, in our example, raised the probability of world war from a low to a high level, while the Archduke's assassination constituted the "final straw" that pushed the probability up to 1.[34] This is a special case of what we shall call *temporal asymmetry*.[35] It involves an assessment of the relative

---

34. The claim that the social conditions raised the probability to a high level implies a comparison with some appropriate counterfactual of what the probability would have been under alternative social conditions.

35. See pp. 160–5 below.

causal potency of the precipitating cause compared to the social context within which that precipitating cause occurred.

In Brenner's case, the asymmetry between demography and class structure is a special case of distribution-dependent primacy. Demographic patterns did not vary sufficiently across the various zones of Europe to explain variations in transitions, whereas class factors of the sort Brenner analyzes did. What this means is that although the demographic factors (interacting symmetrically with class) play an important role in explaining the transition within every society in which the transition occurred, it does not explain *variations* in transition across Europe. Variations must be explained primarily by class factors. Brenner's statement of his core thesis should therefore be revised as follows (changes appear in italics):

> Attempts at economic model-building are necessarily doomed from the start precisely because, most crudely stated, it is *variation in* the structure of class relations, of class power, which will determine the manner and degree to which particular, *relatively universal,* demographic and commercial changes will affect *variations* in long-term trends in the distribution of income and economic growth.

This is an empirical claim about the way in which different causes with different patterns of distribution—one variable across Europe, one relatively invariant—intersected. It is not a claim about qualitative asymmetries.

Functional Asymmetry

Functional asymmetries exist whenever causes are systemically joined as parts of a functionally integrated system. Like contextual asymmetries, functional asymmetries are synchronic.

Consider the famous example of functional explanation in Malinowski's study of fishing rituals among the Trobriand Islanders.[36] Malinowski observed that elaborate fishing rituals only occurred for deep-sea fishing, not for lagoon fishing. Deep-sea fishing was dangerous; lagoon fishing was not. Malinowski concluded that the rituals served the function of reducing the fear caused by the danger, and that the existence and persistence of the fishing rituals could be explained by this function. The structure of his explanation is represented in Figure 7.5.

In this model, fear functionally explains rituals: as fear rises there is

---

36. The use of this example to illustrate functional explanation, and the accompanying diagrammatic representation, come from Arthur Stinchcombe, *Constructing Social Theories* (New York: Harcourt, Brace, Jovanovich and World, 1968).

Figure 7.5 Model of Functional Explanation

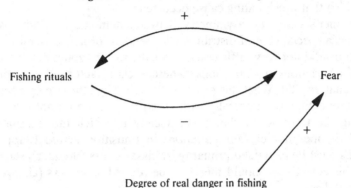

pressure for the social production of rituals. As rituals increase in response to this pressure (through an unspecified search and selection mechanism), fear is reduced. An equilibrium occurs when the level of ritual effectively neutralizes the levels of fear necessary to produce more ritual. So long as the exogenous fear-producing mechanism (the level of danger associated with deep-sea fishing) remains the same, the level of ritual will therefore continue. A variety of feedback mechanisms could regulate such a functional system involving different mixes of conscious search for solutions to fear, trial and error, and social analogues to natural selection.[37] Whatever mechanisms regulate the system, rituals persist because of their functional relation to fear.

In this model, the explanatory asymmetry has a distinctive structure: the two terms—fear and ritual—have reciprocal effects on each other. Fear increases rituals; rituals decrease fear. The asymmetry comes from the functional interconnection of these terms: fear functionally explains rituals but rituals do not functionally explain fear. Thus one would not say that it is the function of fear to produce rituals while it is the function of rituals to reduce fear.[38]

---

37. For a discussion of the problem of specifying causal mechanisms within functional explanations, see G.A. Cohen, *Karl Marx's Theory of History: a Defense* (Princeton, NJ: Princeton University Press, 1978); Jon Elster, "Marxism, Functionalism and Game Theory: the case for methodological individualism", *Theory and Society* 11:4 (1982), pp. 497–512; Philippe Van Parijs *Evolutionary Explanation in the Social Sciences: an emerging paradigm* (Totowa, NJ: Rowan & Littlefield, 1981).

38. It is a truth about the world that the functional explanation in this example runs in one direction only. Imagine the following modification of the story: in the community there are professional ritual producers whose material interests depend upon the proliferation of rituals. They have learned that people are likely to attend rituals more consistently when those rituals are directed towards fearful situations. They therefore design rituals that dramatize the fear in ways that enhance the fear associated with the activity in the absence of the ritual. There would then be a functional symmetry: fear would function to produce rituals while rituals would function to reduce fear.

There is a second way of representing functional explanations, which we discussed in Chapter 3, that perspicuously reveals this asymmetry. G.A. Cohen has argued that functional explanations depend upon "dispositional facts" that pre-exist the establishment of functional relations. Thus, before the development of rituals, it was a dispositional fact of the culture that rituals would be fear reducing. This dispositional fact can then be taken to explain the emergence of the rituals:

(1) *dispositional fact*: [Ritual → reduced fear]
(2) *functional explanation*: [Ritual → reduced fear] → Ritual

While it also is a dispositional fact of the society that fear produces ritual, this second dispositional fact does not explain fear. Thus:

(3) *dispositional fact*: [Fear → increased ritual]
(4) *false functional explanation*: [Fear → increased ritual] → fear.

The fact that (2) is true while (4) is false establishes the functional asymmetry between fear and ritual.

Although we agree with Cohen that one can *represent* a functional explanation in terms of dispositional facts and their effects, we deny that this representation *defines* what a functional claim means. A causal connection can take the form depicted in (2) without entailing a functional claim. Consider a man who is obese; suppose that his obesity causes him not to exercise. The fact that he does not exercise has the consequence that he remains obese. The causal structure can then be represented as follows:

(5) [Obesity → No Exercise] → Obesity.

If a statement of form (2) defined what functional claims mean, it would follow, implausibly, that the function of obesity is to prevent exercise.[39] We thus reject Cohen's analysis of functional claims and we do not offer a proposal of our own. It will suffice, for present purposes, to hold just that functional asymmetries exist whenever the persistence of some social practice is explained by its beneficial effects on something else, and these causes are joined by an appropriate feedback loop.

---

39. This counterexample is due to Christopher Boorse, "Wright on Functions", *Philosophical Review* 85 (1976), pp. 70–86. Boorse uses it to criticize an analysis proposed by Larry Wright in "Functions", *Philosophical Review* 82 (1973), pp. 139–68. Wright's account of functional explanation is essentially what Cohen endorses. Wright's and Boorse's papers are reprinted in Elliott Sober, ed., *Conceptual Issues in Evolutionary Biology* (Cambridge, MA: MIT Press, 1984).

Arguments for functional asymmetry have played an important role in recent Marxist debates. Thus, Cohen's reconstruction of historical materialism is based on a series of arguments about the functional asymmetry of technological development in explaining social change. On Cohen's account, Marx explains the nature of the social relations of production in a given society by the functions they fulfill for the development of the forces of production. In any society there are reciprocal effects of the forces of production on the relations of production and of the relations on the forces. A given technology can reinforce or undermine a set of production relations; the production relations can stimulate or retard (fetter) the development of the forces of production. Given such reciprocal effects, how can there be an asymmetry between forces and relations of production? Cohen argues that in classical historical materialism, this claim is based on a functional asymmetry within this pattern of reciprocal causation: the social relations of production are the way they are because of their beneficial effects on the development of the forces of production and not vice versa.[40] As noted in Chapter 2, this structure can be schematized as follows:

Level of PF → [PR → development of PF] → PR.

where PF = productive forces, and PR = production relations. In other words, the level of development of the forces of production explains which kinds of production relations will further enhance the development of the forces of production, and this (dispositional) fact explains which production relations actually pertain. There is then a qualitative explanatory functional asymmetry between the productive forces and the production relations.

These kinds of functional interactions do constitute a type of qualitative asymmetry in causal arguments. By themselves, however, they do not provide a basis for assigning differential explanatory importance to one or the other terms in the functional relation. In the functional interconnection of fear and rituals described by Malinowski, it makes no sense to say that fear is a "more important" cause of the level of ritual than ritual is of the level of fear. Similarly, in Cohen's reconstruction of historical materialism, it cannot be concluded, *simply by virtue of their functional interconnection*, that the forces of production are a more important cause of the relations of production than the relations of production are of the forces of production.

---

40. Cohen makes a parallel argument for the functional asymmetry of the economic structure with respect to the "superstructure": the superstructure takes the form it does and persists because of its effects on reproducing the economic structure (the "base").

Yet Cohen does argue for what he terms the "Primacy Thesis", the claim that the forces of production determine the relations of production to a greater extent than the relations determine the forces.[41] As argued in Chapter 5, we are sympathetic to the idea the Primacy Thesis expresses: that there exists an endogenous dynamic process in human history that causes some economic structures to be on the historical agenda and others not. But despite what Cohen suggests, this claim, if it is true, is not a consequence of the functional argument he has provided. It follows instead from two possible claims about the relative causal potency of different causes.

First, recall that, for historical materialism, the forces of production have a tendency to develop which ultimately leads them to generate instabilities in the relations of production (i.e. when the relations fetter the forces). Recall too that superstructural forms tend to *reproduce* existing production relations. We thus have two causes each affecting the relations: the forces destabilize the relations (when fettering occurs), the superstructures stabilize the relations. The critical thesis that allows for an epochal trajectory of social forms is that the first of these causal forces is more potent than the second. The Primacy Thesis, properly reconstructed, does not claim explanatory priority for the forces over the relations in consequence of how they are related functionally. It is not even a claim about the greater explanatory importance of the forces relative to the relations. It is strictly a causal potency claim: in general, the forces of production are more powerful than the superstructure *with respect to their effects on the relations of production.*

There is a second and parallel way of reconstructing the primacy thesis. The development of the forces of production is driven by two causes in historical materialism: by human nature (conjoined with scarcity) and by the relations of production. When these two causes contradict each other—when human nature pushes for increases in the forces of production and the relations fetter such development—human nature ultimately prevails. It is a more potent cause. This leads to changes in the relations (because human nature's causal potency is also stronger than the superstructures).

In both of these reformulations, Cohen's statement of the Primacy Thesis—the forces determine the relations to a greater extent than vice versa—is at best elliptical. The real issue is not that in a system of reciprocal causation, X explains Y to a greater extent than Y explains X. Rather, what we have is a structure in which relative causal potency claims are being made either about two causes of the development of the forces of production (human nature and the relations of production) or

---

41. See Chapter 2 above, and Cohen, *KMTH*, p. 134.

about two causes of the relations of production (the forces of production and superstructures). This primacy claim itself requires a functional analysis no more than do corresponding claims about the magnitudes of forces in physics. Cohen's functional proposal, we conclude, while interesting in its own right, is quite separate from the thesis of causal primacy that he advances.[42]

Temporal Asymmetry

We have, to this point, examined qualitatively different ways causes operate at the same point in time. It will often be the case that evidence for such synchronic asymmetries will depend on examining changes over time. For example, to support functional asymmetry claims, it may be necessary to observe the development of a system to a point where functional requirements change. Nevertheless, the asymmetry claim itself is not about the trajectory of development of the system, but about the configurations of causes within the system.[43] We now turn to types of qualitative causal asymmetry—temporal asymmetry and dynamic asymmetry—that are essentially diachronic in character.

Temporal asymmetries obtain between causes in virtue of their location in a temporally ordered sequence culminating in some effect. Temporal asymmetries are characteristic of historical explanations in which an event is explained as the end-point of a chain of events. More generally, they are found wherever a temporal ordering of causes is central to an explanation. Thus, the conventional sociological account of occupational attainment, in which individuals' occupations are held to be directly caused by their education and social background, and in which social background is also a cause of education, involves temporal asymmetry claims.

As a simple statement of temporal ordering, temporal asymmetries

---

42. The independence of the two claims becomes clear if we shift the functional story from social development to living organisms. It is perfectly legitimate to produce a range of functional explanations for the interconnections of the parts of a living organism. This does not imply, however, that when a "contradiction" occurs between various structures and their functions that the structures change to restore functionality; the organism may simply die. When arteries become clogged so that the heart no longer functions to maintain the circulation of the blood, there is nothing that ensures a transformation of the arteries to allow for further survival of the organism. The primacy of the forces of production, therefore, rests on the dynamic claim that they have a tendency to develop in history (the development thesis) joined with a (weakly defended) claim that this tendency is causally more potent than the reproductive tendencies of superstructures on the relations of production.

43. In one sense all causal arguments are "diachronic" in so far as effects temporally follow causes. To speak about a mechanism generating an effect is to talk about a change that occurs in time. We use "synchronic" to describe facts about the relation among simultaneous causes and "diachronic" to describe facts about sequences of causes or sequences of effects of the same cause.

are pervasive and unproblematic in social scientific explanations. What is illegitimate is the identification of such orderings with claims for causal primacy. Thus, in accounts of occupational attainment, it would be a mistake to conclude from the fact that social background is a determinant of both education and current occupation, that it is a more important or more fundamental determinant of current occupation than is education.[44] Earlier causes are not *ipso facto* more important than later ones; they may also be weaker than the causes that follow them temporally.

Perhaps the most frequently encountered argument that moves from temporal ordering to a claim about causal primacy occurs in analyses that assign explanatory importance to the "origins" of particular processes. Sometimes it is held that in a chain of events $X_1 \rightarrow X_2 \rightarrow X_3 \rightarrow X_4$ (where the subscripts are temporally ordered), the first cause is inherently more important simply by virtue of being first. But since, in social science settings, it almost never happens that the links in causal chains are deterministic, there is no reason why earlier causes should be viewed as more important than later causes in either the distribution-dependent or the causal potency sense.[45]

The temptation to regard earlier events as more important than later ones in historical explanations derives from a failure to consider *what might have happened* given the empirical facts present at each stage. Take the simple sequence $X_1 \rightarrow X_2 \rightarrow X_3 \rightarrow X_4$, and suppose that in the

---

44. If social background were not just *a* determinant of education, but *completely* determined education, then it could be argued that it is indeed a more important cause of occupation than education is. It is worth noting, however, that *even if* X completely determines Y, and Y completely determines Z, it is still not assured that X is a *more important* cause of Z than Y is. By transitivity, X does completely determine Z; but Y also completely determines Z. The fact that X determines Z via Y is, of course, crucial for the explanation, but Y is just as important a fact in this causal process as X is.

45. Cf. Richard F. Miller, *Fact and Method: Explanation, Confirmation and Reality in the Natural and Social Sciences* (Princeton, NJ: Princeton University Press, 1987, pp. 98ff). Miller appears to suppose a highly deterministic relation within temporally ordered sets of causes when he distinguishes shallow causes from deeper causes in his analysis of causal depth-as-priority. Miller examines examples in which an immediate, proximate cause of an event—for example, the role of middle-class mobilization in the rise of the Nazis—is viewed as "shallow" if it can be demonstrated that some other cause—in this case, the power and interests of the bourgeoisie in Germany—is, in Miller's words, both "intimately" connected with the outcome and explains the proximate cause itself. The restriction of "intimacy" of connection with the explanandum is introduced to avoid silly infinite regresses, in which distant causes are always given priority over proximate ones. Intimacy, however, really seems to be a criterion of the degree of determination involved in the causal processes under consideration. If a temporally distant cause determined an outcome with a very high level of probability, then it, too, would count as the "deeper" explanation of the outcome than the proximate causes. In any case, such a degree of determinism in a sequence of events is virtually never present in the social sciences. Thus, in contrast with Miller, we believe that the translation of temporal priority into explanatory priority requires an independent argument.

world X_1, X_2, X_3, and X_4 actually did occur. Let us also suppose that once X_2 occurs, X_4 has a very high probability of occurring. It could still be the case that given X_1, the most likely future would be something other than $X_2 \rightarrow X_3 \rightarrow X_4$. But X_2 actually occurred. In such a sequence it would be wrong to claim that of all the events in the chain, X_1 had the greatest causal importance. Because many historians refuse to consider counterfactual trajectories of events, they therefore treat the "origins" of de facto sequences as most important by default.

In some historical explanations it may be plausible to assign causal primacy to causes that can be identified as "origins" of some subsequent trajectory. For example, the particular conditions and conflicts that lead to the founding of a state are sometimes thought to be more important than any subsequent events or conditions in explaining current institutional arrangements. Foundational struggles generate constitutions and other institutional norms and practices that regulate basic political structures and procedures for as long as the state exists. We might say that what goes on at the historical origin of states generates a set of restrictive structural limits within which subsequent causal processes operate as selections. We have already argued that, in general, it is impossible to establish that limits are more important than selections. Nevertheless, when the explanatory objective is to account for the exclusion of specific kinds of historical alternatives, it may well be possible to identify initial processes of institutionalization as "decisive moments" within which important exclusions are created.[46]

Many historical analyses involve "path dependent explanations"— explanations in which, in the extreme case, there is a single path to some result.[47] In such explanations, there is a well-defined meaning to the notion of an "origin": it is that point at which the historical trajectory is set in motion.[48] In as much as getting on the path is a necessary (though

---

46. Arthur Stinchcombe's well-known analysis of the importance of the historical timing of the founding of particular industrial sectors in explaining their current organizational form would be an example. When an industry first becomes consolidated, Stinchcombe argues, it adopts particular institutional forms from the forms historically available at the time. Once these are firmly in place, they are exceedingly difficult to change—i.e. they exclude other possibilities effectively—even if they become suboptimal over time. See Arthur L. Stinchcombe, "Social Structure and Organizations", in James March, ed., Handbook of Organizations (Chicago: Rand McNally, 1965), pp. 142–93.

47. Path-dependent explanations are particularly striking when there is a unique path to some outcome, but more generally such arguments require only that there be switchpoints in which certain "destinations" are ruled out and others ruled in. There may still be more than one route to a given destination.

48. Historical arguments need not encounter an infinite regress of causes, always tracing the explanation of an historical trajectory back to an earlier determinant. Certain steps in an historical chain of causes and effects definitively close off some paths of development and open up others. Such "switchpoints" can be treated as "origins" of subsequent trajectories.

perhaps not sufficient) condition for producing the outcome, there is some justification for treating origins as particularly important.

However, temporal asymmetry arguments, even when they refer to singular causal chains, do not imply that the origins of trajectories are more important than the causes that follow them. Nor do they imply that the distant past is more important than the recent past in explaining particular phenomena.

Suppose that we are trying to explain the occurrence of a revolution. Figure 7.6 illustrates a variety of temporal patterns of causes that could lead to the revolution. The vertical axis represents the probability that the revolution will occur. Since the revolution actually did occur, at the moment it began, t_r, the probability was 1. The question then becomes how this probability developed historically. Let t_0 be some point in the past where we begin our investigation. The probability at t_0 is the probability that a revolution will occur at time t_r, given the existing social conditions at time t_0.[49] Of course, it is extremely unlikely that precise values can be assigned to these evolving probabilities. Nevertheless, patterns of the sort portrayed in this figure are implicit in many historical explanations.

In Figure 7.6(a) the probability of a revolution remained very low until just before the actual revolution occurred. This situation might exist when a series of events, without deep social structural roots, came together in just the right temporal order—e.g. an unexpectedly prolonged stalemate in a war combined with the return from exile of a brilliant and charismatic leader. In Figure 7.6(b), there is no identifiable episode in which the probability of an eventual revolution rapidly increases. In this case, no cause or cluster of causes can be assigned causal primacy. Although models (a) and (b) are implicit in the work of atheoretical historians who are hostile to sociological theory, both none the less embody theories of how the process in question developed. To assign later events heavier weights, or to assign events equal weight, requires just as much a theoretical understanding of causal processes as assigning heavier weights to earlier events.

Figure 7.6(c) represents a theoretical stance opposed to 7.6(a): early

---

49. The precise shape of these temporally ordered probability curves will depend upon how the *explanandum* is defined. The *explanandum* could be the occurrence of the exact revolution that actually occurred (e.g. the American Revolution beginning on July 4, 1776), or it could be the occurrence of a revolution of a given type in a given country in a given period. If the event to be explained is defined in a fine-grained way, then proximate causes often will affect the probability of the event to a much greater extent than if the event is described in a coarse-grained way. Prior to early 1776 the probability of a revolution being launched on July 4, 1776 was undoubtedly far below 1, though the probability of a liberal bourgeois revolution of national independence occurring within the next few years might have already been very close to 1.

Figure 7.6 Historicist Models of the Probabilities of Revolution

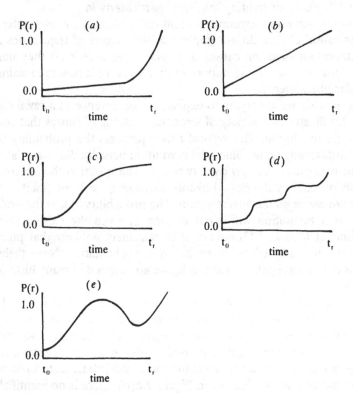

P(r) = Probability of a revolution at time t_r
t_0 = time zero, starting point for the analysis
t_r = time at which the revolution actually occurs

on, a set of conditions was created that rapidly increased the probability of a revolution. There was then an extended period in which the country was "ripe" for revolutionary upheaval; all that was needed was some spark to trigger the event. Figure 7.6(d) represents a trajectory in which there were a number of episodes in which the probability of revolution rapidly increased. In this picture, the middle episode is the "most important" in the sense of increasing the probabilities to the greatest extent (from 0.2 to 0.8). Figure 7.6(e) suggests a more complex historical pattern: after an early period in which the conditions for revolution rapidly increased there was a period in which those probabilities declined. Perhaps political reforms lowered the probability; then a military *coup* launched by a backward-looking ruling class blocked further reforms, restoring the earlier trajectory.

It is clear from these diagrams that the translation of temporal asymmetries in historical explanations into causal primacy claims need not be limited to the explanation of events or phenomena that actually occurred. One could try to explain the likelihoods of revolutions in different countries in the past where revolutions did *not* occur. Or one could equally construct explanations of this form in which the explanandum is the probability of a revolution (or anything else) in the future. Different societies have different probabilities today of having revolutions by the year 2000. These probabilities have evolved through different historical trajectories. An historical analysis of these trajectories should aim to identify the links in the chain in which these probabilities changed most dramatically.[50]

Temporal patterns of probabilities such as those illustrated in Figure 7.6 would have to be derived from substantive arguments about the mechanisms that actually affect probabilities. To argue that the probability of a revolution increased rapidly in the middle of the curve in Figure 7.6(c) requires a theory of social conditions and events conducive to revolutionary change, in addition to the observation that these conditions existed in this period. Such arguments, in turn, depend upon a developed understanding of the relative potency of the causes that enter the trajectory.

Dynamic Asymmetry

As already noted, systemic causes may be distinguished from merely contingent ones. Dynamic asymmetries are systemic in the sense that they operate within particular systems, pushing these systems along a trajectory of social change. Dynamic causes are therefore to be distinguished both from endogenous causes that do not impart any developmental tendency, and also from exogenous causes. In the historical explanations modeled in Figure 7.6, the trajectories of event-probabilities were characterized as consequences of sequences of causal chains. But there was no supposition of any general mechanism that governed the overall sequence itself. The argument was not, therefore, a dynamic argument in our sense. The trajectories depicted were simply consequences of contingent occurrences. For dynamic asymmetries to exist, there must be some underlying mechanism generating a trajectory of development.

In the history of the social sciences, there have been many attempts at

---

50. Ellery Eells (*Probabilistic Causality*, Cambridge: Cambridge University Press, 1991) uses the trajectory of an event's probability to characterize whether the event occurred *because of* or *in spite of* some putative cause.

describing causal processes thought to impart a developmental trajectory to social phenomena: the "iron law of oligarchy" describes a set of mechanisms, embedded in the internal social system of organizations, that leads popular democratic institutions to develop centralized hierarchical institutional forms; the theory of structural differentiation elaborated by Parsons and others tries to explain the long historical pattern of increasing institutional specialization in distinct social "functions" in whole societies; and, perhaps most famously, historical materialism tries to theorize the overall trajectory of human history through an account of the dynamic relationship between forces and relations of production. In each of these cases, the trajectory of social change is not seen as the cumulative effect of *contingently* connected causes. It is determined by underlying, dynamic processes.

Claims for dynamic asymmetry generally occur in explanations that combine *dynamic endogenous* causes with *contingent exogenous* causes or in explanations that postulate a number of endogenous causes, not all implying the same dynamic trajectory. We shall examine dynamic asymmetries in each of these contexts, and then consider the relationship between dynamic asymmetry claims and causal primacy.

Dynamic-systemic Causes vs. Contingent Causes

Suppose we want to explain why animals die. One strategy might be to identify a range of contingent, proximate causes of individual deaths— diseases, accidents, predators, etc. Another approach would be to examine the genetic determinants, if any, of mortality. In so far as animals are "programmed to die", it might be thought that genetic determinants are endogenous dynamic causes of death, even if in a given population, malnutrition causes most actual deaths.[51] In such a case, malnutrition would be the primary cause of death (in the distribution-dependent sense), yet there would nevertheless be genetic mechanisms, dynamic causes, that make death inevitable.

Traditional historical materialist arguments contain a variety of claims that combine dynamic and contingent causes. Consider Marx's account of the systemic contradictions that are supposed to ensure the eventual demise of capitalism. In Marx's view, the process of capital accumulation contains a fundamental and devastating contradiction: each individual capitalist, in seeking to maximize profits, makes innovations that substitute capital for labor. The cumulative effect of these individuals'

---

51. The claim that lifespans are positively programmed genetically is controversial. However, even if lifespans are the result of physiological deterioration due to the failure of the genetic program to repair the organism adequately, rather than the result of a self-destruct mechanism, the causes of aging and death would still be endogenous.

choices raises "the organic composition of capital", the ratio of physical capital to living labor. Since, in his view, only direct, living labor produces value, and since profits derive from *surplus* value, the rising organic composition of capital has the effect, other things being equal, of lowering the average *rate* of profit over time. Given that the rate of profit of actual firms is distributed around this average rate, as the average declines, an increasing number of firms will experience net losses. This situation will lead, in turn, to increasing bankruptcies and eventually to a general economic crisis. Since in such crises capitalists can obtain capital cheaply (by buying up capital equipment from bankrupt capitalists), the conditions of profitability tend to be restored during the trough of a crisis, leading to a renewed period of profitable accumulation. However, because of the long-term tendency for the organic composition of capital to rise, the peak rate of profit in the new cycle will be lower than in previous ones. In the long term, therefore, economic recoveries will be less robust, with weaker booms and more prolonged busts.

If this scenario were correct, eventually capitalism would become an unreproducible social system. In time, the average rate of profit would be so low that capitalism would collapse. Marx, however, did not believe that capitalism would, in fact, last long enough for this final collapse to occur. The popular masses would topple the system before it reached that point. The declining rate of profit—or, more strictly, the deteriorating economic prospects it produces—helps explain why masses of people come to oppose capitalism and to favor socialism—before capitalism becomes unable to reproduce itself for strictly economic reasons. In different countries, for a variety of *contingent* political, cultural and historical reasons, the necessary ideological and political conditions for the overthrow of capitalism might be easier or harder to achieve. But, in the classical Marxist view, the contradictions of capitalism are so profound that eventually workers should be able to transform the system, even under relatively disadvantageous conditions. Like genetically driven aging culminating in death, capitalism is a social system with a built-in self-destruction mechanism. It might therefore seem that this mechanism most fundamentally explains capitalism's inevitable decline and fall, even if the explanation for the demise of actual capitalisms depends more on contingent political and cultural factors.[52]

A partition of causes into systemic and contingent is, however, highly

---

52. Needless to say, few Marxists today would accept this strong dynamic asymmetry argument. Few now believe that the contradictions of capitalism will eventually render capitalism unreproducible or socialism inevitable.

dependent upon how the "system" in which a cause is embedded is described. For example, in the case of death, one could define the system ecologically rather than organismically. The system in which an individual death is explained might then include disease agents and nutrition sources, as well as the genetic endowments of individuals. Within this larger system, diseases and nutrition would not be contingent mechanisms, but fully endogenous ones. It is only when the system or "unit of analysis" is defined as the organism that these causes become contingent and exogenous. The systemic/contingent distinction is thus always relative to descriptions of system-properties.

This fact seems to suggest that the claim that dynamic asymmetries are systemic is essentially arbitrary. This conclusion would indeed follow if there were no criteria for assessing the adequacy of claims that particular sets of causes constitute "systems"—in other words, if there were no sustainable theories of systemically interconnected social processes. Theories show what comprises a system and what does not. To say that A and B are parts of a system, and that C is not, is to say that A and B are causally interconnected in a systematic and reproducible manner, and that C is not connected with A and B in this way. In so far as social scientists succeed in their explanatory objectives, positing and defending a system-description of a set of causes is not arbitrary. It is a theoretical achievement. In the final analysis, progress in social science grounds the systemic/contingent distinction.

One of the long-standing debates in the social sciences involves the question of the extent to which societies can be analyzed as social systems. In so far as social structural configurations are reproduced over time through a set of interconnected causes, and in so far as changes in one institutional site of a society have ramifications for other institutional arrangements, it seems clear that societies are indeed causally integrated systems, albeit of a relatively loosely coupled and open variety.[53] What is more problematic is whether societies should be treated as functionally integrated systems. In any event, what matters in the present context is that unless some degree of systematicity is posited for interconnections among causal mechanisms in social scientific

---

53. Characterizing social systems as "loosely coupled" implies that system*ness* should be viewed as a variable property of causal problems rather than as an all-or-nothing property. While it may be true that "everything is connected to everything else", the explanatory ramifications of such interconnectedness can vary from a situation in which a change in one element generates commensurate changes in all other elements of a system to a situation in which changes in one element have negligible effects on other elements. A parallel point about the concept of individuality in biology is developed by E. Sober, in "Organisms, Individuals, and Units of Selection", in F. Tauber, ed., *Organism and the Origin of Self* (Princeton, NJ: Princeton University Press, forthcoming).

explanations, it is impossible to distinguish contingent from systemic causes—and therefore dynamic endogenous causes from exogenous ones.

Many social scientists are skeptical about the existence of dynamic mechanisms. Anthony Giddens, for example, has insisted that history has no overall determinate trajectory of development—that there is nothing equivalent to an organism's genetic mechanism that explains a society's trajectory. According to Giddens, social transformations can only be retroactively explained by the actual sequence of causal processes that happened to be temporally juxtaposed.[54] Since history has no systematic explanation, it does not make sense to talk about asymmetries between endogenous dynamic factors and exogenous contingent ones. But even if one rejects the possibility of a dynamic account of the overall trajectory of human history, it still is possible that more limited dynamic arguments of this sort can be formulated with respect to specific historical epochs or specific institutions. One could argue, as many Marxists do today, that historical materialism as a general theory of history is unsustainable, but that the Marxist theory of capitalist development is essentially sound.[55]

Dynamic-systemic Causes vs. Structural-systemic Causes

The interaction of dynamic- and non-dynamic-systemic causes plays an important role in a number of on-going discussions among radical social theorists—particularly debates about the state and about gender.

First, consider the state. If we look *statically* at a capitalist society and examine the social structural relationship between its political and economic institutions, it is hard to justify the Marxist idea that the state is "superstructural" on its economic "base" or even to identify any inherent asymmetry between them—structural, contextual or even functional. It is true that the capitalist structure of the economy imposes limits on what states can do, particularly since the state is dependent upon capitalist production for its revenues. But it is equally clear, given the state's role in superintending capitalist economies, that the institutional structure and policies of the state impose limits on what capitalist firms can do. The economy imposes structural limits on the state, but the state imposes structural limits on the economy. One might argue that the limits of capital on state policies are more powerful than the limits of the state on capitalist practices. But, as we have seen, it is unlikely that this intuition can be made sufficiently precise to support a genuine causal primacy claim.

---

54. See Chapter 4.
55. Cf. Chapter 5.

However, there is a case for a causal asymmetry when dynamic and synchronic factors interact. Suppose that the nature and condition of the economy limit state policies, while state policies limit economic forms and initiatives. Supppose too, as Marxists believe, that capitalist economies contain an engine of social change, rooted in capitalist exploitation, competition and accumulation that explains the central tendencies of capitalist development from merchant capitalism to competitive industrial capitalism to multinational global capitalism. Suppose, finally, that there is no systematic engine of change internal to state institutions. While the state grows and develops in particular ways, its course is driven by causes external to it. If this characterization of the dynamic forces operating between the state and economy is correct, then even if it were true that state institutions and economic institutions constrain each other in a systemic way (thereby constituting two interconnected elements in a social system), there would still be a dynamic asymmetry: the trajectory of development of the state and the economy would be driven by dynamic causes operating in the economy, but not by dynamic causes endogenous to the state. This causal pattern is illustrated in Figure 7.7.

A similar explanatory structure pertains to the relation between class and gender. Synchronically, class relations and gender relations each impose limits on many social practices. While in specific cases it may be possible to argue that one or the other is in some sense "more important", it is unlikely that there is a plausible general case to be made for the explanatory primacy of class or gender in purely synchronic terms. But dynamically the situation is different. There appears to be nothing analogous to capital accumulation or the "dialectic of forces and relations of production" that pushes gender relations along a determinate path of development. Attempts at identifying such processes, for example Mary O'Brien's analysis of the dialectic of forces and relations

Figure 7.7 Interaction of Dynamic and Structural Systemic Causes

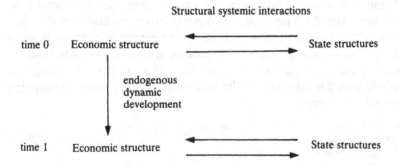

of biological reproduction, have not so far succeeded.[56] However, if even weak historical materialism is right, class does have an endogenous dynamic. In this sense, even if we cannot say in general that class is more important than gender or vice versa with respect to some range of explananda, we can identify a dynamic asymmetry between them.

Two conceivable rejoinders to these conclusions should be noted. First, atheoretical historians and social scientists would deny that class relations have any endogenous dynamic even under capitalism. They would maintain instead that gross changes are just cumulative effect of finer-grained transformations, with no mechanism governing the overall trajectory.[57] Other social scientists might argue, instead, that what appears to be a class dynamic is, in fact, something else: perhaps a technological dynamic. They might then claim that technological change drives the system independently of class, state or gender relations. These factors could, of course, still have synchronic effects on technology; but the dynamic properties of the system would rest on a technological imperative.

It is also conceivable that, in addition to a class dynamic, there are dynamic mechanisms that govern forms of gender relations or forms of the state. As already remarked, to date arguments of this sort have not been very persuasive in the gender case. But the situation is perhaps more promising for the state. Much has been made, in recent years, of the fact that states are embedded in competitive geopolitical state systems. Competition in these systems could function like capitalist market competition as a mechanism driving states to accumulate resources and power. Perhaps this is what Giddens has in mind when he maintains that states accumulate "authoritative resources" in a trajectory of increasing "space–time distanciation".[58] It should also be noted that states are not exactly unitary entities. They are comprised of a myriad of agencies, bureaucracies, branches of government and parties, and also of individual politicians and bureaucrats. Competition and conflict among these corporate and individual actors could drive state institutions along a particular path of development. Thus efforts by individual bureaucracies and agencies to increase their budgets could push the state as a whole along a certain developmental trajectory. If arguments of this kind turn out to be sound, there might not be any dynamic asymmetry between class and the state after all.

---

56. See Mary O'Brien, *The Politics of Reproduction.*
57. See Chapter 4.
58. See Chapter 4. "Space–time distanciation" refers to the geographical and temporal distances over which intentional action can be planned. See A. Giddens, *A Contemporary Critique of Historical Materialism* (Berkeley: University of California Press, 1981).

Dynamic Asymmetry vs. Causal Primacy

There is a temptation with dynamic asymmetries, as with the other qualitative asymmetries we have considered, to regard the asymmetry itself as a basis for a causal primacy claim. However, what we have found to be the case for other qualitative asymmetries holds here too: there is no reason to consider dynamic endogenous processes more important than contingent causes or synchronic systemic causes *simply because they are dynamic and endogenous.*

When it seems that dynamic causes are more important than other causes, it is often only because, consciously or not, the explanandum has been construed in a tendentious way. Consider our example of the death of animals. One might seek to explain why, for a given type of animal, a particular distribution of lifespans occurs. Alternatively, one might wish to explain why particular animals cannot continue to exist for longer than some specified time. Genetic upper bounds on the number of cell divisions might be the most important cause of the latter phenomenon, but not important at all in the former case. Even if we wanted to explain not lifespans but the overall trajectory of an animal's development—an explanandum for which genetic mechanisms are often very important— there would still be aspects of the trajectory that might be more heavily determined by contingent factors than by the genetic growth dynamic. *Variations* across human populations in the timing of the development of secondary sex characteristics, for example, may be more influenced by variations in nutrition levels than by variations in endogenous dynamic causes. The fact that the dynamic cause propels growth in all human beings does not imply that *variations* in the dynamic cause explain *variations* in growth across the human population. Similarly, the endogenous dynamic of capitalist economies might be the fundamental determinant of the broad contours of their trajectory of development and of the high probability of the eventual collapse of capitalism, without explaining very much about finer-grained aspects of capitalist development or the actual demise of any particular capitalist society.

Shift of explananda are particularly evident in discussions of the relation between class and gender. If we want to explain the massive expansion of women's labor force participation in the post-Second World War period in all capitalist countries, the most plausible explanation is likely to revolve around the dynamics of capitalist development in these societies and the ways in which this dynamic has dramatically changed labor force requirements. This dynamic, however, probably has little to do with explaining why women were the principal source of the untapped available labor supply, or why there are variations in the labor force participation rates of women across capitalist societies at roughly equal levels of economic development. Perhaps these variations are best explained by differences in patriarchal ideologies linked to religious institutions and kinship structures. This suggestion is entirely compatible with the idea that the principal cause of the fact that women's labor force participation is expanding in advanced capitalist countries is a dynamic internal to the capitalist mode of production.

Even if class is very important in the explanation of many phenomena having to do with gender relations, it does not follow that it is important in the explanation of all explananda somehow connected with gender. The same conclusion holds, of course, for gender-based mechanisms. In general, the fact that some explanandum can be explained in a certain way does not imply anything about how closely related explananda are best explained.

Conclusion

Three principal lessons may be drawn from this analysis of causal asymmetries.

First, causal primacy claims, if correct, should be recast as *quantitative* asymmetry claims. It is therefore unlikely, in most explanatory contexts, that causal primacy claims can be sustained with precision. In order to validate claims about quantitative asymmetries, one either must establish the relative importance of different causes within an empirical distribution of causes or else devise a strategy for comparing the potencies of causes. The latter task is especially difficult because of the incommensurability of the units in which causes are calibrated.

Second, it is illegitimate to infer explanatory importance directly from the fact of qualitative asymmetry: limits are not inherently more important than selections; functional asymmetries do not imply causal primacy; there is no general reason to regard earlier links in causal chains as more important than later ones; and endogenous dynamic causes are not in themselves more important than contingent or non-dynamic systemic causes. In every case, if one cause actually is more important than another, it is only because it is quantitatively more important, regardless of their qualitative relationship.

Finally, it is crucial that investigators have a clear sense of the explanatory problem under consideration before they attempt to resolve disputes about quantitative or qualitative causal asymmetries. Ambiguities in these matters afflict social scientific practice generally. In particular, we are convinced that many of the controversies among radical social theorists—including debates about the relative importance of class and gender, or class and the state—are confounded by shifts in explananda. If these disputes are to be successfully adjudicated—indeed if they are genuine disputes at all—it is not enough that they address the same *topic.* Contending explanations must literally have the same explanandum.

Our conclusions suggest that for many of the most interesting problems in social science, it is unlikely that fine-grained assessments of the relative importance of different causes can be made. While it may be relatively easy to distinguish between important and minor causes, it will generally be very difficult to make nuanced judgments about the relative importance of causes within these broad categories. Thus, if both the institutional properties of the state and the nature of class relations systematically shape state policy formation, it is unlikely that either can be said to be more important *in general.* Assessments of relative importance *among important causes,* even if they can be made rigorously in particular instances, are likely to be so affected by the precise characterization of the explananda and by the range of variation allowed for different causes, that generalizations are likely to be vulnerable to small changes in the specification of the problem.

Nevertheless, many of the most durable debates in the social sciences—and many contemporary debates among radical social theorists—do revolve around problems of causal asymmetry and, especially, causal primacy. In traditional Marxism, at least in its Hegelian versions, claims for the global primacy of class were embedded in a conception of society as an integrated "totality". If societies were tightly integrated systems, organized through some singular "essence" that stamped all the "parts" of the whole with a specific function and character, and if that essence were identified with class relations, then there indeed would be grounds for according class explanatory primacy *in general.* Class primacy within this sub-tradition of Marxism therefore amounted to a claim for class *reductionism*: whatever was explanatory in particular instances was ultimately a form of appearance of class. Virtually no Marxist today would accept this reductionist perspective. Societies are understood to contain a variety of irreducibly distinct causal mechanisms. While there are asymmetries among causes, including asymmetries that justify causal primacy claims, there is no principle that warrants the conclusion that class considerations always comprise the primary determinants of social phenomena.

Once the presumption that class is the singular determinant of the social totality is abandoned and a range of distinct, causally efficacious mechanisms is admitted, the sweeping, global claims to causal primacy characteristic of much of the Marxist tradition are unsustainable. We think it is very likely that class considerations are of great explanatory importance for many well-defined explananda. But we also believe that it is unlikely that this conclusion—or anything like it—could possibly hold for "society" in general.

It is wise, therefore, to shift discussion away from causal primacy to causal importance, and to focus on the systematic impact of a given set of causes. We shall suggest in Chapter 8 that the mechanisms identified in class analysis have considerable importance across a wide range of explanatory problems; and therefore that Marxist class analysis sustains a case for the causal *pervasiveness* of class, though not for its global primacy. Claims for causal pervasiveness, to be plausible, must be grounded in a specific explanatory agenda. We therefore must ask whether Marxism in fact has a coherent explanatory program and whether the mechanisms traditionally identified with Marxist explanations really do play an important explanatory role in Marxism's explanatory projects. To ask these questions is to investigate "the Marxist agenda". This is the topic of the next chapter.

PART III

Conclusion

8

Prospects for the Marxist Agenda

For more than a century "Marxism" has designated a vital current in the political culture and intellectual life, first of Western Europe and then of the entire world. For many people today, however, including many who would have called themselves Marxists not long ago, this tradition seems largely spent. As a political tendency, Marxism is so deeply in crisis that many erstwhile Marxists nowadays eschew even the label. And after two decades of analytical scrutiny, Marxist theory has emerged shorn of nearly everything that once appeared to distinguish it methodologically from rival views and deflated in its explanatory pretensions. It is therefore appropriate to ask what, if anything, remains of what once seemed the principal alternative to "bourgeois" theory and practice.

We believe that a great deal remains. Thus in focusing on Marxist themes in preceding chapters, our aim was not, as Marx said of his own critique of Left Hegelianism in *The German Ideology*, "to settle accounts" with a no longer tenable tradition. Rather, in clearing away what evidently cannot be sustained, our intent has been to expose, as Marx might also have said, the "rational kernel" that remains. By way of conclusion, we shall try to specify how this "rational kernel" points towards a reconstructed Marxist agenda.

Two stylized analogies between Marxism as an intellectual tradition and medicine will be useful in framing our discussion. The first concerns the distinction between medicine as clinical practice and medicine as scientific research; the second involves the distinction between disciplines within medicine that are organized primarily around organic systems and those that are organized around diseases.

Clinical vs. Scientific Marxism

Clinical practitioners treat illnesses by relying on available accounts of the mechanisms that generate disease symptoms. They are "scientific" in the sense that they apply scientific knowledge. But as clinicians they are not primarily concerned with advancing or transforming the theories they deploy. Instead, they use existing theories to understand disease and to cure or treat ill patients. It may be that, for some ailments, no existing theories are of much use. Such failures in clinical practice provide a powerful motivation for new discoveries. But clinical medicine *per se* does not aim at the generation of new knowledge. Clinicians regard existing theories as tools in their clinical practice, not as objects of interest in their own right.

Scientific medicine, in contrast, is committed to advancing understanding. To this end scientists typically seek out cases that do not fit the predictions of existing theories. Observations that constitute *anomalies* for existing knowledge provide a basis for reconstructing—and advancing—received views. To this end, rather than looking for the theory that best "fits" the data, as in clinical medicine, the task is to look for data that challenges the best available theories.[1]

By analogy, we can distinguish *clinical* from *scientific* Marxism as analytically distinct poles of Marxist theoretical practice. Clinical Marxism attempts to diagnose and address the "pathologies" of social situations using the tools in the Marxist medicine bag. While clinical Marxism employs the achievements of scientific Marxism—and is therefore "scientific" in the way that clinical medicine is—it does not aim to develop or reconstruct Marxist theory, but to understand the (class) forces and (systemic) constraints at work in specific cases, and to prescribe treatments and, where possible, cures. Scientific Marxism, in contrast, is concerned precisely with the development and reconstruction of Marxist theory. As scientific Marxists, theorists actively look for cases that pose problems for existing theory. To this end, anomalies are challenges indispensable for deepening theoretical insight, not embarrassments to be denied or willfully ignored.

The distinction between scientific and clinical Marxism is not identical to the distinction between academic and political Marxism. There are many academic Marxists whose scholarship is essentially clinical in nature. When a Marxist historian or sociologist, for example, studies a

---

1. Thus when there are well-formulated, contending theories of specific diseases, it is well to look for data that discriminate between the rival explanations. Adjudication between rival theories consists, in part, in finding data that constitute an anomaly with respect to one explanation but not another.

particular revolution or labor movement, and tries to understand why it occurred and why it succeeded or failed, much of the work uses the repertoire of Marxist concepts and theories to diagnose the facts of a particular case. As with doctors diagnosing the illness of a patient, the academic clinical Marxist may learn a great deal *about* the particular case in question, without learning very much of a more general nature *from* the case.

Marxism espoused the ideal that these clinical and scientific modes should mutually reinforce and enrich each other. The clinical practice of Marxism, particularly when it is deployed politically in the actual practice of socialist movements, helps to identify anomalies, failures of the scientific theory to diagnose social situations adequately. These anomalies provoke reconstructions of the theory through the scientific practice of Marxism. And the reconstructed theory is then applied more effectively in future struggles. This "dialectic of theory and practice" should engender an open and creative dialogue between these two sides of Marxist practice. However, as already remarked, Marxists have often tended to deny or ignore anomalies. Even Marxists who proclaimed allegiance to scientific norms typically defended existing theory with a zeal more characteristic of religion than science.

This tendency towards dogmatism was due in part to the peculiar institutional relationship between the scientific and clinical practices of Marxism. Imagine a medical system in which clinicians controlled both clinical and scientific medicine and in which their power and privileges institutionally depended upon the production of particular diagnoses and the implementation of particular treatments. In such a situation one would predict suppression of anomalies and theoretical stagnation.

The Marxist tradition has been subjected to just such pressures. Throughout much of the twentieth century, clinical Marxists, or, more precisely, the political elites in state socialist societies and Communist parties who were the official guardians of clinical Marxism, have institutionally dominated scientific Marxism. The result has not only compromised the scientific status of Marxism, but has also undermined the usefulness of scientific Marxism for clinical practitioners.[2]

The contemporary renaissance of scientific Marxism is, in part, a consequence of the greater autonomy accorded the development of Marxist theory as the role of Marxist officialdom has waned. It is difficult to imagine the theoretical advances within Marxism of the 1970s

---

2. It does not follow, of course, that all of the diagnoses clinical Marxists have produced are wrong. Because of the explanatory power of even dogmatic, "vulgar" Marxism, it has been a useful tool for clinical Marxism in at least some settings (e.g. in highly class polarized third world societies).

and 1980s occurring if Marxist theoretical work had been produced primarily within the organizational structures of political parties that required party discipline of their members. The heightened autonomy of Marxist scientific practice from direct subordination to political requirements has contributed to the opening up of Marxist discourse to wider theoretical influences and debates. This is strikingly the case in the emerging school of analytical Marxism, which self-consciously engages a variety of traditions of "bourgeois" social science and philosophy. But even among Marxists critical of analytical Marxism, there is a much less intimate relationship between the production of Marxist theory and active participation in Marxist political parties than in earlier periods, and this has facilitated the new directions that theoretical developments have taken.

To understand the nature of these new developments it will be useful to turn to our second analogy between Marxism and medicine: the distinction between disciplines rooted in independent variables and those designed by dependent variables.

Independent- vs. Dependent-variable Marxisms

Compare endocrinology and oncology. Endocrinology is defined by its study of a particular organ system in the body—the endocrine system. Endocrinologists investigate and treat the glands that comprise this system, and anything else—from personality to human growth, from cancer to sexuality—in which the endocrine system plays a role. For some of these concerns, the hormones produced by the endocrine system play an important role; for others, their effects are peripheral. While most research by endocrinologists revolves around problems for which it is already known that the endocrine system is important, there is no embarrassment in investigating issues in which hormones turn out to be only marginally involved. Progress in endocrinology results, in part, from demarcating precisely the causal range of the endocrine system, and from understanding its effects even in cases where hormones play only a small role.

Oncology, on the other hand, is defined by the collection of ailments it investigates and treats—cancers. Oncologists explore processes implicated in the generation and development of cancer: from genetic factors to environmental pollution, from viruses to smoking. Some of these determinants may be massively important for some cancers and not others; some may be relatively unimportant for any. While most research on the causes of cancer revolves around causes that are already known to be important, there is no embarrassment in investigating causes that turn out to be relatively unimportant. Progress in oncology involves understanding the specificity of the impact of both more important and less important causes.

These two kinds of medical specialities could be called, respectively, "independent-variable" and "dependent-variable" disciplines. A similar distinction is implicit in the Marxist tradition.

Independent-variable Marxism

Independent-variable Marxism is defined, in the first instance, by its preoccupation with a particular cluster of interconnected mechanisms: class, property relations, exploitation, mode of production, economic structure. This list might be expanded or contracted, but at the core is the concept of class, understood in a distinctively Marxist way. Thus, independent-variable Marxism can be called *Marxism as class analysis*.

In addition to studying the internal properties of these phenomena, Marxism as class analysis investigates a variety of problems in which class is thought to be consequential. Thus there are Marxist class analyses of religion, art, social conflict, war, poverty, electoral politics, the trajectory of capitalist development, and many other topics. For some of these explananda, class, understood in the Marxist way, turns out to be massively important; for others class is important along with a range of other causes; and for still others, class is not very important at all. The progress of Marxism as class analysis comes, in part, from understanding the scope and limits of the explanatory capacity of class.

What, it might be asked, justifies the use of the term "Marxism" juxtaposed to "class analysis"? There are, after all, a variety of non-Marxist traditions of class analysis in sociology, each anchored in the study of a particular cluster of explanatory mechanisms. Marxism as class analysis is distinguished from these other class analyses on two grounds: first, because of the way class is conceptualized, and second, because of the substantive theory of the effects of class.[3]

"Class" is a contested term in social science. For some sociologists, class simply designates rungs on a socioeconomic status ladder; for others, classes are any social groups that stand in a relation of authoritative domination and subordination. Marxism as class analysis is grounded in a distinctive way of conceptualizing class: classes are

---

3. To say that Marxism as class analysis implies a substantive commitment to contested theoretical positions somewhat weakens the analogy with disciplines within medicine. In medicine, one can treat endocrinology as a *topic*, a subject matter defined by its concern with a particular causal system, since it is not highly contested whether this causal mechanism exists. Marxism as class analysis cannot plausibly be viewed simply as a topic of inquiry.

defined *relationally*; those relations are *antagonistic*; those antagonisms are rooted in *exploitation*; and exploitation is based on the social relations of production (or, as is sometimes said, on social property relations).[4]

The justification for using the term "Marxism" in Marxism as class analysis also derives from substantive theoretical commitments about the effects of class. If one believed that class, defined in the above way, had little or no explanatory importance for any of the problems traditionally studied by Marxists, it would be odd to identify the resulting class analysis with Marxism simply because of the formal conceptual criteria used to define class. *Marxism* as class analysis (as opposed to class analysis that uses class concepts with a Marxist bent) implies some commitment to positions that bear a conceptual affinity with traditional Marxist theses about the causal importance of class and related concepts for understanding social change and social reproduction.

In these terms one might want to distinguish between three degrees of commitment to the Marxist content of class analysis:

Orthodox Marxist class analysis approaches specific problems with the presumption that class and related concepts are the *most important* causal processes at work. An orthodox Marxist need not insist dogmatically that class is always of paramount importance, but will be surprised when it is not.

Neo-Marxist class analysis adopts the presumption that class and related concepts are *important*, but not necessarily the most important, causes. A neo-Marxist will not be surprised, in general, to find that other causes have considerable importance for some problems, but will be surprised if class is of only marginal relevance.

Post-Marxist class analysis presumes only that class is a *relevant* factor in any analysis; there is no general expectation that it has considerable importance.

In all of these forms of Marxist class analysis, the *concept* of class is understood in the distinctively Marxist way, but the presumptions about

---

4. For discussion of these conceptual parameters, see Erik Olin Wright, *Classes* (London: Verso, 1985), pp. 34–7. John Roemer has questioned whether, even within a strictly Marxist concept of class, "exploitation" is an essential element. However, Roemer's principal concern is with the relevance of exploitation to the normative indictment of capitalism, not with the explanatory role exploitation plays in class analysis. See Roemer, "Should Marxists be Interested in Exploitation?" *Philosophy and Public Affairs* 14:1 (1985), pp. 30–65.

the explanatory importance of class differ. In these terms, one can, without inconsistency, be an orthodox Marxist with respect to certain questions, a neo-Marxist with respect to others, and a post-Marxist with respect to still others. Post-Marxism can be an exit-point from Marxism altogether, but unlike anti-Marxism it does not summarily reject the explanatory importance of Marxist class concepts.

To define Marxism in terms of its use of class as an independent variable does not mean that Marxist explanations are restricted to class. Even Marxism's core explanatory concepts involve factors that are not simply derivations from class. Consider, for example, the term "economic structure", which appears in many Marxist explanations. Typically, references to economic structures are not restricted to the set of class relations within production. The distribution of employment across industrial sectors, the geographical distribution of different kinds of production, the relative importance of import-oriented and export-oriented firms, and the size of units of production are all aspects of economic structure that figure in Marxist explanations. Nevertheless, what gives the use of these concepts a distinctively *Marxist* character is the focus on their linkage to the class aspects of a society's economy.

Dependent-variable Marxism

Dependent-variable Marxism is defined by its concern with explaining the reproduction and transformation of class relations in different kinds of societies. More specifically, dependent-variable Marxism attempts to explain the developmental trajectory of capitalism as a particular kind of class-based economic system in order to understand the possibilities for socialism, and eventually communism. To employ a somewhat tendentious expression, but one with a venerable history in the Marxist tradition, dependent-variable Marxism is *Marxism as scientific socialism.*

Like Marxism as class analysis, Marxism as scientific socialism cannot be defined apart from its substantive theoretical commitments. In particular, Marxists as scientific socialists subscribe to a distinctively Marxist view of capitalism, socialism and perhaps also communism as forms of society within the historical materialist trajectory. To be sure, Marxists in this sense need not be *strong* historical materialists (as defined in Chapter 5). But they must endorse an historical materialist view of the possibilities confronting humankind and of the obstacles in the way of epochal historical transformations. Proponents of *weak restricted* historical materialism are therefore still scientific socialists. But those who hold positions that depart more radically from the theory of history Marx proposed—to the degree that they deny altogether the existence of the historical dynamic Marx purported to identify—would not count as "Marxists" in this sense.

The distinction between orthodox Marxism, neo-Marxism and post-Marxism is also reflected in Marxism as scientific socialism. Orthodox Marxists believe that socialism (and eventually communism) are virtually inevitable because of the contradictions within capitalism and the dynamic postulated within historical materialism. Neo-Marxists reject the inevitability of the historical materialist trajectory, but nevertheless see socialism as a probable outcome of the dynamics of capitalism. Post-Marxists see socialism as merely a possibility. Orthodox, neo- and post-Marxists are "Marxists" because they see socialism as a possible product of the materialist dynamics and contradictions of capitalism. However, they disagree about how predictable the outcome of these processes is.[5]

It might be thought that this characterization of dependent-variable Marxism is too restricted. Marxists, after all, investigate state policies, forms of consciousness, wars, imperialism—indeed, a host of phenomena ostensibly distinct from the epochal transformation of class structures. Still, what gives these explananda a distinctively Marxist character is their connection to historical materialist themes; it is the dynamic properties of capitalist societies and the prospects for transforming them in a socialist direction that motivate Marxist inquiries. Thus Marxists characteristically study state policies because of their effects on social relations of production; not for their own sake or for reasons distinct from historical materialist concerns. Policies that do not bear on these issues do not constitute distinctively Marxist objects of explanation. They may, of course, be of interest to a more diffuse *radical* social analysis, and Marxism as class analysis may play a role in their explanation. Nevertheless, what gives an explanandum—in contrast to an explanans—its Marxist character is its bearing on the reproduction and transformation of social relations of production.

The Link between Independent-variable Marxism and Dependent-variable Marxism

Until recently, within the Marxist tradition, independent- and dependent-variable Marxism were inextricably linked. Marxism as class analysis was thought to explain the distinctive explananda of Marxism as scientific socialism. This conviction was hardly surprising for Marxists who evinced an extraordinary—and unrealistic—faith in the explanatory

---

5. Thus one could be a non-Marxist scientific socialist if one believed, for example, that socialism becomes possible not because of any materialist dynamic, but because of the cultural logic of moral development.

powers of class analysis. But even for Marxists who had abandoned strong historical materialism, class analysis was still seen as providing the core explanations for Marxism as scientific socialism.

Today, the unity of class analysis and scientific socialism can no longer be taken for granted. On the one hand, class analysts are more aware than before of the importance of interactions between class and other factors in the generation of social phenomena, even including class conflicts themselves. On the other hand, few theorists still believe that class analysis by itself can provide an adequate theoretical basis for transforming capitalist societies towards socialism and communism. If the current tension between class analysis and scientific socialism were to develop into a complete rupture, it might no longer be appropriate to describe either class analysis or scientific socialism (if it continued to exist at all) as "Marxist". The Marxist pedigree of certain questions and concepts would, of course, remain beyond dispute, but Marxism as a coherent theoretical project would effectively cease to exist.

Is this tension between class analysis and scientific socialism something to be regretted by those still committed to Marxism? Or is it an opportunity for significant intellectual advance within a broadly Marxist framework? To address these questions, we need to introduce one more dimension to the discussion: Marxism as an emancipatory project.

Marxism as an Emancipatory Theory

Our discussions in this book have centered on Marxism as a social science, not as a normative theory. We have seen how longstanding beliefs about an unalterable opposition between Marxist and "bourgeois" social science are deeply flawed; how Marxism is not, as was once believed, a "paradigm" incompatible with all aspects of mainstream social science. Nevertheless, we have argued that there is a distinctively Marxist explanatory apparatus and a distinctively Marxist focus on certain social phenomena.

In much the same way, until quite recently it was generally assumed that Marxist normative theory, if it existed at all, was at odds with liberal social philosophy and perhaps even, in crucial respects, incommensurable with it. However, in light of recent work by analytical Marxists and liberal social philosophers, this understanding too has been put into question.

The term "Marxism" has always led a double life: designating both a theoretical project for understanding the social world and a political project for changing it. Traditionally, these objectives were thought to be complementary: Marxist theory was to direct political practice, and

Marxist politics was to direct the orientation and perhaps even the content of Marxist theory. In this sense, historically, Marxism has always had an "emancipatory" dimension. In its subject matter and its explanatory apparatus, it aimed to comprehend aspects of human oppression and, by theorizing the conditions for eliminating this oppression, to advance the struggle for human freedom.

"Oppression", however, is a normatively contentious idea. Is a particular form of inequality or domination an instance of oppression and therefore an impediment to human emancipation? Or is it an inevitable condition of human life or a by-product of normatively neutral (or perhaps even desirable) arrangements? Any theoretical practice with emancipatory objectives must eventually confront such questions.

Different emancipatory theories can be defined by the different forms of oppression that they seek to understand and transform: feminism constitutes a tradition of emancipatory theory built around gender oppression; Marxism around class oppression. Some Marxists have claimed that Marxism constitutes a fully general emancipatory theory, not simply a theory of the transformation of class oppression as such, but of all forms of socially constituted oppression. As we discussed in Chapter 7, such arguments usually take the form of insisting that class oppression is the "most fundamental" and that other forms of oppression—based on gender, race, nationality, religion, etc.—are themselves either directly explained by class, usually via a functionalist form of reasoning, or operate within limits narrowly circumscribed by class considerations. We do not think that there is any reason, in general, to support such comprehensive claims of class primacy, and in any case, the legitimacy of the distinctively Marxist emancipatory project does not depend on class oppression's being more "fundamental" than other forms of oppression.

The core normative ideal underlying the Marxist emancipatory project is *classlessness*, or radical egalitarianism with respect to the control over society's productive resources and the socially produced surplus. We believe that this ideal underlies Marx's claim that under communism the distribution of the social product will proceed to each according to need, from each according to ability. We shall not attempt to provide philosophical foundations for this value here, but the essential idea is that the existence of classes is a systematic impediment to human freedom, since it deprives most people of control over their destiny, both as individuals and as members of collectivities. In these terms, class relations in general, and capitalism in particular, violate values of *democracy*, in so far as the existence of classes blocks the ability of communities to allocate social resources as they see fit, and they violate values of individual *liberty* and *self-realization*, in so far as class inequalities deprive many individuals of the resources necessary to pursue their life plans.

While, traditionally, the philosophical defense of this emancipatory project was relatively underdeveloped, nevertheless, it is an integral part of the Marxist tradition. We can thus view Marxism as a whole as containing three interdependent theoretical nodes: Marxism as class analysis (independent-variable Marxism), Marxism as scientific socialism (dependent-variable Marxism), and Marxism as class emancipation (normative Marxism). These form a kind of triad.

Marxism as class emancipation

Marxism as class analysis   Marxism as scientific socialism

In classical Marxism, these three elements mutually reinforced each other. Marxism as class emancipation identified the disease in the existing world. Marxism as class analysis provided the diagnosis of its causes. Marxism as scientific solution identified the cure. Without class analysis and scientific socialism, the emancipatory critique would simply be a moral condemnation, while without the emancipatory objective, class analysis would simply be an academic speciality.

The enormous appeal of Marxism came in part from the unity of these three elements, for together they provided a basis for the belief that eliminating the miseries and oppressions of the existing world was not simply a utopian fantasy, but a practical political project. The dissolution of that unity is an important part of the "crisis of Marxism".

The Crisis of Marxism and the Prospects for the Marxist Agenda

The expression "the crisis of Marxism" nowadays designates two distinct realities: the political, economic and ideological crisis of states and political parties that adopted Marxism as an official ideology; and the crisis within the intellectual tradition of Marxism. The first of these crises is rooted in the stagnation and decay of authoritarian state socialist societies.[6] The second, however, comes not from the stagnation of Marxism as a theoretical tradition, but has accompanied a period of considerable vitality, openness to new ideas and theoretical progress within each of the three poles of the Marxist tradition—class analysis, scientific socialism and class emancipation. Class analysis has registered plain and durable successes, but the idea that social science in general ought to devolve into class analysis no longer appears plausible. The jury is still out on Marxism as scientific socialism, but it is now beyond dispute that the strong historical materialism that formerly motivated Marxist concerns with capitalism, socialism and communism is untenable. The jury is out too on socialism's and communism's place in the broader struggle for human emancipation.

More tellingly, the link between these theories, once unquestioned, can no longer be assumed. We have already discussed the disjunction between Marxism as class analysis and Marxism as scientific socialism. It is now plain that a similar disjunction also looms between these dimensions of Marxism and Marxism as an emancipatory theory.

Classical Marxism was a marvelously ambitious endeavor. It aspired, first of all, for unity between theory and practice. Theory was to guide practice; practice was to transform theory. Its clinical and scientific aspects were inextricably interdependent. In addition, classical Marxism aimed to construct an integrated and comprehensive framework for the analysis of social phenomena. This framework was no eclectic combination of distinct theoretical elements rooted in different explanatory principles; it was a unified theory with a fully integrated conceptual structure. Thus classical Marxism embodied a unity of class analysis and scientific socialism, forged around a general emancipatory project.

This vision of Marxism can no longer be maintained. The disjunction between Marxism as class analysis and Marxism as scientific socialism has fractured the prospects for a "unified field theory" of emancipatory possibilities, and the high degree of autonomy between clinical and scientific Marxism that has developed since the 1960s has eroded the "unity of theory and practice". For better or worse, Marxist theory today

---

6. It is ironic that the collapse of authoritarian state socialisms should be a stimulus for proclamations of the "end of Marxism" as a social theory by anti-Marxists, and for self-doubt by Marxists and their sympathizers. From the perspective of *classical* Marxism, the collapse of these regimes and their return to a "normal" path of capitalist development is eminently predictable. If anything, the long detour from the Bolshevik Revolution to *perestroika* was a challenging anomaly to historical materialism. The restoration of capitalist property relations in relatively underdeveloped industrial economies, on the other hand, actually corroborates the theory. *If* Marx was right, socialism is not achievable until the forces of production have developed massively under capitalism, and further development is fettered by capitalist property relations. The attempt to construct revolutionary socialism by an act of will in violation of this "law of history" was therefore doomed from the start.

is seldom directed by immediate political exigencies, and institutional links with political parties or movements have declined along with those parties and movements themselves.

While the traditional model no longer seems tenable, even in principle, many Marxist intellectuals are unhappy with the emerging alternative—a social theory with less ambitious explanatory scope and with less certainty about its explanatory capabilities. The sense of crisis that results reflects a deep ambivalence over the implications of this transformation of a comprehensive emancipatory theory to a more restricted account of particular social processes and tendencies.

It is clear that a retreat to earlier Marxist aspirations is no longer possible. The world has changed and those earlier forms are irretrievable. The fragmentation of the once unitary triad of Marxist theory undoubtedly erodes its appeal as an ideology. Yet in many respects these three components of the old Marxist triad have flourished as their interconnections have weakened. We are optimistic that a reconstructed Marxism, even if less integrated, is feasible and that what is now experienced as a crisis will come to be seen as unavoidable growing pains.

Bibliography

Albert, Michael and Robin Hahnel, *Marxism and Socialist Theory* (Boston: South End Press, 1981).

Alford, Robert and Roger Friedland, *The Powers of Theory* (Cambridge: Cambridge University Press, 1985).

Althusser, Louis and Etienne Balibar, *Reading Capital* (London: New Left Books, 1970).

Althusser, Louis, "Ideology and Ideological State Apparatuses", in *Lenin and Philosophy* (London: New Left Books, 1971).

Althusser, Louis, *For Marx* (London: New Left Books, 1969).

Anderson, Perry, *Lineages of the Absolutist State* (London: New Left Books, 1974).

Anderson, Perry, *Considerations on Western Marxism* (London: New Left Books, 1976).

Ashton, T.H. ed., *The Brenner Debate: Agrarian Class Structure and Economic Development in Pre-Industrial Europe* (Cambridge: Cambridge University Press, 1985).

Bachrach, Peter and Morton S. Baratz, "The Two Faces of Power", *American Political Science Review* 51 (December 1962), pp. 947–52.

Balibar, Etienne, "The Fundamental Concepts of Historical Materialism", in L. Althusser and E. Balibar, *Reading Capital* (London: New Left Books, 1970).

Barrett, Michèle, *Women's Oppression Today*, revised edition (London: Verso, 1989).

Beauchamp, Tom, ed., *Philosophical Problems of Causation* (Encino and Belmont: Dickenson Publishing Co., 1974).

Beckner, Morton, *The Biological Way of Thought* (Berkeley: University of California Press, 1959).

Bergmann, Gustav, *Philosophy of Science* (Madison: University of Wisconsin Press, 1957).

Boorse, Christopher, "Wright on Functions", *Philosophical Review* 85 (1976), pp. 70–86.

Bowles, Sam and Herbert Gintis, *Democracy and Capitalism* (New York: Basic Books, 1986).

Boyd, R., "Materialism without Reductionism", in N. Block, ed., *Readings in Philosophy of Psychology* (Cambridge, MA: Harvard University Press, 1980).

Brenner, Johanna and Maria Ramas, "Rethinking Women's Oppression", *New Left Review* 144 (1984).

Brenner, Robert, "Agrarian Class Structure and Economic Development in Pre-Industrial Europe", *Past and Present* 70 (February 1976).

Brenner, Robert, "The Agrarian Roots of European Capitalism", in T.H. Ashton and C.H.E. Philpon, eds, *The Brenner Debate*, (Cambridge: Cambridge University Press, 1985), pp. 213–327.

Burge, Tyler, "Individualism and Psychology", *Philosophical Review* 95 (1986), pp. 3–43.

Carling, Alan, "Rational Choice Marxism", *New Left Review* 160 (1986).

Cartwright, Nancy, "Causal Laws and Effective Strategies", *Nous* 13 (1979), pp. 419–37.

Chodrow, Nancy, *Mothering* (Berkeley: University of California Press, 1978).

Cohen, G.A., "Functional Explanation, Consequence Explanation and Marxism", *Inquiry* 25 (1982), pp. 27–56.

Cohen, G.A., *History, Labour and Freedom: themes from Marx* (Oxford: Clarendon Press, 1988).

Cohen, G.A., *Karl Marx's Theory of History: a defense* (Princeton: Princeton University Press, 1978).

Cohen, G.A., "The Labor Theory of Value and the Concept of Exploitation", *Philosophy and Public Affairs* 8, 2 (1979), pp. 338–60.

Cohen, G.A., "Reply to Elster", *Political Studies* xxviii, 1 (1980).

Cohen, G.A., "Reply to Elster, 'Marxism, Functionalism and Game Theory'", *Theory and Society* 11 (1982), pp. 483–96.

Cohen, G.A., "Restricted and Inclusive Historical Materialism", *Irish Philosophical Journal* 1 (1984), pp. 3–31; reprinted (with modifications) in G.A. Cohen, *History, Labour and Freedom: Themes from Marx* (Oxford: Clarendon Press, 1988).

Cohen, Jean, *Class and Civil Society* (Amherst: University of Massachusetts Press, 1982).

Cohen, Joshua and Joel Rogers, *On Democracy* (Harmondsworth: Penguin, 1983).

Cohen, Joshua, "Review of *KMTH*", *The Journal of Philosophy* LXXXV, 4 (1983).

Crenson, Matthew A., *The Unpolitics of Air Pollution: a study of non-decision-making in the cities* (Baltimore: Johns Hopkins Press, 1971).

d'Encausse, Hélène Carrere and Stuart Schram, *Marxism and Asia* (London: Allen Lane, 1969).

Dobb, Maurice, *Studies in the Development of Capitalism* (London: 1946, repr. 1963, 1972).

Eberhard, Wolfram, *Conquerors and Rulers: Social Forces in Medieval China* (Leiden: E.E. Brill, 1970).

Eells, Ellery, *Probabilistic Causality* (Cambridge: Cambridge University Press, 1991).

Elster, Jon, "Cohen on Marx's Theory of History", *Political Studies*, XXVIII: 1 (March 1980), pp. 121-8.

Elster, Jon, *Logic and Society* (New York: John Wiley, 1978).

Elster, Jon, *Making Sense of Marx* (Cambridge: Cambridge University Press, 1985).

Elster, Jon, "Marxism, Functionalism and Game Theory", *Theory and Society* 11 (1982), pp. 453-82.

Elster, Jon, *Ulysses and the Sirens: Studies in Rationality and Irrationality* (Cambridge and Paris: Cambridge University Press and Edition de la Maison des Sciences de l'Homme, 1979).

Fisher, R.A., *The Genetical Theory of Natural Selection* (Oxford: Oxford University Press, 1930).

Fodor, Jerry, *The Language of Thought* (New York: Thomas Crowell, 1975).

Giddens, Anthony, *Central Problems in Social Theory* (Berkeley, University of California Press, 1979).

Giddens, Anthony, *A Contemporary Critique of Historical Materialism* (Berkeley: University of California Press, 1981).

Giddens, Anthony, *The Nation State and Violence* (Berkeley: University of California Press, 1985).

Glymour, Clark, R. Scheines and P. Spirtes, *Discovering Causal Structure* (Orlando, Fl: Academic Press, 1987).

Godelier, Maurice, "La notion de 'mode de production asiatique,'" in CERM, *Sur le "Mode de production asiatique"* (Paris: Editions Sociales, 1969).

Gould, Stephen J. and Richard C. Lewontin, "The Spandrels of San Marco and the Panglossian Paradigm: A Critique of the Adaptationist Programme", *Proceedings of the Royal Society, London* 205 (1978), pp. 581-98 (reprinted in Elliott Sober, ed., *Conceptual Issues in Evolutionary Biology* (Cambridge: Bradford/MIT Press, 1984), pp. 252-70).

Habermas, Jürgen, *Communication and the Evolution of Society* (Boston: Beacon Press, 1979).

Hartman, Heidi, "The Unhappy Marriage of Marxism and Feminism", in Lydia Sargent, ed., *Women and Revolution* (Boston: South End Press, 1981).

Hempel, Carl, *Aspects of Scientific Explanation* (New York: The Free Press, 1965).

Hindess, Barry and Paul Q. Hirst, *Marx's Capital and Capitalism Today* (London: Routledge & Kegan Paul, 1977).

Hindess, Barry and Paul Q. Hirst, *Pre-Capitalist Modes of Production* (London: Routledge & Kegan Paul, 1975).

Hobbes, Thomas, *Leviathan*, ed., M. Oakshott (Oxford: Basil Blackwell, 1946).

Hodgson, Geoff, "The Theory of the Falling Rate of Profit", *New Left Review* 84 (March/April 1974).

Hull, David, *Philosophy of Biological Science* (Englewood Cliffs, NJ: Prentice-Hall, 1974).

Hume, David, *A Treatise of Human Nature* ed., L.A. Selby-Bigg ed., (Oxford: Oxford University Press, 1960).

Hume, David, *An Enquiry Concerning the Principles of Morals* (Indianapolis: Hackett, 1977).

Lachman, Richard, "An Elite Conflict Theory of the Transition to Capitalism", *American Sociological Review* 55, 3, (June 1990).

Laclau, Ernesto and Chantal Mouffe, in *Hegemony and Socialist Strategy: towards a radical democratic politics* (London: Verso, 1985).

Levine, Andrew, "Althusser's Marxism", *Economy and Society* 10, 1981, 3, pp. 243–83.

Levine, Andrew, *Arguing for Socialism* (London: Routledge & Kegan Paul, 1984; second edition, Verso, 1988).

Levine, Andrew, *The End of the State* (London: Verso, 1987).

Lewontin, Richard, "Adaptation", *Scientific American* 239(3) (1978), pp. 156–69.

Lewontin, Richard, "The Analysis of Variance and the Analysis of Causes", *American Journal of Human Genetics* 26 (1974), pp. 400–11.

Lewontin, Richard, "Is Nature Probable or Capricious?", *Bioscience* 16, (1966), pp. 25–6.

Lewontin, R. and R. Levins, *The Dialectical Biologist* (Cambridge, MA: Harvard University Press, 1985).

Lukes, Stephen, *Power: a Radical View* (London: Macmillan, 1974).

Macdonald, Graham and Philip Pettit, *Semantics and Social Science* (London, Routledge & Kegan Paul, 1981).

Marx, Karl, *Capital*, vol. I (London: Penguin Books, 1976).

Marx, Karl, *Critique of Hegel's Philosophy of Right*, ed. Joseph O'Mally (Cambridge: Cambridge University Press, 1971).

Marx, Karl, *Pre-Capitalist Economic Formations*, ed. Eric J. Hobsbawm (New York: International Publishers, 1964).

Marx, Karl, Preface to *A Contribution to the Critique of Political Economy* (1859).

Mayr, Ernst, "Lamarck Revisited", in *Evolution and the Diversity of Life* (Cambridge, MA: Harvard University Press, 1975), pp. 444–535.

McMurtry, John, *The Structure of Marx's World View* (Princeton, NJ: Princeton University Press, 1978).

Merleau-Ponty, Maurice, *The Adventures of the Dialectic*, trans. Joseph Bien (Evanston, Ill.: Northwestern University Press, 1973).

Miller, Richard F., *Fact and Method: Explanation, Confirmation and Reality in the Natural and Social Sciences* (Princeton, NJ: Princeton University Press, 1987).

Miller, Richard W., *Analyzing Marx: morality, power and history* (Princeton, NJ: Princeton University Press, 1984).

Munson, Ronald, ed., *Man and Nature* (New York: Delta Books, 1971). Quoted in Hull (1974).

Nagel, Ernest, *The Structure of Science* (London: Routledge & Kegan Paul, 1961).

O'Brien, Mary, *The Politics of Reproduction* (London: Routledge & Kegan Paul, 1983).

Offe, Claus, "Structural Problems of the Capitalist State: class rule and the political system. On the selectiveness of political institutions", in von Beyme, ed., *German Political Studies*, vol. I (Sage, 1974).

Orloff, Ann and Theda Skocpol, "Why Not Equal Protection? Explaining the Politics of Public Social Spending in Britain, 1900–1911, and the United States, 1880s–1920", *American Sociological Review* 49:6 (1984), pp. 726–50.

Poulantzas, Nicos, *Political Power and Social Classes* (London: New Left Books, 1973).

Przeworski, Adam, "Social Democracy as an Historical Phenomenon", *New Left Review* 122 (1980).

Przeworski, Adam, "The Challenge of Methodological Individualism to Marxist Analysis", *Politics & Society* 10:3 (1982).

Przeworski, Adam, *Capitalism and Social Democracy* (Cambridge: Cambridge University Press, 1985).

Putnam, Hilary, "The Meaning of 'Meaning'", *Mind, Language and Reality* (Cambridge: Cambridge University Press, 1975).

Rader, Melvin, *Marx's Interpretation of History* (Oxford: Oxford University Press, 1979).

Roemer, John, *A General Theory of Exploitation and Class* (Cambridge, MA: Harvard University Press, 1982).

Roemer, John, *Analytical Foundations of Marxian Economic Theory* (Cambridge: Cambridge University Press, 1981).

Roemer, John, "Should Marxists be Interested in Exploitation?" *Philosophy and Public Affairs* 14:1 (1985), pp. 30–65.

Rosenberg, A., "The Supervenience of Biological Concepts", in E. Sober, ed., *Conceptual Issues in Evolutionary Biology* (Cambridge, MA: MIT Press, 1984).

Salmon, Wesley, *Scientific Explanation and the Causal Structure of the World* (Princeton, NJ: Princeton University Press, 1984).

Shaw, William H., *Marx's Theory of History* (Palo Alto: Stanford University Press, 1979).

Skocpol, Theda, "Bringing the State Back in: False Leads and Promising Starts in Current Theories and Research", in Peter Evans, Dietich Rueschemeyer and Theda Skocpol, eds, *Bringing the State Back in* (Cambridge: Cambridge University Press, 1985), pp. 3–37.

Skocpol, Theda, "Political Response to Capitalist Crisis: Neo-Marxist Theories of the State and the Case of the New Deal", *Politics & Society* 10:2 (1980).

Sober, Elliott, "Apportioning Causal Responsibility", *Journal of Philosophy* 85 (1988) pp. 303–18.

Sober, Elliott, ed., *Conceptual Issues in Evolutionary Biology* (Cambridge, MA: MIT Press, 1986).

Sober, Elliott, *The Nature of Selection: Evolutionary Theory in Philosophical Focus* (Cambridge: Bradford/MIT Press, 1984).

Sober, Elliott, "Organisms, Individuals, and Units of Selection", in F. Tauber, ed., *Organism and the Origin of Self* (Dordrecht: Kluwer, 1991).

Steedman, Ian, *Marx after Sraffa* (London: New Left Books, 1977), Chapter 9.

Stinchcombe, Arthur L., "Social Structure and Organizations", in James March, ed., *Handbook of Organizations* (Chicago: Rand McNally, 1965), pp. 142–93.

Stinchcombe, Arthur, *Constructing Social Theories* (New York: Harcourt Brace Jovanovich, 1968).

Sweezy, Paul M., *The Theory of Capitalist Development: Principles of Marxian Political Economy* (New York: Monthly Review Press, 1942).

Sweezy, Paul et al., *The Transition from Feudalism to Capitalism* (New York and London: Verso, 1978).

Therborn, Goran, *The Power of Ideology and the Ideology of Power* (London: NLB/Verso, 1982).

Therborn, Goran, *What Does the Ruling Class Do When it Rules?* (London: NLB, 1978).

Van Parijs, Philippe, *Evolutionary Explanation in the Social Sciences: an emerging paradigm* (Totowa, NJ: Rowan and Littlefield, 1981).

Van Parijs, Philippe, "Marxism's Central Puzzle", in T. Ball and J. Farr, eds., *After Marx* (Cambridge: Cambridge University Press: 1984).

Van Parijs, Philippe, "A Revolution in Class Theory", *Politics & Society* 15, 4 (1986–87), reprinted in Erik Olin Wright et al., *The Debate on Classes* (London: Verso, 1990).

Wallerstein, Immanuel, *The Modern World-System: Capitalist Agriculture and the Origins of the European World-Economy in the Sixteenth Century* (New York and London: Academic Press, 1974).

Williams, George C., *Adaptation and Natural Selection* (Princeton, NJ: Princeton University Press, 1966).

Wittfogel, Karl A., *Oriental Despotism* (New Haven, CT: Yale University Press, 1963).

Wolfe, Richard and Stephen Resnick, *Knowledge and Class* (Chicago: University of Chicago Press, 1988).

Wood, Allen, *Karl Marx* (London: Routledge & Kegan Paul, 1981).

Wright, Erik Olin, *Class, Crisis and the State* (London: Verso, 1978).

Wright, Erik Olin, *Classes* (London: Verso, 1985).

Wright, Larry, "Functions", *Philosophical Review*, 82 (1973) pp. 139–68.

Index

Cohen, G. 2, 12, 13, 16ff, 53, 64, 81, 93–4, 100, 156, 158
Cohen, J. 3
commodity fetishism 42
communism 11, 91
communist parties 1, 4, 15, 32, 181
Compatibility Thesis 19, 21, 26, 28, 33, 35
consumerism 34ff, 42
contradiction 6–7, 20, 35, 44, 91, 166
  see also Compatibility Thesis
Contradiction Thesis 25, 29, 37ff, 52
correlation 140
Cutler, A. 86

Darwin, C, 47
D'Encausse, H. 37
Derrida, J. 5
Development Thesis 23, 31, 36ff, 83, 89
dialectics 6, 59, 106
dispositions 18, 64, 157
Dobbs, M. 152
Dobzhansky, T. 49
domination 68, 74

egoism 123
Eells, E. 165
Elster, J. 2, 6, 7, 53, 64ff, 107, 108ff, 124, 156
emergent properties 119
Engels, F. 81
evolution 48, 51, 54, 62, 64, 76, 78, 86, 90, 98, 112, 118
explanation
  and causality 131–2
  coarse-grained and fine-grained 55, 150, 163, 172
  of differences 71
  see also causality, individualism, holism, relational properties
exploitation 73

feminism 130–1, 171 see also gender
fettering 19, 26ff, 31, 35, 41, 82, 90
  see also contradiction

feudalism 22, 38, 39, 57, 72, 93, 152
  see also capitalism
Fisher, R. 50
Fodor, J. 116
Foucault, M. 5
Frankfurt School 3, 4
free-rider problem 44, 123 see also game theory
Friedland, R. 130
functional explanation 17, 62ff, 76ff, 95, 114, 155 see also explanation, teleological theories of history

game theory 44, 122ff
gender 67, 73, 105, 143, 170 see also feminism
Giddens, A. 61ff, 169, 171
Gintis, H. 2
Glymour, C. 131
Godelier, M. 37
Gould, S. 57

Habermas, J. 86
Hahnel, R. 86
Hartman, H. 131
Hayek, F. von 107
Hegelian theories of history 114
Hempel, C. 132
Hindess, B. 37, 86, 129
Hirst, P. 37, 86, 129
historians, atheoretical 55, 57
historical concepts 49
historical directionality 11, 50, 55, 58, 75, 78ff, 83, 85, 90, 169 see also sticky downwards
historical materialism, 52, 58, 60, 77, 80, 89, 96
  inclusive versus restricted 94, 96, 185
  limited 93
  orthodox 11, 15, 22, 31, 32, 38, 45, 52
  politics of 98
  strong versus weak 96, 99, 185
Hobbes, T. 24
Hodgson, G. 34

Printed in the United States
by Baker & Taylor Publisher Services